MORAVIAN
DAILY
TEXTS

*Bible Texts with Hymn Verses
and Prayers for Every Day
in the Year*

2016

Two Hundred Eighty-Sixth Year

The Moravian Church in North America
1021 Center St., Bethlehem, PA 18018
459 S. Church St., Winston-Salem, NC 27101
www.moravian.org

Moravian Daily Texts 2016

Verse translation by Erdmute Frank. Compilation and copy editing by Renee Schoeller, with assistance from Mike Riess.

Cover photo: Detail from fabric produced for Moravians in Tanzania. Thanks to the Rev. Mary Kategile of the Moravian Church of Western Tanzania for permission. Photo by Mike Riess, IBOC.

Book design: Sandy Fay, Laughing Horse Graphics, Inc., Doylestown, Pa.

Printed by McNaughton & Gunn, Inc., Saline, Mich.

Printed in the United States of America

ISBN: 978-1-933571-61-4 large print edition

INTERPROVINCIAL BOARD
OF COMMUNICATION

MIX
Paper from responsible sources
FSC
www.fsc.org   FSC® C011935

NEW EVERY MORNING

"The steadfast love of the Lord never ceases, his mercies never come to an end; they are new every morning."
Lamentations 3:22,23

The first printed edition of the *Daily Texts* (Losungen) was published in Herrnhut, Saxony, in 1731. The title page of that edition quoted the passage from Lamentations and promised a daily message from God that would be new every morning. It was an outgrowth of a spiritual renewal of the Moravian Church (Unitas Fratrum) that dated from August 13, 1727.

In 1722 refugees from Bohemia and Moravia began arriving at the estate of Count Nicholas Ludwig von Zinzendorf (1700-1760), where he gave them a welcome and land on which to establish the settlement of Herrnhut ("Watch of the Lord").

Each day the settlers came together for morning and evening devotions, consciously placing their lives in the context of God's Word. On May 3, 1728, during the evening service, Count Zinzendorf gave the congregation a "watchword" for the next day. It was to be a "Losung" (watchword) to accompany them through the whole day.

Thereafter one or more persons of the congregation went daily to each of the 32 houses in Herrnhut to bring them the watchword for the day, and engage the families in pastoral conversations about the text.

From this oral tradition, the *Daily Texts* soon became fixed in printed form. Zinzendorf compiled 365 watchwords for the year and the first edition of the Losungen was published for 1731.

Even in the first editions there appeared the characteristic coupling of a Bible verse and hymn stanza. Zinzendorf called the hymns "collects" and considered them to be the answer of the congregation to the Word of God. The *Daily Texts* would be a great deal poorer without the mixture of God's Word and our human response.

The watchword soon became accompanied by a "doctrinal" text. The idea of an additional text grew out of a number of collections of texts from the Bible that were put together by Zinzendorf. Such additional lists (some of them for children) were used for special study within the groups in the community, and they came to be referred to as doctrinal texts.

For the *Daily Texts,* as for the whole Moravian Church, Count Zinzendorf's death (May 9, 1760), was a turning point.

His co-workers sensed the uniqueness of Zinzendorf's watchwords, textbooks, and lessons and had them published at Barby-on-the-Elbe in a four-volume collection 1762.

From then on the watchwords and doctrinal texts are distinguished by the way they are selected each year. The watchwords are chosen from various verse collections and, since 1788, they have been drawn by lot from a collection of around 2,000 suitable Old Testament texts. The doctrinal texts are not chosen by lot but are selected. The difference between the watchwords and doctrinal texts was explained in 1801 as follows: "The watchword is either a promise, an encouragement, an admonition or word of comfort; the doctrinal text contains a point of revealed doctrine."

By 1812 it was established that all watchwords would be drawn by lot from a selection of Old Testament texts, and the doctrinal texts would be selected from the New Testament. No doctrinal text is used more than once in a given year. By the end of the nineteenth century, the custom was established to relate the two texts in theme or thought.

Into all the world

Another characteristic of the *Daily Texts* that was already apparent in the early years of its publication was its worldwide distribution. Missionaries who went as "messengers" from Herrnhut after 1732 had a *Daily Texts (Losungen)* in their luggage. They felt united with their home congregation through the daily contemplation of the same Scripture passages.

The *Daily Texts* of 1739 lists a multitude of places around the globe where messengers were witnessing for the Savior. The introduction read:

"The Good Word of the Lord, 1739, From all the Prophets for His congregations, and servants at Herrnhut, Herrnhaag, Herrendijk [Holland], Pilgerruh [Denmark], Ebersdof, Jena, Amsterdam, Rotterdam, London, Oxford, Berlin, Greenland, St. Croix, St. John and St. Thomas [Virgin Islands], Berbice [Guyana], Palestine, Surinam, Savannah in Georgia, among the Moors in Carolina, with the wild Indians in Irene [an island in the Savannah River in Georgia], in Pennsylvania, among the Hottentots [South Africa], in Guinea, in Latvia, Estonia and Lithuania, Russia, on the White Sea, in Lappland, Norway, in Switzerland, [Isle of] Man, Hittland [Scotland], in prison, on pilgrimage, to Ceylon, Ethiopia, Persia, on visitation to the missionaries among the heathen, and elsewhere on land and sea."

This distribution of the Moravians into every continent in the known world seems all the more amazing when you consider that the settlement at Herrnhut was only 17 years old, and the first missionaries had gone out only seven years earlier in 1732.

Present membership of the worldwide Moravian Church is more than 1 million in 21 provinces. The *Daily Texts* has a press run of more than 1 million copies in the German language alone. This far surpasses the 25,000 members of the Moravian Church in all of Europe. Other language editions bring the total circulation of this small devotional book to over 1.5 million copies. The *Daily Texts* is now published in more than 50 languages and dialects.

The physical form of the *Daily Texts* varies considerably from country to country. Some, like this North American edition, have a separate page for the verses, hymns, and prayers of each day. Others have several days' texts printed on one page, which makes a thin, pocket-size volume. Some are beautiful examples of the printing and bookbinding arts. Others are simply photocopied and stapled together.

These external nonessentials pale beside the fact that this little book is probably the most widely read devotional guide in the world, next to the Bible. It forms an invisible bond between Christians on all continents, transcending barriers of confession, race, language, and politics. In its quiet way it performs a truly ecumenical service for the whole of Christendom.

North American editions
The printing of the *Daily Texts* in North America dates back at least to 1767, when the Losungen was printed "at Bethlehem on the Forks of the Delaware by Johan Brandmuller." The printer's imprint bears the date of 1767 as well and may have been an extra printing for the German version done at Barby-

on-the-Elbe in Germany, where most of the printing was done for the Moravian Church those days.

During the crucial days of the Revolution, the German-language edition was printed in Philadelphia by Heinrich Miller, who had worked for Benjamin Franklin when he first came to America. The daily text for July 4, 1776, was from Isaiah 55:5 —"Behold, you shall call nations that you know not, and nations that knew you not shall run to you" (RSV).

English versions were printed in London as early as 1746, and the title page bears the imprint of "James Hutton near the Golden Lion in Fetter Lane." Hutton was the well-known London printer associated with the Moravian Church who was a friend of John and Charles Wesley in the formative years of their ministry.

The 1850s were crucial years for the Moravian Church in North America as the congregations established in the United States broke away from direct control from the Moravian headquarters in Europe. Both German and English editions of the Daily Texts were regularly printed in Philadelphia or Bethlehem, Pennsylvania, and in a few years the custom was established to include the statistics of the provinces and districts of the Moravian Church in North America.

The biblical texts for each day are chosen in Herrnhut, Germany, and then sent around the world to those who prepare the different language editions. Since 1959 the edition published in the United States has included a prayer for each day. For this North American edition, the hymns are chosen or written, and the prayers are written by Moravian clergy and laypersons from the United States and Canada. Each month is prepared by a different individual or couple, of a variety of ages, so that the prayers reflect the great diversity of devotion in the Moravian Church.

DAILY TOPICS FOR PRAYER

On August 27, 1727, certain members of the Moravian Church in Herrnhut, Saxony, formed a remarkable prayer union known as the "Hourly Intercession." This provided that, for every hour of the day and night, one of the volunteer intercessors would, for one hour in private, bear on his or her heart and mind the interests and hopes of the Kingdom of God in the world. This wonderful intercession continued for over 100 years.

On August 27, 1872, a Moravian Prayer union was formed in England as a form of resuscitation of the Hourly Intercession, and today its members are found in all areas of the Moravian world. You are invited to join in this prayer covenant. The following prayer suggestions may be helpful:

Sunday: The Church At Worship. For her purity and peace, unity and power. For the congregation to which we belong or with which we worship. For the ministry of the word of God. For the winning of people into fellowship with Christ. For all church schools, youth ministries, and other church groups at work.

Monday: The Church At Work. For the church in its mission next door and in other lands. For new congregations and specialized ministries. For the workers and leaders in these endeavors. For the worker volunteers to carry out the mission of the church.

Tuesday: Home and School. For households. For the Christian education of the young, and that our children may be led to give themselves to Christ. For all schools and teachers. For young people enrolled in colleges and universities. For the training of ministers in theological seminaries.

Wednesday: For Those In Need. For all in special need, whether as aged, sick, poor, or homeless. For those in prison. For all victims of famine, oppression, aggression, and war.

Thursday: Our Nation and Our World. For those who govern and for those who are governed. For the guidance of God to all who are in authority. For unity of nations and all agencies for peace. For the whole human family and equal rights for all. For the guidance and blessing of God as humanity enters the future.

Friday: Our Own Church Fellowship. For the purity, zeal, and practice of the church as a witnessing fellowship of the love of God. That the church may be a light to the world wherever its congregations are found, and that it may be active in redeeming mission in these communities.

Saturday: The Witness of Christians. That all who confess the name of Christ may grow in the grace and knowledge of Jesus Christ as Lord and Savior.

"O thou King of kings and Lord of lords, who desirest that all people should dwell together in unity, let thy will be known and done among the nations; guide their feet into the way of peace. Remember us and all humanity in thy mercy. Deliver us from the sins which give rise to war and conflict, and strengthen within our hearts the will to establish righteousness and justice in the earth. Give unto us and to all who worship thee the sincere desire to live in peaceful and loving fellowship with all people. Fix our minds and hearts upon thine eternal purposes for your children on earth."

— A Prayer for Peace

THE *DAILY TEXTS* IN FAMILY WORSHIP

Almost from the very beginning the *Daily Texts* has been used as a guide for family worship as well as for private and personal devotions. The use of the *Daily Texts* in family worship will vary depending on the time available and the age of the children. One of the values of the *Daily Texts* is that it is adaptable to numerous patterns of use.

One pattern followed by many families is to begin the meal (usually breakfast or the evening meal) with the reading of the texts of the day and the accompanying hymn stanzas. After this, the family joins in the blessing or table grace. A suitable blessing may be chosen from among the following:

Come, Lord Jesus, our Guest to be,
and bless these gifts bestowed by thee.
Bless thy dear ones everywhere,
and keep them in thy loving care.

Be present at our table, Lord;
be here and everywhere adored;
from thine all-bounteous hand our food
may we receive with gratitude.

The worship of the family can then close with a prayer offered in the leader's own words or in those of the printed prayer offered in the *Daily Texts*. As a part of free prayer by the leader or in connection with the printed prayer, use can be made from day to day of the subjects of the Daily Topics for Prayer as given in the preceding pages.

HOW TO USE THE *DAILY TEXTS*

The strength of the *Daily Texts* lies in presenting the Scripture unhindered by illustration. The texts are left to stand alone and to speak to each reader in his or her life. This also allows the *Daily Texts* to be adaptable to different patterns of devotion and study.

Contents For Each Day

54   FEBRUARY

1 **Tuesday, February 23 — Psalm 29**
Genesis 50; Matthew 18:1–14

2 **For as the earth brings forth its shoots, so the Lord God will cause righteousness and praise to spring up before all the nations. Isaiah 61:11**

3 Plenteous grace with thee is found,   724
grace to cover all my sin;
let the healing streams abound;
make and keep me pure within.
Thou of life the fountain art,
freely let me take of thee;
spring thou up within my heart,
rise to all eternity.

4 **He who supplies seed to the sower and bread for food will supply and multiply your seed for sowing and increase the harvest of your righteousness. 2 Corinthians 9:10**

3 We thank you, our Creator,   453
for all things bright and good,
the seedtime and the harvest,
our life, our health, our food;
accept the gifts we offer
for all your love imparts,
and what you most would treasure—
our humble, thankful hearts.

5 While winter still holds fast to our world, it is spring in our hearts. Your Son shines warm, life-giving light upon your children, helping us to grow in faith and love for you. Feed that faith and nurture it, so that we may follow you. Amen.

1. **SCRIPTURE LESSONS:** At the top of each page for ongoing study. Not related to the printed texts. Monday through Saturday are part of a plan to read through the Psalms in one year and the rest of the Bible in two. Sundays and special days are the assigned lessons for that day of the church year from the Moravian Revised Common Lectionary, also common to many denominations.

2. **WATCHWORD FOR THE DAY:** From the Old Testament, the first printed text. It is to be a "watchword" to accompany you throughout the day. Usually a promise, encouragement, admonition, or comfort.

3. **HYMN VERSES:** Broken down by meter and usually related to the watchword or theme for the day. It is a devotional response or commentary on the text. Can be used for prayers.

4. **DOCTRINAL TEXT:** From the New Testament. Usually contains some point of Christian doctrine to expand on the watchword.

5. **PRAYER:** A response to God of praise, confession, thanksgiving, or intercession in light of the texts and hymn verses.

• Every Sunday and some church holidays, the *Daily Texts* page will include the **WATCHWORD FOR THE WEEK/ HOLIDAY**. Like the daily watchword, the weekly/holiday text is to accompany the reader throughout the week or holiday and is related to the events of the church year. These differ every year based upon the lectionary cycle.

Devotions
The printed texts, hymn verses, and prayers are the heart of the devotional guide. Their purpose is to help the reader get more closely in touch with God and to meditate upon the Word of God. When reading the texts, hymns and prayers, feel the encouragement found in them. Hear any word or correction for your life; ponder the great message of faith; meditate upon the hymn verses and prayers; feel God's presence surrounding you in faith; and in silence, hear God's word speaking to you.

These texts can also be the center of a daily spiritual diary where you keep a journal of your daily meditations and their meaning in your life.

ACKNOWLEDGMENTS

Bible texts in this publication are quoted from the *New Revised Standard Version Bible,* © 1989 by the Division of Christian Education of the National Council of the Churches of Christ in the United States of America, and are used by permission. Verses marked NIV are taken from *The Holy Bible New International Version®,* NIV®, © 1973, 1978, 1984, 2011 by Biblica, Inc.® Used by permission. All rights reserved worldwide. Verses marked NASB are taken from the *New American Standard Bible®,* © 1960, 1962, 1963, 1968, 1971, 1972, 1973, 1975, 1977, 1995 by The Lockman Foundation. Used by permission. Verses marked ESV are taken from *The Holy Bible, English Standard Version,* © 2001 by Crossway. Verses marked NKJV are taken from the *New King James Version®* © 1982 by Thomas Nelson, Inc. Used by permission. All rights reserved. Verses marked GNT are taken from the *Good News Translation,* ©1992 by the American Bible Society.

Sunday readings are taken from the *Revised Common Lectionary,* © 1992 by the Consultation on Common Texts (CCT).

Unless otherwise noted, hymn stanzas found in the *Daily Texts* are taken from the *Moravian Book of Worship,* 1995. The number found to the right of each stanza designates the source of the stanza in that hymnal. If the number is preceded by a p the hymn used is from one of the liturgies and the p designates the page number. The letter b after a number denotes the Hymnal and Liturgies of the Moravian Church Unitas Fratrum, 1920. The letter r after a number denotes the Hymnal of the Moravian Church, 1969. The letter s after a number denotes a hymn or song from *Sing to the Lord A New Song, A New Moravian Songbook,* 2013. When hymns are copyrighted, information is given at the bottom of the page; we gratefully acknowledge permission to use copyrighted material.

Hymn stanzas are broken down by meter except when space would not allow.

The Scripture readings for Monday through Saturday are part of a plan to read through the Old and New Testaments in two years and the Psalms in one year.

Friday, January 1 — Psalm 1
Genesis 1:1–2:3; Matthew 1:1–17

O give thanks to the Lord of lords, who alone does great wonders, for his steadfast love endures forever. Psalm 136:3–4

> Pardon for sin and a peace that endureth,   460*
> thine own dear presence to cheer and to guide;
> strength for today and bright hope for tomorrow,
> blessings all mine, with ten thousand beside!
> Great is thy faithfulness! Great is thy faithfulness!
> Morning by morning new mercies I see;
> all I have needed thy hand hath provided;
> great is thy faithfulness, Lord, unto me!

Now to him who by the power at work within us is able to accomplish abundantly far more than all we can ask or imagine, to him be glory in the church and in Christ Jesus to all generations, forever and ever. Amen. Ephesians 3:20–21

> Gracious Lord, gracious Lord,   528
> blessed is our lot indeed
> in your ransomed congregation;
> here we on your merits feed,
> and the well-springs of salvation,
> all the needy to revive and cheer,
> stream forth here, stream forth here.

Lord, through you all things are possible. As we sit at the precipice of a new year, may we look upon it with hope and expectation of what you will enable us to do in your name and through your love. Amen.

Saturday, January 2 — Psalm 2
Genesis 2:4–25; Matthew 1:18–25

He guides me along the right paths for his name's sake. Psalm 23:3 (NIV)

> He leadeth me: O blessed thought!   787
> O words with heav'nly comfort fraught!
> Whate'er I do, where'er I be,
> still 'tis God's hand that leadeth me.
> He leadeth me, he leadeth me;
> by his own hand he leadeth me,
> his faithful foll'wer I would be,
> for by his hand he leadeth me.

Jesus Christ says, "My sheep hear my voice. I know them, and they follow me." John 10:27

> Jesus makes my heart rejoice,   662
> I'm his sheep and know his voice;
> he's a Shepherd, kind and gracious,
> and his pastures are delicious;
> constant love to me he shows,
> yea, my very name he knows.

Guiding Spirit, may we recognize your voice as you call us by name into your wonderful kingdom: the kingdom you claim here on earth and the one where we will join you in heaven. Amen.

Second Sunday after Christmas

Watchword for the Week — God has made known to us the mystery of his will, according to his good pleasure that he set forth in Christ. Ephesians 1:9

Sunday, January 3 — Jeremiah 31:7–14; Psalm 147:12–20 Ephesians 1:3–14; John 1:(1–9),10–18

O come, let us worship and bow down, let us kneel before the Lord, our Maker! Psalm 95:6

> Praise to the Lord,   530
>   who will prosper your work and defend you;
> surely his goodness and mercy shall daily attend you.
> Ponder anew what the almighty can do
> if with his love he befriend you.

He called you out of darkness into his marvelous light. 1 Peter 2:9

> O come, O bright and morning star,   274
> and bring us comfort from afar!
> Dispel the shadows of the night,
> and turn our darkness into light.
> Rejoice! Rejoice!
> Immanuel shall come to you, O Israel!

Lord of light and love, we praise you for not only giving us life in your creation, but for also bringing the light of your love into the darkness of our lives. Amen.

Monday, January 4 — Psalm 3
Genesis 3,4; Matthew 2:1–12

**Search me, O God, and know my heart; test
me and know my thoughts. See if there is any
wicked way in me, and lead me in the way
everlasting. Psalm 139:23–24**

> Come now, O Lord,   742
>   and search each inmost thought.
> Ask if we love and serve you as we ought.
> Do we attempt to do your holy will?
> Does constant love for you our poor hearts fill?

**Christ may dwell in your hearts through faith.
Ephesians 3:17**

> Faith finds in Christ our ev'ry need   700
> to save or strengthen us indeed;
> we now receive the grace sent down,
> which makes us share his cross and crown.

Forgiving Lord, test our hearts and guide us in your
ways. May the sins in our hearts be expelled by
your love and may your righteousness inspire our
faith. Amen.

Tuesday, January 5 — Psalm 4
Genesis 5; Matthew 2:13–23

Satisfy us early with your mercy, that we may rejoice and be glad all our days! Psalm 90:14 (NKJV)

Praise him for his grace and favor   529
to his people in distress.
Praise him, still the same forever,
slow to chide, and swift to bless.
Alleluia! Alleluia!
Glorious in his faithfulness!

All the people would get up early in the morning to listen to him in the temple. Luke 21:38

O Word of God Incarnate,   p23
O Wisdom from on high,
O Truth unchanged, unchanging,
O Light of our dark sky;
we praise you for the radiance
that from the Scripture's page,
a lantern to our footsteps,
shines on from age to age.

Lord of mercy, all that you say and do is inscribed upon the hearts of the faithful. May we know the joy of your mercy and your call for our lives. Amen.

Epiphany of the Lord

Watchword for the Epiphany — Arise, shine; for your light has come, and the glory of the Lord has risen upon you. Isaiah 60:1

Wednesday, January 6 — Psalm 5
Genesis 6:1–7:10; Matthew 3

Epiphany of the Lord — Isaiah 60:1–6; Psalm 72:1–7,10–14
Ephesians 3:1–12; Matthew 2:1–12

The heavens are yours, the earth also is yours; the world and all that is in it—you have founded them. The north and the south—you created them. Psalm 89:11–12

Praise the Lord! You heav'ns, adore him,   454
praise him, angels in the height;
sun and moon, rejoice before him;
praise him, all you stars and light.
Praise the Lord! For he has spoken;
worlds his mighty voice obeyed;
laws which never shall be broken
for their guidance he has made.

In Christ all things in heaven and on earth were created, things visible and invisible, whether thrones or dominions or rulers or powers—all things have been created through him and for him. Colossians 1:16

His sov'reign pow'r without our aid   455
formed us of clay and gave us breath;
and when like wand'ring sheep we strayed,
he saved us from the pow'r of death.

Creative Lord, we are blessed to be a part of your creation. May we be guided and inspired by your creative acts. May all that we do be done for your glory. Amen.

Thursday, January 7 — Psalm 6
Genesis 7:11–8:22; Matthew 4:1–11

All the nations you have made shall come and bow down before you, O Lord, and shall glorify your name. Psalm 86:9

Immortal, invisible, God only wise,   457
in light inaccessible hid from our eyes,
most blessed, most glorious, O Ancient of Days,
almighty, victorious, your great name we praise.

The grace of God has appeared, bringing salvation to all. Titus 2:11

Hail, all hail, victorious Lord and Savior,   p82
you have burst the bonds of death,
grant us, as to Mary, the great favor
to embrace your feet in faith:
you have in our stead the curse endured,
and for us eternal life procured;
joyful, we with one accord
hail you as our risen Lord.

In this seemingly broken world, O Lord, your divine love shines through. Guide the nations into peace and understanding and help us to trust in your salvation and not in our own works. Amen.

Friday, January 8 — Psalm 7:1–9
Genesis 9; Matthew 4:12–25

Break up your fallow ground, for it is time to seek the Lord until he comes to rain righteousness on you. Hosea 10:12 (NASB)

> Lord God, with shame I now confess   p32
> I've turned away from you;
> forgive me all my sin today,
> my heart and soul renew.

Do not be conformed to this world, but be transformed by the renewing of your minds, so that you may discern what is the will of God—what is good and acceptable and perfect. Romans 12:2

> They live to him who bought them   516
>   with his blood,
> baptized them with his Spirit, pure and good;
> and in true faith and ever-burning love,
> their hearts and hopes ascend to seek above
> th'eternal good.

Loving Lord, you call us into repentance, a moment for us to be honest with you. Let the false luster of our lives be transformed by the beauty of your kingdom. May we be renewed by your Spirit in order to live the life to which you call us. Amen.

Saturday, January 9 — Psalm 7:10–17
Genesis 10:1–11:9; Matthew 5:1–16

The Lord is a stronghold for the oppressed, a stronghold in times of trouble. Psalm 9:9

A mighty fortress is our God,   788*
a sword and shield victorious;
he breaks the cruel oppressor's rod
and wins salvation glorious.
The old satanic foe
has sworn to work us woe!
With craft and dreadful might
he arms himself to fight.
On earth he has no equal.

Paul wrote: I am content with weaknesses, insults, hardships, persecutions, and calamities for the sake of Christ. 2 Corinthians 12:10

While life's dark maze I tread,   705
and griefs around me spread,
O, be my guide;
make darkness turn to day,
wipe sorrow's tears away,
nor let me ever stray
from you aside.

Sustaining Creator, in our weakness you give us strength; in hardship, an oasis; in persecution or calamities, protection. You are everything to us, dear Lord. Beyond our temporal concerns you bring love and hope. May we be such beacons in the lives of others. Amen.

* © 1978 by *Lutheran Book of Worship*. Reprinted by permission of Augsburg Fortress.

First Sunday after the Epiphany

Watchword for the Week — God says, "Do not fear, for I have redeemed you; I have called you by name, you are mine." Isaiah 43:1

Sunday, January 10 — Isaiah 43:1–7; Psalm 29
Acts 8:14–17; Luke 3:15–17,21–22

I will remove the heart of stone from their flesh and give them a heart of flesh, so that they may follow my statutes and keep my ordinances and obey them. Ezekiel 11:19–20

I, the Lord of snow and rain,   641*
I have borne my people's pain.
I have wept for love of them,
they turn away.
I will break their hearts of stone,
give them hearts for love alone.
I will speak my word to them.
Whom shall I send?

If anyone is in Christ, there is a new creation: everything old has passed away; see, everything has become new! 2 Corinthians 5:17

Your dying cleansed the world of sin,   333**
and all who die with you are clean,
washed in your blood, we lose our stains,
and with your cross you break our chains.

You, O Lord, revel in a repentant heart. Teach us the value of humility before your throne and cleanse us from all unrighteousness. May we be dressed in the white robes of your salvation. Amen.

* © 1981 by Daniel L. Schutte and New Dawn Music, PO Box 13248, Portland, OR 97213. All rights reserved. Used with permission.

** Text by Jaroslav J. Vajda © 1983 Concordia Publishing House. Used with permission. www.cph.org.

Monday, January 11 — Psalm 8
Genesis 11:10–12:9; Matthew 5:17–26

Take delight in the Lord, and he will give you the desires of your heart. Psalm 37:4

Sincerely I have sought you, Lord,   510
O let me not from you depart;
to know your will and keep from sin,
your word I cherish in my heart.

Whatever you ask for in prayer, believe that you have received it, and it will be yours. Mark 11:24

Have we trials and temptations?   743
Is there trouble anywhere?
We should never be discouraged;
take it to the Lord in prayer!
Can we find a friend so faithful
who will all our sorrows share?
Jesus knows our ev'ry weakness;
take it to the Lord in prayer!

What should be the benefit of prayer, O God, but that we are able to speak to you, to know that you care so deeply to listen to our needs, sorrows, and joys? May we always be willing to take everything to you in prayer. Amen.

Tuesday, January 12 — Psalm 9:1–10
Genesis 12:10–13:18; Matthew 5:27–42

One who rules over people justly, ruling in the fear of God, is like the light of morning, like the sun rising on a cloudless morning. 2 Samuel 23:3–4

> Savior, blessed Savior,   778
> listen while we sing,
> hearts and voices raising
> praises to our King.
> All we have to offer,
> all we hope to do,
> body, soul, and spirit,
> all we yield to you.

Keep watch over yourselves and over all the flock, of which the Holy Spirit has made you overseers. Acts 20:28

> Chosen flock, your faithful Shepherd follow,   444
> who laid down his life for you;
> all your days unto his service hallow,
> each to be disciples true;
> evermore rejoice to do his pleasure,
> be the fullness of his grace your treasure;
> should success your labor crown,
> give the praise to him alone.

Gentle Shepherd, you grant us your authority of love. In every way that we find ourselves in authority over others, let us take your example and lead in gentleness and love. Amen.

Wednesday, January 13 — Psalm 9:11–20
Genesis 14,15; Matthew 5:43–6:4

The Lord says, "I will be with them in trouble, I will rescue them and honor them." Psalm 91:15

> O God, our help in ages past,   461
> our hope for years to come,
> our shelter from the stormy blast,
> and our eternal home!

Through death Jesus might free those who all their lives were held in slavery by the fear of death. Hebrews 2:15

> Fear not, children, joyful stand   789
> on the borders of your land;
> Jesus Christ, your Father's Son,
> bids you undismayed go on.

O, to be free, dear Lord! We are no longer slaves to our sins and death but to the joy you offer us in serving you. Call us into the service of your love. Amen.

Thursday, January 14 — Psalm 10:1–11
Genesis 16,17; Matthew 6:5–18

No inhabitant will say, "I am sick;" the people who live there will be forgiven their iniquity. Isaiah 33:24 ·

> Blessed inhabitants of Zion,   522
> washed in the Redeemer's blood!
> Jesus, whom their souls rely on,
> makes them kings and priests to God;
> 'tis his love his people raises
> in his courts to reign as kings,
> and as priests, his solemn praises
> each for a thank-off'ring brings.

Jesus said to the paralytic, "Son, your sins are forgiven." Mark 2:5

> Much forgiven, may I learn   779
> love for hatred to return;
> then my heart assured shall be
> you, my God, have pardoned me.

Too often, loving Lord, we fall victim to the sickness of sin. We allow ourselves to become complacent. Heal us with your forgiving love. Inspire us to lead a life of joy in your service. Amen.

Friday, January 15 — Psalm 10:12–18
Genesis 18; Matthew 6:19–34

**You know me, O Lord; you see me; and you
examine my heart's attitude toward you.
Jeremiah 12:3 (NASB)**

> Grant by guidance from above   586
> that obedience, faith, and love
> show our hearts to you are giv'n,
> that our treasure is in heav'n.

**Do not pronounce judgment before the time,
before the Lord comes, who will bring to light
the things now hidden in darkness and will
disclose the purposes of the heart. Then each one
will receive commendation from God.
1 Corinthians 4:5**

> Show'rs of blessing, show'rs of blessing   636
> from the Lord proceed,
> strength supplying, strength supplying
> in the time of need;
> for no servant of our King
> ever lacked for anything.
> He will never, he will never
> break the bruised reed.

O Lord, we open our hearts to you. May they be
found not wanting, but ideal for your kingdom here
on earth and your home in heaven. While we walk
in your creation, may all that we do be pleasant in
your sight. Amen.

Saturday, January 16 — Psalm 11
Genesis 19:1–29; Matthew 7:1–12

You shall have no other gods before me.
Exodus 20:3

> Most gracious God and Lord,   488
> the world's almighty Savior,
> worthy to be adored by all,
> both now and ever!
> Those souls are blessed indeed
> who cling to you in faith,
> as you for us were laid
> low in the dust of death.

No one can serve two masters. Matthew 6:24

> Jesus, Master, whose I am,   614
> purchased yours alone to be,
> by your blood, O spotless Lamb,
> shed so willingly for me,
> let my heart be all your own,
> let me live to you alone.

Heavenly Lord, use us! We are your own! Amen.

Second Sunday after the Epiphany

Watchword for the Week — Now there are varieties of gifts, but the same Spirit; and there are varieties of services, but the same Lord. 1 Corinthians 12:4–5

Sunday, January 17 — Isaiah 62:1–5; Psalm 36:5–10 1 Corinthians 12:1–11; John 2:1–11

My people shall be satisfied with my bounty, says the Lord. Jeremiah 31:14

Come, let us all with gladness raise　　　519
a joyous song of thanks and praise
to God who rules the heav'nly host,
God, Father, Son, and Holy Ghost.

God is able to provide you with every blessing in abundance, so that by always having enough of everything, you may share abundantly in every good work. 2 Corinthians 9:8

Only be still and wait his pleasure　　　712
in cheerful hope with heart content.
He fills your needs to fullest measure
with what discerning love has sent;
doubt not our inmost wants are known
to him who chose us for his own.

Fill us, O Lord. Fill us with your grace to fullest measure that we may have it in abundance, that it may grow through our spirits, and that it may be an offering unto you and a gift to all whom we serve in your love. Amen.

Monday, January 18 — Psalm 12
Genesis 19:30–20:18; Matthew 7:13–23

The Lord makes a way in the sea, a path in the mighty waters. Isaiah 43:16

> Refresh your people on their toilsome way;   p139
> lead us from night to never-ending day;
> fill all our lives with heav'n-born love and grace,
> until at last we meet before your face.

Jesus said, "Do not fear, only believe." Mark 5:36

> We walk by faith and not by sight;   713
> no gracious words we hear from Christ,
> who spoke as none e'er spoke;
> but we believe him near.

Lead on, lead on, O glorious Lord. Lead us on the path of righteousness! Turn not back to see if we follow; we follow you! Amen.

Tuesday, January 19 — Psalm 13
Genesis 21; Matthew 7:24–8:4

Do not put the Lord your God to the test. Deuteronomy 6:16

> This is our Father's world: 456
> O let us not forget
> that though the wrong is often strong,
> God is the ruler yet.
> He trusts us with his world,
> to keep it clean and fair—
> all earth and trees, all skies and seas,
> all creatures ev'rywhere.

Jesus Christ says, "If you love me, you will keep my commandments." John 14:15

> Blessed be the tie that binds   680
> our hearts in Christian love;
> the fellowship of kindred minds
> is like to that above.

Heavenly Lord, too often our actions could press you toward anger, yet you act out of love and concern for us. Guide us ever in lives of your love. Amen.

Wednesday, January 20 — Psalm 14
Genesis 22; Matthew 8:5–22

We also will serve the Lord, for he is our God. Joshua 24:18

> To serve the present age,   645
> my calling to fulfill,
> O may it all my pow'rs engage
> to do my Master's will.

Think of us in this way, as servants of Christ and stewards of God's mysteries. 1 Corinthians 4:1

> The task your wisdom has assigned   638
> here let me cheerfully fulfill,
> in all my work your presence find
> and prove your good and perfect will.

In us, O Lord, you have entrusted a sacred obligation. To us you have shown the great mysteries of your love; in humility you find greatness, in weakness you find strength, in self-giving you find abundance, and in death you find life. May we always be guided by the mystery of your love. Amen.

Thursday, January 21 — Psalm 15
Genesis 23:1–24:25; Matthew 8:23–34

**Then we your people, the flock of your pasture, will give thanks to you forever; from generation to generation we will recount your praise.
Psalm 79:13**

> Join we all with one accord;   525
> praise we all our common Lord;
> for we all have heard his voice,
> all have made his will our choice.
> Join we with the saints of old,
> no more strangers in the fold,
> one the Shepherd who us sought,
> one the flock his blood has bought.

**With joy give thanks to the Father, who has made you fit to have your share of what God has reserved for his people in the kingdom of light.
Colossians 1:12 (GNT)**

> Hear us, O Lord, as we now pray,   536*
> dedicate us to your way;
> lead us to work that bears your fruit,
> giving knowledge of your truth.
> Open our door and enter in,
> rescue from darkness and from sin.
> Strengthen according to your might,
> share with us the promised life.

Great Shepherd, we are your flock, honored to hear our names called by you. You, Lord, give us green pastures to lie down in and still waters to walk beside. In you we find all that we need for true purpose for our lives. Call on us; we are yours. Amen.

* © 1991 by Beth E. Hanson

Friday, January 22 — Psalm 16:1–6
Genesis 24:26–66; Matthew 9:1–13

O give thanks to the Lord, call on his name, make known his deeds among the peoples. Psalm 105:1

Thanks we give and adoration   p36
for the gospel's joyful sound;
may the fruits of your salvation
in our hearts and lives abound;
may your presence, may your presence,
with us evermore be found.

Paul wrote: We may proclaim the good news in lands beyond you. 2 Corinthians 10:16

We've a message to give to the nations,   621
that the Lord who's reigning above
has sent us his Son to save us,
and show us that God is love,
and show us that God is love.
For the darkness shall turn to dawning,
and the dawning to noonday bright;
and Christ's great kingdom shall come on earth,
the kingdom of love and light!

We find comfort in your message and purpose in its proclamation, heavenly Savior, but too often we feel like we are in a world that doesn't want to listen. Remind us that it is your message that we are called to share, not our own. Help us to take ourselves out of the message and share only your true light. Amen.

Saturday, January 23 — Psalm 16:7–11
Genesis 25; Matthew 9:14–26

Anxiety weighs down the human heart, but a good word cheers it up. Proverbs 12:25

Other refuge have I none;   724
hangs my helpless soul on thee;
leave, ah, leave me not alone,
still support and comfort me.
All my trust on thee is stayed,
all my help from thee I bring;
cover my defenseless head
with the shadow of thy wing.

Let your gentleness be known to everyone. The Lord is near. Philippians 4:5

Take my hands, Lord Jesus,   578*
    let them work for you,
make them strong and gentle, kind in all I do;
let me watch you, Jesus, 'til I'm gentle too,
'til my hands are kind hands, quick to work for you.

Lord of love and kindness, help us to show your true power. May we seek not our own joy but to bring happiness to others; not our own security but to help others find hope; not our own peace but a harmony that brings others together. Grant us your love. Amen.

Third Sunday after the Epiphany

Watchword for the Week — Let the words of my mouth and the meditation of my heart be acceptable to you, O Lord, my rock and my redeemer. Psalm 19:14

Sunday, January 24 — Nehemiah 8:1–3,5–6,8–10; Psalm 19
1 Corinthians 12:12–31a; Luke 4:14–21

When I felt secure, I said, "I will never be shaken," but when you hid your face, I was dismayed. Psalm 30:6–7 (NIV)

My soul before you prostrate lies;   721
to you, its Source, my spirit flies;
O turn to me your cheering face;
I'm poor, enrich me with your grace.

God opposes the proud, but gives grace to the humble. Humble yourselves therefore under the mighty hand of God, so that he may exalt you in due time. Cast all your anxiety on him, because he cares for you. 1 Peter 5:5–7

Give deep humility;   750
the sense of godly sorrow give,
a strong desiring confidence
to hear your voice and live.

Lord of all blessings, we often become content with our lives, thinking we will never be shaken; but when hardship arises we fear losing you. You are never far from us and we need only to reach out with humble spirits, acknowledging your grace and love even in the most difficult times. Amen.

Monday, January 25 — Psalm 17:1–7
Genesis 26; Matthew 9:27–38

He will bless those who fear the Lord, both small and great. Psalm 115:13

Bless, O Lord, we pray, your congregation;   445
bless each home and family;
bless the youth, the rising generation;
blessed may your dear children be;
bless your servants, grant them help and favor;
you to glorify be their endeavor.
Lord, on you we humbly call;
let your blessing rest on all.

Come; for everything is ready now. Luke 14:17

Ready, Lord, I'm ready, Lord,   601*
to follow where you lead.
Show me, Lord, just show me, Lord,
the service you will need.
Ready, Lord, I'm ready, Lord,
I'm ready, come what may,
so call me, Lord, just call me, Lord,
and I'll be on your way.

Gracious Lord, through your blessings we become
ready for all things. We are strengthened with your
grace and guided by your Spirit. We hope for every
opportunity to show that we are ready to answer
your call. Amen.

Tuesday, January 26 — Psalm 17:8–15
Genesis 27:1–29; Matthew 10:1–16

The whole earth is filled with awe at your wonders; where morning dawns, where evening fades, you call forth songs of joy. Psalm 65:8 (NIV)

Let the whole creation cry,   p127
"Glory to the Lord on high!"
Heav'n and earth awake and sing,
"Praise to our almighty King!"
Praise God, angel hosts above,
ever bright and fair in love;
sun and moon, lift up your voice;
night and stars, in God rejoice.

The jailer and his entire household rejoiced that he had become a believer in God. Acts 16:34

And can it be that I should gain   773
an int'rest in the Savior's blood?
Died he for me, who caused his pain—
for me, who caused his bitter death?
Amazing love! How can it be
that you, my Lord, should die for me?
Amazing love! How can it be
that you, my Lord, should die for me?

From the first morning of our lives to the last evening that falls upon us, we live in your joy, Creator God. It is a blessing to be one with you, and with all those who serve you. As we continue our journeys here in your creation, may we hold each moment dearly. Amen.

Wednesday, January 27 — Psalm 18:1–6
Genesis 27:30–28:9; Matthew 10:17–25

Lord, you gave your good spirit to instruct our ancestors. Nehemiah 9:20

Move in our midst, O Spirit of God.   489
Go with us down from your holy hill.
Walk with us through the storm and the calm.
Spirit of God, now go with us still.

We have received not the spirit of the world, but the Spirit that is from God, so that we may understand the gifts bestowed on us by God. 1 Corinthians 2:12

Spirit of God, who dwells within my heart,   490
wean it from sin, through all its pulses move.
Stoop to my weakness, mighty as you are,
and make me love you as I ought to love.

Loving Spirit, we rejoice because you have called us into relationship with God. You have opened to us God's word which proclaims the wonders of God's work. You make us aware of all God's miracles surrounding us each day. Amen.

Thursday, January 28 — Psalm 18:7–15
Genesis 28:10–29:14; Matthew 10:26–42

The Lord said to Moses, "You shall speak all that I command you." Exodus 7:1,2

God, grant me strength to do   615
with ready heart and willing,
whatever you command,
my calling here fulfilling;
and do it when I ought,
with zeal and joyfulness;
and bless the work I've wrought,
for you must give success.

And now, Lord, grant to your servants to speak your word with all boldness. Acts 4:29

Lord, have mercy, Lord, have mercy   636
on each land and place
where your servants, where your servants
preach the word of grace;
life and pow'r on them bestow,
them with needful strength endow,
that with boldness, that with boldness
they may you confess.

In a world that needs your message of love so dearly, Lord, give us words to share and strength to share them. Make our lives your message to all with whom you bring us into contact. May they hear your words in all that we do. Amen.

Friday, January 29 — Psalm 18:16–24
Genesis 29:15–30:24; Matthew 11:1–10

Justice, and only justice, you shall pursue, so that you may live. Deuteronomy 16:20

From search for wealth and power   683*
and scorn of truth and right,
from trust in bombs that shower
destruction through the night,
from pride of race and station
and blindness to your way,
deliver ev'ry nation,
eternal God, we pray.

Pursue righteousness, godliness, faith, love, endurance, gentleness. 1 Timothy 6:11

Take my motives and my will,   647
all your purpose to fulfill.
Take my heart—it is your own;
it shall be your royal throne.

Lord of righteousness, make all your treasures our
pursuit. You brought into the turmoil of this world
all good and great joy. Help us to focus our lives
on all that you have given us. Guide us to live lives
that show the joy of your creation. Amen.

Saturday, January 30 — Psalm 18:25–29
Genesis 30:25–31:21; Matthew 11:11–24

Let us go with you, for we have heard that God is with you. Zechariah 8:23

> O that with yonder sacred throng   403
> we at his feet may fall;
> we'll join the everlasting song,
> and crown him Lord of all.

Now among those who went up to worship at the festival were some Greeks. They came to Philip, who was from Bethsaida in Galilee, and said to him, "Sir, we wish to see Jesus." John 12:20–21

> Fairest Lord Jesus! King of creation!   470
> Son of God and Son of man!
> Truly I'd love thee, truly I'd serve thee,
> light of my soul, my joy, my crown.

O, they wish to see Jesus; how we have longed
for the same thing, Lord! We forget that you are
all around us: in a child's smile, in a loved one's
embrace, in outstretched hands, in every kind word.
"Sir, they wish to see Jesus;" may they see you in us.
Amen.

Fourth Sunday after the Epiphany

Watchword for the Week — For now we see in a mirror, dimly, but then we will see face to face. 1 Corinthians 13:12

Sunday, January 31 — Jeremiah 1:4–10; Psalm 71:1–6
1 Corinthians 13:1–13; Luke 4:21–30

**From the least to the greatest of them, everyone is greedy for unjust gain; and from prophet to priest, everyone deals falsely. They have treated the wound of my people carelessly, saying, "Peace, peace," when there is no peace.
Jeremiah 6:13–14**

Cure your children's warring madness,   751*
bend our pride to your control;
shame our wanton, selfish gladness,
rich in things and poor in soul.
Grant us wisdom, grant us courage,
lest we miss your kingdom's goal,
lest we miss your kingdom's goal.

**Paul wrote: I am not seeking my own good but the good of many, so that they may be saved.
1 Corinthians 10:33 (NIV)**

Minds to think and hearts to love—   649
God's good gifts to me and you;
minds and hearts he gave to us
to help each other the whole day through.

Generous Lord, infuse our spirits with your love and compassion that we might see the broken spirits of others and respond as you have shown us. Where there is need, help us to meet it with your kindness. May all that is good be seen in us, your children. Amen.

*   Used by permission of Elinor Fosdick Downs

Monday, February 1 — Psalm 18:30–36
Genesis 31:22–55; Matthew 11:25–12:8

Lord God, do not destroy the people who are your very own possession, whom you redeemed in your greatness. Deuteronomy 9:26

> Church, rejoice! Raise your voice,   631
> sing Jehovah's worthy praise;
> extol his name forever;
> laud him, our God and Savior;
> proclaim to ev'ry nation
> the tidings of salvation;
> bear the witness to his greatness;
> spread the story of his glory
> to the earth's remotest bounds.

Paul wrote: I am confident of this, that the one who began a good work among you will bring it to completion by the day of Jesus Christ. Philippians 1:6

> And so, good Savior, now we pray: 18s*
> grant us your Spirit's pow'r
> as in the past, so in our day
> and ev'ry future hour:
> with hope may our lives testify
> that you all needful gifts supply
> to serve the world and unify
> your church for life on high.

Gracious God, your greatness redeems us. Guide us as we work to bring others to you, so they too can know you. In your name we pray. Amen.

* C. Daniel Crews (1999). © 2013 by Interprovincial Board of Communication and Moravian Music Foundation.

Tuesday, February 2 — Psalm 18:37–45
Genesis 32:1–21; Matthew 12:9–21

The earth feared and was still when God rose up to establish judgment, to save all the oppressed of the earth. Psalm 76:8–9

> Heal division; love renew;   521*
> help us all to turn to you.
> Mighty Shepherd, gather near
> all your sheep oppressed by fear:
> have mercy, Lord.

The eyes of the Lord are on the righteous, and his ears are open to their prayer. But the face of the Lord is against those who do evil. 1 Peter 3:12

> Had I the grace to seek his face   596
> in any trying hour!
> Help from none will he withhold
> who implores his power.

Heavenly Savior, yours is the true power over evil. Hear us as we bring our prayers for the oppressed of this world. Shine your light and power on those in desperate need of your love and care. Amen.

*   © 1994 by C. Daniel Crews

Wednesday, February 3 — Psalm 18:46–50
Genesis 32:22–33:20; Matthew 12:22–32

The Lord of hosts has planned, and who will annul it? His hand is stretched out, and who will turn it back? Isaiah 14:27

On this, our festive day,   633
your people here adore you;
we come to sing and pray
and lay our gifts before you.
Your hand has helped us on
through ev'ry passing year;
now, Father, Spirit, Son,
our grateful praises hear!

If God is for us, who is against us? Romans 8:31

O Jesus, you have promised   603
to all who follow you
that where you are in glory
your servants shall be too.
And Jesus, I have promised
to serve you to the end;
O give me grace to follow,
my master and my friend.

Holy Protector, forgive us for those times when we believe we can handle this world on our own. Your mighty yet gentle hand guides us through both the good and trying times of our lives. Know that we are for you. Amen.

Thursday, February 4 — Psalm 19:1–6
Genesis 34; Matthew 12:33–45

The Lord is just in all his ways, and kind in all his doings. Psalm 145:17

Come now, Incarnate Word,   555
our just and mighty Lord,
our prayer attend.
Come and your people bless
and give your word success;
strengthen your righteousness,
Savior and Friend!

Lord, who will not fear and glorify your name? For you alone are holy. All nations will come and worship before you, for your judgments have been revealed. Revelation 15:4

Rejoice, all those in Christ's command!   24s*
Again, we say, rejoice!
With hearts and minds and adoration,
proudly lift your voice.
Declare good news to all the world;
from mountains, shout and sing!
With ev'ry breath, give all you are
to Christ, our Lord and King!

O Savior and Friend, we join the nations in singing
your praise and living our lives in your glory.
Help us to follow your way and heed your kind
judgments. In your name we pray. Amen.

*   © 2009 by Zachariah D. Bailey

Friday, February 5 — Psalm 19:7–14
Genesis 35:1–36:8; Matthew 12:46–13:9

Take care what you do, for there is no perversion of justice with the Lord our God, or partiality, or taking of bribes. 2 Chronicles 19:7

Because the Lord our God is good,   539
his mercy is forever sure.
His truth at all times firmly stood,
and shall from age to age endure.

While Jesus was having dinner at Matthew's house, many tax collectors and sinners came and ate with him and his disciples. Matthew 9:10 (NIV)

Holy Spirit, ever working   495
through the church's ministry;
quick'ning, strength'ning, and absolving,
setting captive sinners free;
Holy Spirit, ever binding
age to age and soul to soul
in communion never ending,
you we worship and extol.

Father, we come to you as sinners. You know our deepest faults and wayward deeds. Yet, you invite us to your table, welcome us as disciples, and forgive us our trespasses. For these mercies, we thank you every day. Amen.

Saturday, February 6 — Psalm 20
Genesis 36:9–43; Matthew 13:10–23

David said to his son Solomon, "The Lord God is with you. He will not fail you or forsake you, until all the work for the service of the house of the Lord is finished." 1 Chronicles 28:20

> Blessed are the strong but gentle,   595
> trained to serve a higher will,
> wise to know th'eternal purpose
> which their Father shall fulfill.
> Blessed are they who with true passion
> strive to make the right prevail,
> for the earth is God's possession
> and his purpose will not fail.

The Lord will give you understanding in all things. 2 Timothy 2:7

> O teach us all your perfect will   734
> to understand and to fulfill:
> when human insight fails, give light;
> this will direct our steps aright.

Gracious Lord, you give us greater knowledge of our world. Your light and grace lead us to a place of hope and love. May we have the courage to follow. Amen.

Last Sunday after the Epiphany
Transfiguration of our Lord

Watchword for the Week — And when they looked up, they saw no one except Jesus himself alone. Matthew 17:8

Sunday, February 7 — Exodus 34:29–35; Psalm 99
2 Corinthians 3:12–4:2; Luke 9:28–36,(37–43)

Trust in the Lord with all your heart, and do not rely on your own insight. In all your ways acknowledge him, and he will make straight your paths. Proverbs 3:5–6

> Thus may we, as your anointed,   716
> walk with you in truth and grace
> in the path you have appointed,
> 'til we reach your dwelling-place.

Christ says, "Abide in me as I abide in you. Just as the branch cannot bear fruit by itself unless it abides in the vine, neither can you unless you abide in me." John 15:4

> Those in Jesus Christ abiding,   717
> and from self-dependence free,
> in none else but him confiding
> walk in true simplicity.

O Redeemer, today we remember how Jesus' face shone like the sun and his clothes became dazzling white as you prepared to save the world through him. May your bright light continue to shine on us always. Amen.

Monday, February 8 — Psalm 21
Genesis 37; Matthew 13:24–35

They went home, joyful and glad in heart for all the good things the Lord had done for his servant David and his people Israel. 1 Kings 8:66 (NIV)

O then with hymns of praise   517
these hallowed courts shall ring;
our voices we will raise
the Three in One to sing,
and thus proclaim in joyful song
both loud and long that glorious name.

Yes, everything is for your sake, so that grace, as it extends to more and more people, may increase thanksgiving, to the glory of God. 2 Corinthians 4:15

We thank you then, O Father,   p162
for all things bright and good,
the seedtime and the harvest,
our life, our health, our food;
help us show thanksgiving
for all you freely give;
to love you in our neighbor,
and by the way we live.
All good gifts around us
are sent from heav'n above;
Then thank the Lord,
O thank the Lord for all his love.

Lord, the good you do for our sake fills our hearts with joy. Teach us to bring that joy to others, so they too may behold your love and grace. In your name we pray. Amen.

Tuesday, February 9 — Psalm 22:1–8
Genesis 38; Matthew 13:36–46

The eyes of all look to you, and you give them their food in due season. You open your hand, satisfying the desire of every living thing. Psalm 145:15–16

> Lord, be ever my protector;   568
> with me stay, all the day,
> ever my director.
> Holy, holy, holy giver
> of all good, life and food,
> reign adored forever.

Look at the birds of the air; they neither sow nor reap nor gather into barns, and yet your heavenly Father feeds them. Are you not of more value than they? Matthew 6:26

> This is gift of sweetest savor,   419*
> feast bestowed by heaven's favor,
> miracle and meal in union,
> wondrous grace of our communion.

Lord Jesus, in all we see and do, we recognize your life-giving touch. We thank you for feeding our hearts, our souls, and our minds. May we give ourselves entirely to you. Amen.

*   © by Dirk French

Ash Wednesday

Wednesday, February 10 — Psalm 22:9–21
Genesis 39; Matthew 13:47–58

Ash Wednesday — Joel 2:1–2,12–17; Psalm 51:1–17
2 Corinthians 5:20b–6:10; Matthew 6:1–6,16–21

In the morning, Lord, you hear my voice; in the morning I lay my requests before you and wait expectantly. Psalm 5:3 (NIV)

> Come now, O Lord, and teach us how to pray.   742
> Teach us to ask ourselves from day to day
> if we are yours and yours alone will be
> through earthly days and through eternity.

In the morning, while it was still very dark, Jesus got up and went out to a deserted place, and there he prayed. Mark 1:35

> For us he prayed; for us he taught;   485
> for us his daily works he wrought:
> by words and signs and actions thus
> still seeking not himself but us.

Holy Father, as we begin our Lenten journey, guide us to pray as you prayed. Help us to hear your voice during this season of preparation. Despite the dark days to come, we know that light and life await us come Easter. Amen.

Thursday, February 11 — Psalm 22:22–28
Genesis 40:1–41:16; Matthew 14:1–14

I will sing to the Lord, because he has dealt bountifully with me. Psalm 13:6

Our heav'nly Father, Source of love,   p38
to you our hearts we raise.
Your all-sustaining power we prove,
and gladly sing your praise.

Mary said, "My soul magnifies the Lord, and my spirit rejoices in God my Savior." Luke 1:46–47

Know that the Lord is God indeed;   539
he formed us all without our aid.
We are the flock he comes to feed,
the sheep who by his hand were made.
O enter then his gates with joy;
within his courts his praise proclaim.
Let thankful songs your tongues employ;
O bless and magnify his name.

Gracious God, lifting our voices and singing your praise bring us closer to you. Hear us as we rejoice, thanking you for all the goodness and strength you bring to us and to the world. In your name we pray. Amen.

Friday, February 12 — Psalm 22:29–31
Genesis 41:17–57; Matthew 14:15–24

In the place where it was said to them, "You are not my people," it shall be said to them, "Children of the living God." Hosea 1:10

> Children of the heav'nly King,   789
> as you journey, sweetly sing;
> sing your Savior's worthy praise,
> glorious in his works and ways.

To all who received him, who believed in his name, he gave power to become children of God. John 1:12

> As twig is bent, so grows the tree.   78s*
> As child is nurtured, she will be.
> Within each soul a servant sleeps;
> awake the love that childhood keeps.

Heavenly Father, we come to you as strangers, yet are welcomed as your children. Enfold your loving arms around us, protect us from evil and show us the right path to follow. With hope, we pray. Amen.

* John D. Rights (2009). © 2009 by Mary White Rights.

Saturday, February 13 — Psalm 23
Genesis 42; Matthew 14:25–15:9

Judgment will again be righteous, and all the upright in heart will follow it. Psalm 94:15 (NASB)

> Let justice roll on like the rivers of time,   56s*
> and righteousness flow in continuous stream,
> that we in God's wisdom and love may abide
> and live in community, not selfish pride.

Blessed are those who hunger and thirst for righteousness, for they will be filled. Matthew 5:6

> I love to tell the story,   625
> for those who know it best
> seem hungering and thirsting
> to hear it, like the rest.
> And when, in scenes of glory,
> I sing the new, new song,
> I'll sing the old, old story
> that I have loved so long.
> I love to tell the story;
> I'll sing this theme in glory
> and tell the old, old story
> of Jesus and his love.

Righteous One, help us to see right from wrong and good from evil in the world around us. Fill us with your Spirit, and lead us to lives of wisdom, justice, and understanding. In your name we pray. Amen.

* E. Artis W. Weber (2002). © 2013 by Interprovincial Board of Communication and Moravian Music Foundation.

First Sunday in Lent

Watchword for the Week — No one who believes in Christ will be put to shame. Romans 10:11

Sunday, February 14 — Deuteronomy 26:1–11; Psalm 91:1–2,9–16 Romans 10:8b–13; Luke 4:1–13

The Lord is the stronghold of my life; of whom shall I be afraid? Psalm 27:1

Open now the crystal fountain   790
where the healing waters flow;
let the fire and cloudy pillar
lead me all my journey through.
Strong deliv'rer, strong deliv'rer,
ever be my strength and shield;
ever be my strength and shield.

I can do all things through him who strengthens me. Philippians 4:13

Grateful that God dared to rescue   19s*
me from dusty, deep despair,
joyful I go where God leads me,
bold good news and call to share.
God has sought us! God has found us!
Live God's love, a gift so rare.

Protector God, our strength for meeting life's trials comes from you. You are our Shield, our Foundation, our Guardian, and our Friend. Help us to stay strong in faith, hope, and love so that we may serve others in your name. Amen.

* © 2010 by M. Lynnette Delbridge

Monday, February 15 — Psalm 24
Genesis 43; Matthew 15:10–20

Shall we receive the good at the hand of God, and not receive the bad? Job 2:10

> Lord, I would clasp thy hand in mine,   787
> nor ever murmur nor repine,
> content, whatever lot I see,
> since 'tis my God that leadeth me.
> He leadeth me, he leadeth me;
> by his own hand he leadeth me,
> his faithful foll'wer I would be,
> for by his hand he leadeth me.

God is faithful, and he will not let you be tested beyond your strength, but with the testing he will also provide the way out so that you may be able to endure it. 1 Corinthians 10:13

> God is our strength and song,   531
> and his salvation ours;
> then be his love in Christ proclaimed
> with all our ransomed pow'rs.

Heavenly Father, this world tests our resolve and our faith in you. Too many times we feel the fear and heartache of a life without you. Yet, your smiling face and gentle hand remind us of your love and give us the power to live lives of goodness and hope. Amen.

Tuesday, February 16 — Psalm 25:1–7
Genesis 44; Matthew 15:21–28

I will make with you an everlasting covenant. Isaiah 55:3

Remembering what our fathers told   399
you did in their young day,
this solemn jubilee we hold.
May we, as then did they,
ourselves in covenant now bind
with soul and strength, with heart and mind,
through life, in death, on land, o'er sea
to you disciples be.

The Lord Jesus took the cup also, after supper, saying, "This cup is the new covenant in my blood." 1 Corinthians 11:25

One the name in which we pray,   525
one our Savior day by day;
with one cup and with one bread
thus one cov'nant way we tread.
One in spirit, one in life,
one amid earth's frequent strife,
one in faith and one in love,
one in hope of heav'n above.

Lamb of God, with your shed blood you saved us
all. When we drink from the cup, we remember
your sacrifice and affirm the covenant that binds us
to you. May we be one with you forever. Amen.

Wednesday, February 17 — Psalm 25:8–22
Genesis 45; Matthew 15:29–16:4

May the Lord, who is good, pardon everyone who sets their heart on seeking God.
2 Chronicles 30:18–19 (NIV)

> Did you not bid us love you, God and King,   490
> love you with all our heart and strength and mind?
> I see the cross—there teach my heart to cling.
> O let me seek you and O let me find!

A man was there by the name of Zacchaeus; he was a chief tax collector and was wealthy. He wanted to see who Jesus was. Luke 19:2–3 (NIV)

> Into the world, Christ Jesus sends us   74s*
> to love like he loved wherever we go:
> just down the street, into the cities,
> crossing the borders of culture as though
> nothing, but nothing, could keep us away.
> This is the challenge of our mission.

Gracious King, every day we seek your love and grace. We are pilgrims—sometimes lost, sometimes on the right path, sometimes tired of traveling—yet we always hope to see your face throughout our journey and at its end. Amen.

*   © 1999 by Christine Sobania Johnson

Thursday, February 18 — Psalm 26
Genesis 46:1–27; Matthew 16:5–20

Declare his glory among the nations, his marvelous works among all the peoples. Psalm 96:3

Glory, praise, and royal might 521*
to our God of endless light,
who is perfect, three in one,
and unites us in the Son:
have mercy, Lord.

Paul and Barnabas related all that God had done with them, and how he had opened a door of faith for the Gentiles. Acts 14:27

Unseal our lips to sing your praise 561
in endless hymns through all our days;
increase our faith and light our minds;
and set us free from doubt that blinds.

Lord, your goodness and light fills all the world. As believers, we see that light and feel that goodness, yet many do not. Help us to open the door of faith to welcome those who desire your love. In your name we pray. Amen.

* © 1994 by C. Daniel Crews

Friday, February 19 — Psalm 27:1–6
Genesis 46:28–47:31; Matthew 16:21–28

A father of the fatherless and a judge for the widows is God in his holy habitation. God makes a home for the lonely; he leads out the prisoners into prosperity. Psalm 68:5–6 (NASB)

Wind of God, O earth-stirring Spirit,   499*
yours the passion we need this day.
Yours the thirst for peace and for justice,
yours the yearning, the will, the way.
Source of righteousness, source of power,
source of light in the world's dark hour,
the poor, the lonely know you as friend.
Stir us to action, O holy wind.

Jesus Christ says, "Truly I tell you, just as you did it to one of the least of these who are members of my family, you did it to me." Matthew 25:40

In the just reward of labor,   449**
God's will is done.
In the help we give our neighbor,
God's will is done.
In our worldwide task of caring
for the hungry and despairing,
in the harvest we are sharing,
God's will is done.

Father most holy, you teach us to feed the hungry, comfort the sick, clothe the naked, and welcome the stranger. Help us to see these as everyday occurrences, not occasional efforts, so that through you we can improve our world. In your name we pray. Amen.

Saturday, February 20 — Psalm 27:7–14
Genesis 48; Matthew 17:1–13

Do not be frightened or dismayed, for the Lord your God is with you wherever you go. Joshua 1:9

Yea, though I walk in death's dark vale,   720
yet will I fear no ill;
for thou art with me, and thy rod
and staff me comfort still;
for thou art with me, and thy rod
and staff me comfort still.

God did not give us a spirit of cowardice, but rather a spirit of power and of love and of self-discipline. 2 Timothy 1:7

The young, the old inspire   376
with wisdom from above,
and give us hearts and tongues of fire
to pray and praise and love.
O light of light, explore
and chase our gloom away,
with luster shining more and more
unto the perfect day.

Gracious God, the world presents us with many
fears and worries. But in you we have one who
makes us brave in the face of these fears. May your
spirit of love and power strengthen and protect us
all the days of our lives. Amen.

Second Sunday in Lent

Watchword for the Week — The Lord is my light and my salvation; whom shall I fear? Psalm 27:1

Sunday, February 21 — Genesis 15:1–12,17–18; Psalm 27 Philippians 3:17–4:1; Luke 13:31–35

There is a river whose streams make glad the city of God, the holy dwelling places of the Most High. God is in the midst of her, she will not be moved. Psalm 46:4–5 (NASB)

Glorious things of you are spoken,   522
Zion, city of our God;
he whose word cannot be broken
formed you for his own abode;
on the rock of ages founded,
what can shake your sure repose?
With salvation's walls surrounded
you may smile at all your foes.

In Jesus Christ you also are being built together for a dwelling place of God in the Spirit. Ephesians 2:22 (NKJV)

What splendid rays of truth and grace,   596
all other light excelling!
This I know when he in love
makes my heart his dwelling!

Benevolent Creator, you have built a home for us in you. Through the Spirit of your Son, help us to welcome into your house those seeking your love and forgiveness this and every Sunday. We worship you and give you thanks. Amen.

Monday, February 22 — Psalm 28
Genesis 49; Matthew 17:14–27

**For we are aliens and transients before you,
as were all our ancestors; our days on the earth
are like a shadow, and there is no hope.
1 Chronicles 29:15**

> Lord, our God, Lord, our God,   506
> may your precious saving word,
> 'til our days on earth are ended,
> light unto our path afford;
> then, among your saints ascended,
> we for your redeeming love shall raise
> ceaseless praise, ceaseless praise.

**Here we have no lasting city, but we are looking
for the city that is to come. Hebrews 13:14**

> My God will lead me to a spot   794
> where, all my cares and griefs forgot,
> I shall enjoy sweet rest.
> As pants for cooling streams the hart,
> I languish for my heavenly part,
> for God, for God, my Refuge blessed.

Lord of light, many in your world wander without
direction or hope. They do not hear your word or
feel your touch. Guide them through your strength
and wisdom to find the road to you. Direct them
home and welcome them always. Amen.

Tuesday, February 23 — Psalm 29
Genesis 50; Matthew 18:1–14

For as the earth brings forth its shoots, so the Lord God will cause righteousness and praise to spring up before all the nations. Isaiah 61:11

> Plenteous grace with thee is found,   724
> grace to cover all my sin;
> let the healing streams abound;
> make and keep me pure within.
> Thou of life the fountain art,
> freely let me take of thee;
> spring thou up within my heart,
> rise to all eternity.

He who supplies seed to the sower and bread for food will supply and multiply your seed for sowing and increase the harvest of your righteousness. 2 Corinthians 9:10

> We thank you, our Creator,   453
> for all things bright and good,
> the seedtime and the harvest,
> our life, our health, our food;
> accept the gifts we offer
> for all your love imparts,
> and what you most would treasure—
> our humble, thankful hearts.

While winter still holds fast to our world, it is spring in our hearts. Your Son shines warm, life-giving light upon your children, helping us to grow in faith and love for you. Feed that faith and nurture it, so that we may follow you. Amen.

Wednesday, February 24 — Psalm 30:1–5
Exodus 1:1–2:10; Matthew 18:15–35

Do not cast me away from your presence, and do not take your holy spirit from me. Psalm 51:11

Create in me a clean heart, O God,   p79
and renew a right Spirit within me.
Cast me not away from your presence,
and take not your Holy Spirit from me.
Restore unto me the joy of salvation;
anoint me with your Sprit free.
Create in me a clean heart, O God,
and renew a right Spirit within me.

God has destined us not for wrath but for obtaining salvation through our Lord Jesus Christ. 1 Thessalonians 5:9

Holy Trinity, we confess with joy   p197
that our life and whole salvation
flow from Christ's blessed incarnation
and his death for us
on the shameful cross.

Gracious Lord, keep us close, even as we doubt and sin. While we may not be worthy, we hope and trust that your spirit will always be with us. Through your love, help us to stand in your presence and serve you, we pray. Amen.

Thursday, February 25 — Psalm 30:6–12
Exodus 2:11–3:22; Matthew 19:1–12

Even before a word is on my tongue, O Lord, you know it completely. Psalm 139:4

Still, Lord, too often we miss your vision;　　　81s*
that we have failed you we must confess:
we confuse service with our ambition;
only your leading brings true success.

When you are praying, do not heap up empty phrases as the Gentiles do; for they think that they will be heard because of their many words. Your Father knows what you need before you ask him. Matthew 6:7–8

Keep me from saying words　　　　　　615
that later need recalling;
guard me, lest idle speech
may from my lips be falling;
but when, within my place,
I must and ought to speak,
then to my words give grace,
lest I offend the weak.

Heavenly Father, you know our hearts and minds even better than we do. You understand our needs and you are there for us. Help us to express our love and thankfulness directly from the heart, unfiltered and true. In your name we pray. Amen.

* C. Daniel Crews (1999). © 2013 by Interprovincial Board of Communication and Moravian Music Foundation.

Friday, February 26 — Psalm 31:1–5
Exodus 4:1–5:9; Matthew 19:13–22

Woe to those who are wise in their own eyes and clever in their own sight. Isaiah 5:21 (NIV)

> Restrain me lest I harbor pride,   733
> lest I in my own strength confide;
> though I am weak, show me anew
> I have my pow'r, my strength from you.

If I understand all mysteries and all knowledge, and if I have all faith, so as to remove mountains, but do not have love, I am nothing. 1 Corinthians 13:2

> Lead on, O King eternal,   753
> 'til sin's fierce war shall cease,
> and holiness shall whisper
> the sweet amen of peace;
> for not with sword's loud clashing,
> nor roll of stirring drums,
> but deeds of love and mercy,
> the heav'nly kingdom comes.

Omnipotent God, though we may think ourselves wise, there are many mysteries to which only you know the answers. Help us to have faith in your knowledge and grant us understanding in ways that enlighten and enhance our lives and strengthen our love for all. Amen.

Saturday, February 27 — Psalm 31:6–9
Exodus 5:10–6:12; Matthew 19:23–30

You have blessed it, O Lord, and it shall be blessed forever. 1 Chronicles 17:27 (NKJV)

> At your feet, our God and Father,   310
> who has blessed us all our days,
> we with grateful hearts would gather
> to begin the year with praise—
> praise for light so brightly shining
> on our steps from heav'n above,
> praise for mercies daily twining
> round us golden cords of love.

Do not repay evil for evil or abuse for abuse; but, on the contrary, repay with a blessing. It is for this that you were called—that you might inherit a blessing. 1 Peter 3:9

> Blessed to be a blessing,   582*
> privileged to care,
> challenged by the need
> apparent ev'rywhere,
> where the world is wanting
> fill the vacant place,
> be the means through which
> the Lord reveals his grace.

Righteous Redeemer, as you have blessed us with your love and power, teach us how to be blessings to those around us. Through those blessings, help us to make your world a more peaceful, grateful, loving, and glorious place. Amen.

* © 1975 by The Evangelical Covenant Church

Third Sunday in Lent

Watchword for the Week — Seek the Lord while he may be found, call upon him while he is near. Isaiah 55:6

Sunday, February 28 — Isaiah 55:1–9; Psalm 63:1–8
1 Corinthians 10:1–13; Luke 13:1–9

I, the Lord your God, hold your right hand; it is I who say to you, "Do not fear, I will help you." Isaiah 41:13

Amazing grace, how can it be   77s*
that God to us is true,
that we are precious in God's sight,
despite the things we do?
Creator, former, shaper,
making real what we have known,
that God's love is dependable,
and names us as God's own.

Simon's mother-in-law was in bed with a fever, and they told Jesus about her at once. He came and took her by the hand and lifted her up. Then the fever left her. Mark 1:30–31

Always giving and forgiving,   544
ever blessing, ever blessed,
wellspring of the joy of living,
ocean depth of happy rest!
Loving Father, Christ our brother,
let your light upon us shine;
teach us how to love each other,
lift us to the joy divine.

Benevolent Healer, you know the illnesses within your children. Take our hands, make us whole, help us face our fears. Heal us so that we may live the lives that you set forth for us with happiness and health. Amen.

* © 2007 by Judith M. Ganz

Monday, February 29 — Psalm 31:10–20
Exodus 6:13–7:24; Matthew 20:1–16

Correct me, O Lord, but in just measure; not in your anger, or you will bring me to nothing. Jeremiah 10:24

As we answer to God's calling,   70s*
humbly gather, humbly pray;
humbly let us seek forgiveness
when we err or go astray.
In our faith we are united;
in our love we are made one.
We partake to bring remembrance
of his death until he come.

No discipline seems pleasant at the time, but painful. Later on, however, it produces a harvest of righteousness and peace for those who have been trained by it. Hebrews 12:11 (NIV)

Hence, all thoughts of sadness!   722
For the Lord of gladness,
Jesus, enters in.
Those who love the Father,
though the storms may gather,
still have peace within;
and, whatever I must bear,
still in you lies purest pleasure,
Jesus, priceless treasure!

Teacher, we know that we are far from perfect. We stumble, we waiver, we doubt and do wrong. Yet in your eyes, and with your forgiveness, perfection is not required. We thank you for your saving grace and righteousness. Amen.

*   © 2011 by June Edwards

March 1, 1457:
Beginning of the Unity of the Brethren in Bohemia

Tuesday, March 1 — Psalm 31:21–24
Exodus 8; Matthew 20:17–28

Be strong, and let your heart take courage, all you who wait for the Lord. Psalm 31:24

Ev'ry day will be the brighter 310
when your gracious face we view;
ev'ry burden will be lighter
when we know it comes from you.
Spread your love's broad banner o'er us;
give us strength to serve and wait,
'til the glory breaks before us
through the city's open gate.

The one who endures to the end will be saved. Mark 13:13

God of church and God of hist'ry, 637*
pour your blessings on our deeds.
Grant endurance for our ventures,
give us strength to serve and lead.
Alleluia! Our Creator,
Christ and Spirit—this our creed.

Lord God, help us to make patience and waiting a part of our Lenten disciplines, knowing that all who wait on you renew their strength. In patience we experience that all things do good work for those who love you. Amen.

* © 1992 by Willard R. Harstine

Wednesday, March 2 — Psalm 32
Exodus 9; Matthew 20:29–21:11

**How beautiful on the mountains are the feet
of those who bring good news, who proclaim
peace, who bring good tidings, who proclaim
salvation, who say to Zion, "Your God reigns!"
Isaiah 52:7 (NIV)**

> Sing praise to God who reigns above,　　　　537
> the God of all creation,
> the God of pow'r, the God of love,
> the God of our salvation.
> My soul with comfort rich he fills,
> and ev'ry grief he gently stills:
> to God all praise and glory!

**As shoes for your feet put on whatever will
make you ready to proclaim the gospel of peace.
Ephesians 6:15**

> Proclaim to ev'ry people, tongue, and nation　　618
> that God, in whom they live and move, is love;
> tell how he stooped to save his lost creation,
> and died on earth that we might live in love.
> Publish glad tidings, tidings of peace,
> tidings of Jesus, redemption, and release.

O God, the good news of Jesus Christ is to be neither
hoarded nor withheld. Give us, we ask, the courage
to be your witnesses for love, justice, and peace by
our words, our actions, and our examples to others.
Amen.

Thursday, March 3 — Psalm 33:1–5
Exodus 10; Matthew 21:12–22

It is I, speaking in righteousness, mighty to save. Isaiah 63:1 (ESV)

Mine is the sin, but yours the righteousness;   421
mine is the guilt, but yours the cleansing blood;
here is my robe, my refuge, and my peace,
your blood, your righteousness, O Lord, my God.

Just as one man's trespass led to condemnation for all, so one man's act of righteousness leads to justification and life for all. Romans 5:18

You only are true life—   486*
to know you is to live
the more abundant life
that earth can never give.
O risen Lord! we live in you:
in us each day your life renew!

Wondrous Creator, we seek the transformation that takes away our resentments, prejudices, and fears, so that we may live life more fully, always seeking ways in which we can be good neighbors and advocates for the voiceless. Through Christ our Lord we pray. Amen.

Friday, March 4 — Psalm 33:6–11
Exodus 11:1–12:20; Matthew 21:23–32

Only you know what is in every human heart. 1 Kings 8:39

Spirit of God, who dwells within my heart,   490
wean it from sin, through all its pulses move.
Stoop to my weakness, mighty as you are,
and make me love you as I ought to love.

Now may our Lord Jesus Christ himself and God our Father, who loved us and through grace gave us eternal comfort and good hope, comfort your hearts and strengthen them in every good work and word. 2 Thessalonians 2:16–17

How good the name of Jesus sounds   487
to all believing ears!
It soothes our sorrows, heals our wounds,
and drives away our fears.
It makes the wounded spirit whole,
and calms the troubled mind;
his manna for each hungry soul,
the lost and weary find.

We open our hearts to you, dearest Friend; purify them with the refiner's fire, tenderize them with awareness of the needs of others, and stimulate them so that we may reach out in compassion to answer the calls of our neighbors' distress. Amen.

Saturday, March 5 — Psalm 33:12–22
Exodus 12:21–51; Matthew 21:33–46

I said, "I have toiled in vain, I have spent my
strength for nothing and vanity; yet surely
the justice due to me is with the Lord, and my
reward with my God." Isaiah 49:4 (NASB)

> We hail you as our Savior, Lord,   267
> our refuge and our great reward;
> without your grace we waste away
> like flow'rs that wither and decay.

Jesus said, "The kingdom of God is as if someone
would scatter seed on the ground, and would
sleep and rise night and day, and the seed would
sprout and grow, he does not know how. The
earth produces of itself, first the stalk, then
the head, then the full grain in the head."
Mark 4:26–28

> As grows the hidden seed   653*
> to fruit that serves our need,
> your kingdom grows.
> So let our toil be used,
> no gift of yours abused,
> no humble task refused
> your love bestows.

O Master Gardener, if the soil of our lives is to be
receptive to the seed of your word, our lives must be
fertilized with your love and grace to promote good
and healthy spiritual growth. We want to produce
good fruit for your kingdom. Amen.

Fourth Sunday in Lent

Watchword for the Week — If anyone is in Christ, there is a new creation: everything old has passed away; see, everything has become new! 2 Corinthians 5:17

Sunday, March 6 — Joshua 5:9–12; Psalm 32
2 Corinthians 5:16–21; Luke 15:1–3,11b–32

God has power to help or to overthrow.
2 Chronicles 25:8

> I bind unto myself today   p237
> the power of God to hold and lead,
> his eye to watch, his might to stay,
> his ear to hearken to my need,
> the wisdom of my God to teach,
> his hand to guide, his shield to ward;
> the word of God to give me speech,
> his heavenly host to be my guard.

Christ Jesus is our hope. 1 Timothy 1:1

> He came singing hope   580*
> and he lived singing hope;
> he died, singing hope.
> He arose in silence.
> For the hope to go on
> we must make it our song;
> you and I be the singers

Savior of the world, enable our voices to be in harmony with all who share a common faith in you; let the volume of what unites us overpower any discord between us. Amen.

Monday, March 7 — Psalm 34:1–7
Exodus 13:1–14:18; Matthew 22:1–14

Honor your father and your mother.
Exodus 20:12 (NIV)

As it was without beginning,   458
so it lasts without an end;
to their children's children ever
shall God's righteousness extend:
unto such as keep God's cov'nant
and are steadfast in his way,
unto those who still remember
the commandments and obey.

Children and grandchildren must first learn
to practice piety in regard to their own family
and to make some return to their parents;
for this is acceptable in the sight of God.
1 Timothy 5:4 (NASB)

For the joy of human love,   538
brother, sister, parent, child,
friends on earth, and friends above,
pleasures pure and undefiled,
Lord of all, to you we raise
this our hymn of grateful praise.

Passing before our windows are faces of family, friends, and neighbors who have given our faith journey meaning and purpose. Thanks be to you, O God, for placing them in our paths. Amen.

Tuesday, March 8 — Psalm 34:8–18
Exodus 14:19–15:21; Matthew 22:15–22

The Lord says, "I will be gracious to whom I will be gracious, and will show mercy on whom I will show mercy." Exodus 33:19

> Because the Lord our God is good,   539
> his mercy is forever sure.
> His truth at all times firmly stood,
> and shall from age to age endure.

Paul wrote: I am grateful to Christ Jesus our Lord, who has strengthened me, because he judged me faithful and appointed me to his service, even though I was formerly a blasphemer, a persecutor, and a man of violence. But I received mercy. 1 Timothy 1:12–13

> Praise, my soul, the King of heaven,   529
> to his feet your tribute bring.
> Ransomed, healed, restored, forgiven,
> evermore his praises sing.
> Alleluia! Alleluia!
> Praise the everlasting King!

Make us more merciful people, Lord, especially when we are quick to judge and ready to condemn. Too often we jump hastily to conclusions. As you have been merciful to us, so may we be to those around us, through your help and strength, O God. Amen.

Wednesday, March 9 — Psalm 34:19–22
Exodus 15:22–16:36; Matthew 22:23–40

For as the new heavens and the new earth, which I will make, shall remain before me, says the Lord, so shall your descendants and your name remain. Isaiah 66:22

Whatever God ordains is right;   718*
all that he does is for us.
He heals our souls and gives us sight
and puts no ill before us.
Our God is true; he makes us new;
our lives are built upon his rock,
our cornerstone and building block.

Jesus said, "The gates of Hades will not prevail against my church." Matthew 16:18

Jesus, still lead on   799
'til our rest be won;
heavn'ly leader, still direct us,
still support, console, protects us,
'til we safely stand
in the promised land.

Lord Jesus, though your church faces struggles, conflicts within, and attacks from without, remind us that it is still your Church. Help us to rise beyond institutional trappings to live as the body of Christ in all we think, do, or say. In your name we pray. Amen.

* © 1978 by *Lutheran Book of Worship*. Reprinted by permission of Augsburg Fortress.

Thursday, March 10 — Psalm 35:1–10
Exodus 17:1–18:6; Matthew 22:41–23:12

Joseph said to his master's wife, "How then could I do this great wickedness, and sin against God?" Genesis 39:9

My Father, I have wandered 763*
and hidden from your face;
in foolishness have squandered
your legacy of grace.
But now, in exile dwelling,
I rise with fear and shame,
as distant but compelling,
I hear you call my name.

Christ was faithful over God's house as a son. Hebrews 3:6

While a helpless infant still, 336**
he had to flee his foes,
and, in time, rejected by
the people whom God chose;
yet he came to seek and serve
the wayward and the lost,
faithful to his Father's will
and heedless of the cost.

Heavenly Father, we are to be counted among the wayward and lost, ones who wander and squander. We confess to you specific sins of omission and commission, seeking your forgiveness through Jesus Christ our Lord. Amen.

Friday, March 11 — Psalm 35:11–18
Exodus 18:7–19:9; Matthew 23:13–22

I am the Lord, and there is no other. I form light and create darkness, I make weal and create woe; I the Lord do all these things. Isaiah 45:6–7

> Praise to the Lord, 530
>   who o'er all things is wondrously reigning,
> shelt'ring you under his wings,
>   O, so gently sustaining.
> Have you not seen all you have needed has been
> met by his gracious ordaining.

God, who said, "Let light shine out of darkness," made his light shine in our hearts to give us the light of the knowledge of God's glory displayed in the face of Christ. 2 Corinthians 4:6 (NIV)

> I heard the voice of Jesus say, 606
> "I am this dark world's Light;
> look unto me, your morn shall rise,
> and all your day be bright."
> I looked to Jesus, and I found
> in him my Star, my Sun;
> and in that Light of life I'll walk,
> 'til trav'ling days are done.

Jesus, Savior, pilot us over the rough waters of each day's living. Help us to find and hold a steady course, looking for the guiding lights of community, sacrament, and word. Hear our prayer in the name of the Christ. Amen.

Saturday, March 12 — Psalm 35:19–28
Exodus 19:10–20:21; Matthew 23:23–32

God, from the depths of the earth you will bring me up again. You will increase my honor, and comfort me once again. Psalm 71:20–21

"Comfort, comfort now my people;   264
tell of peace!" So says our God.
Comfort those who sit in darkness
bowed beneath oppression's load.
To God's people now proclaim
that God's pardon waits for them!
Tell them that their war is over;
God will reign in peace forever!

When Peter noticed the strong wind, he became frightened, and beginning to sink, he cried out, "Lord, save me!" Matthew 14:30

Lord, when the tempest rages,   791*
I need not fear;
for you, the Rock of Ages,
are always near.
Close by your side abiding,
I fear no foe,
for when your hand is guiding,
in peace I go.

O Jesus, we respond to your invitation to step out onto the water, but it doesn't take long before our confidence wavers and our fears set in. We extend our hands to you, knowing that you will grasp them and save us. We praise you for your constant faithfulness. Amen.

Fifth Sunday in Lent

Watchword for the Week — Forgetting what lies behind and straining forward to what lies ahead, I press on toward the goal for the prize of the heavenly call of God in Christ Jesus. Philippians 3:13–14

Sunday, March 13 — Isaiah 43:16–21; Psalm 126
Philippians 3:4b–14; John 12:1–8

Lord, to you I have committed my cause. Jeremiah 11:20

O God, my faithful God,   615
O fountain ever flowing,
without whom nothing is,
all perfect gifts bestowing,
grant me a faithful life,
and give me, Lord, within,
commitment free from strife,
a soul unhurt by sin.

Christ left you an example, so that you should follow in his steps. When he was abused, he did not return abuse; when he suffered, he did not threaten; but he entrusted himself to the one who judges justly. 1 Peter 2:21,23

Jesus taught both by example   665*
and with words of lasting worth;
Christ has given ways to sample
hints of heaven here on earth!
In the same way Christian teachers
model true humanity,
demonstrating in their witness
glimpses of eternity!

Ever-present God, when the urge to retaliate is strong, when bitterness easily rises up from inner places and we desire to hurt as we have been hurt, help us to face down temptation with strength and follow each footstep of Christ. Amen.

* © 1994 by John A. Dalles

Monday, March 14 — Psalm 36
Exodus 20:22–21:27; Matthew 23:33–39

It is better to take refuge in the Lord than to put confidence in mortals. Psalm 118:8

> Then e'en in storms I shall you know,   721
> my sure support and refuge too;
> In ev'ry trial I shall prove
> assuredly that God is love.

Let us approach the throne of grace with boldness, so that we may receive mercy and find grace to help in time of need. Hebrews 4:16

> Jesus, great High Priest of our profession,   400
> we in confidence draw near;
> grant us, then, in mercy, the confession
> of our grateful hearts to hear;
> you we gladly own in ev'ry nation,
> Head and Master of your congregation,
> conscious that in ev'ry place
> you are giving life and grace.

O listening God, as you have been our refuge and help in times past, we trust that in and with you we can still find safety, respite, and restoration. Our confidence is in you and to you we will turn to satisfy our needs. Thanks be to you, living God. Amen.

Tuesday, March 15 — Psalm 37:1–6
Exodus 21:28–22:24; Matthew 24:1–25

Like an eagle that stirs up its nest, that hovers over its young, the Lord spread his wings and caught his people, he carried them on his pinions. Deuteronomy 32:11 (NASB)

> The Lord is never far away,   537
> but through all grief distressing,
> an ever-present help and stay,
> our peace, and joy, and blessing.
> As with a mother's tender hand,
> he leads his own, his chosen band.
> To God all praise and glory!

The peace of God, which surpasses all understanding, will guard your hearts and your minds in Christ Jesus. Philippians 4:7

> The Lord bless and keep you in his favor   446
> as his chosen, cherished heir;
> the Lord make his face shine on you ever
> and enfold you in his care.
> The Lord lift his countenance upon you,
> may where'er you go his Spirit lead you,
> and his peace on you bestow;
> Amen, amen, be it so.

O God, when we think we can fly like eagles we come crashing back to earth; when we trust in the ways of the world, the battle increases. We race to your side for comfort and care. Help us rise to new heights of faith, hope, and love. Amen.

Wednesday, March 16 — Psalm 37:7–15
Exodus 22:25–23:26; Matthew 24:26–35

Do not plan harm against your neighbor who lives trustingly beside you. Proverbs 3:29

Blessed are the brave and peaceful,   595
bringing peace where'er they live,
God shall own them as his children
and through them his peace will give.
All for love and truth who suffer,
in your God rejoice and sing;
he, the end of all your striving,
he, your Father, Lord, and King.

As we have opportunity, let us do good to all people. Galatians 6:10 (NIV)

Teach us to love in truth,   801*
to give and to receive
with joyful and with open hearts,
with all that we believe;
to seek another's good,
to honor what is right,
to let our will and our desire
be held in holy light.

Keep us, Lord, from the snare of spiritual arrogance; teach us to listen to what others believe, seeking to understand and respect their thoughts, and to find our common ground in relationship with Christ. In his name we pray. Amen.

*   © 1993 by United Church Press/Pilgrim Press, Cleveland, OH. Used by permission.

Thursday, March 17 — Psalm 37:16–22
Exodus 23:27–25:9; Matthew 24:36–44

Do not be far from me, for trouble is near and there is no one to help. Psalm 22:11

Sometimes 'mid scenes of deepest gloom,   787
sometimes where Eden's bowers bloom,
by waters calm, o'er troubled sea,
still 'tis his hand that leadeth me.
He leadeth me, he leadeth me;
by his own hand he leadeth me,
his faithful foll'wer I would be,
for by his hand he leadeth me.

Christ says, "Do not let your hearts be troubled. Believe in God, believe also in me." John 14:1

Lord of all, of church and kingdom,   564*
in an age of change and doubt
keep us faithful to the gospel;
help us work your purpose out.
Here, in this day's dedication,
all we have to give, receive;
we, who cannot live without you,
we adore you! We believe!

Saving God, when we are caught in raging waters,
when vicious winds toss us about, when demeaning
actions and statements come from even those we
love, throw us the lifeline of your mercy, love, and
grace. Amen.

* © 1979 by Hope Publishing Company. All rights reserved. Used by permission.

Friday, March 18 — Psalm 37:23–26
Exodus 25:10–40; Matthew 24:45–51

As the rain and the snow come down from heaven, and do not return there until they have watered the earth, making it bring forth and sprout, giving seed to the sower and bread to the eater, so shall my word be that goes out from my mouth. Isaiah 55:10–11

> Upon your precepts and your ways   510
> my heart will meditate with awe;
> your word shall be my chief delight,
> and I will not forget your law.

Christ said, "Those are the ones on whom seed was sown on the good soil; and they hear the word and accept it and bear fruit." Mark 4:20 (NASB)

> God's word in Christ is seed;   501*
> good soil its urgent need;
> for it must find, in humankind
> the fertile soil in heart and mind.
> Good soil! A human field!
> A hundred-fold to yield.

Lord God, as we plan for this year's garden, help us cultivate within our own lives fertile and receptive soil, so that our witness to your love and grace will be bold, far-reaching, and impacting. In Christ's name we pray. Amen.

*   © 1976 by Norman P. Olson

Saturday, March 19 — Psalm 37:27–33
Exodus 26; Matthew 25:1–13

Do not fear disgrace; you will not be humiliated. Isaiah 54:4 (NIV)

You have kindly led us   p205
through our joys and tears;
now accept our praises
and remove our fears.
Grant us all with gladness
to obey your voice;
let your will and pleasure
be our only choice.

If any of you suffers as a Christian, do not consider it a disgrace, but glorify God because you bear this name. 1 Peter 4:16

Praise the Lord! For he is glorious;   454
never shall his promise fail;
God has made his saints victorious;
sin and death shall not prevail.
Praise the God of our salvation;
hosts on high, his pow'r proclaim;
heav'n and earth and all creation,
praise and glorify his name.

Understanding God, you have created us in your image, saying "It is good." Even when there are threats to our dignity, when we are spiritually bullied, we commit to walking with you through the coming Holy Week, at Jesus' side and in your Spirit. Amen.

Palm Sunday

Watchword for the Week — Let those who fear the Lord say, "His steadfast love endures forever." Psalm 118:4

Sunday, March 20 — Isaiah 50:4–9a; Psalm 118:1–2,19–29
Philippians 2:5–11; Luke 19:28–40

Our transgressions indeed are with us, and we know our iniquities: transgressing, and denying the Lord. Isaiah 59:12–13

This holy word exposes sin,   509
convinces us that we're unclean,
points out the wretched, ruined state
of humankind, both small and great.

When the goodness and loving kindness of God our Savior appeared, he saved us, not because of any works of righteousness that we had done, but according to his mercy. Titus 3:4–5

Prepare the royal highway;   344*
the King of kings is near!
Let ev'ry hill and valley
a level road appear!
Then greet the King of glory
foretold in sacred story:
Hosanna to the Lord
for he fulfills God's word!

Lord Jesus Christ, in this Holy Week we are among those shouting "Hosanna!" Save us, we ask you; grant us strength to remain at your side now and beyond, committed, faithful, and obedient, grateful for our salvation. Amen.

Monday, March 21 — Psalm 37:34–40
Exodus 27:1–28:14; Matthew 25:14–30

This is God, our God forever and ever. He will be our guide. Psalm 48:14

Touch now our hands to lead us aright.   489
Guide us forever, show us your way.
Transform our darkness into your light.
Spirit of God, still lead us today.

Lift your drooping hands and strengthen your weak knees, and make straight paths for your feet. Hebrews 12:12–13

O Lord, who through this holy week   348
did suffer for us all,
the sick to heal, the lost to seek,
to raise up them that fall.
Your feet the path of suff'ring trod;
your hand the vict'ry won;
what shall we render to our God
for all that he has done?

Approachable God, worthy of our trust in all things and places, strengthen us when we are tempted to choose the path of least resistance, seeking peace at any price, putting on blinders instead of binoculars. We want to please and honor you now and always. Amen.

Tuesday, March 22 — Psalm 38:1–8
Exodus 28:15–43; Matthew 25:31–46

Yours is the kingdom, O Lord, and you are exalted as head above all. 1 Chronicles 29:11

> Father, your name be praised,   575
>   your kingdom given,
> your will be done on earth as 'tis in heaven;
> keep us in life, forgive our sins,
>   deliver us now and ever.

We do see Jesus now crowned with glory and honor because of the suffering of death. Hebrews 2:9

> What language shall I borrow   345
> to thank you, dearest friend,
> for this, your dying sorrow,
> your mercy without end?
> Lord, make me yours forever,
> a loyal servant true,
> and let me never, never
> outlive my love for you.

Precious God, when we consider the things we exalt in this life, the things we honor, the things that receive our homage and devotion, too often they are less than worthy and are not what would please you. We make this confession, seeking your forgiveness. Amen.

Wednesday, March 23 — Psalm 38:9–16
Exodus 29:1–30; Matthew 26:1–13

O that today you would listen to his voice! Do not harden your hearts. Psalm 95:7–8

O let me hear you speaking   603
in accents clear and still,
above the storms of passion,
the murmurs of self-will.
O speak to reassure me,
to hasten or control;
and speak to make me listen,
O guardian of my soul.

Be doers of the word, and not merely hearers. James 1:22

With gratitude and humble trust   650*
we bring our best today
to serve your cause and share your love
with all along life's way.
O God, who gave yourself to us
in Jesus Christ your Son,
help us to give ourselves each day
until life's work is done.

God of the living word, you have commanded us to be still, to wait patiently, and to listen more attentively for your voice. Help us to slow down, put on the brakes, shift into neutral, and remain in place awaiting your call through Jesus. Amen.

Maundy Thursday

Watchword for Maundy Thursday — He has gained renown by his wonderful deeds; the Lord is gracious and merciful. Psalm 111:4

Thursday, March 24 — Psalm 38:17–22
Exodus 29:31–30:16; Matthew 26:14–30

God has made me fruitful in the land of my misfortunes. Genesis 41:52

By pain and sorrow undeterred,   393*
I shall proceed in gladness:
we who rely on God's own word
see past this mortal sadness.
When cloudy and difficult winter is past,
God will work our great restoration.
Take heart in the coming of springtime at last!
Take heart in glad anticipation!

Jesus said to his disciples, "I am deeply grieved, even to death; remain here, and keep awake." Mark 14:34

My Redeemer, overwhelmed with anguish,   346
went to Olivet for me;
there he kneels, his heart does heave and languish
in a bitter agony;
fear and horror seize his soul and senses,
for the hour of darkness now commences;
ah, how he does weep and groan
our rebellion to atone.

Lord Jesus Christ, you command that we gather at your table in your name and Spirit. Just as we are, we come to receive the signs of your mercy and the evidence of your grace. Thanks be to you, Lord Jesus Christ. Amen.

* © 1994 by Madeleine Forell Marshall

Good Friday

Watchword for Good Friday — For God so loved the world that he gave his only Son, so that everyone who believes in him may not perish but may have eternal life. John 3:16

Friday, March 25 — Psalm 39:1–6
Exodus 30:17–31:11; Matthew 26:31–35

I will sing of your steadfast love, O Lord, forever; with my mouth I will proclaim your faithfulness to all generations. Psalm 89:1

O wondrous love,   351
   whose depth no heart has sounded,
that brought you here,
   by foes and thieves surrounded,
conquer my heart, make love its sole endeavor
henceforth forever!

God was reconciling the world to himself in Christ, not counting people's sins against them. And he has committed to us the message of reconciliation. 2 Corinthians 5:19 (NIV)

Paschal Lamb, by God appointed,   330
all our sins on you were laid;
by almighty love anointed,
you have full atonement made.
All your people are forgiven
through the virtue of your blood;
opened is the gate of heaven;
we are reconciled to God.

O God, there was much about Good Friday that does not seem good: your Son's betrayal, denial, and crucifixion. But we understand that your all-encompassing love is what brought Jesus to the cross: to die for us—but not only for us—for all. Amen.

Great Sabbath

Saturday, March 26 — Psalm 39:7–13
Exodus 31:12–32:29; Matthew 26:36–46

O Lord, let your ear be attentive to hear the prayer of your servant that I now pray before you day and night. Nehemiah 1:6

> O dearly, dearly has he loved,   353
> and we must love him too,
> and trust in his redeeming blood,
> and try his works to do.

Jesus prays, "Holy Father, protect them in your name that you have given me, so that they may be one, as we are one." John 17:11

> May we all your loved ones be,   352
> all one holy family,
> loving, since your love we see:
> hear us, holy Jesus.

Watching God, like your followers in times before, we sometimes cower behind closed and locked doors in fear and desperation. We long for signs, for assurance that sin and death are not the final answer. Break the grip of grief and fear with the coming announcement of the Life. Amen.

Easter

Watchword for the Week — Why do you look for the living among the dead? Jesus is not here, but has risen. Luke 24:5

Sunday, March 27 — Acts 10:34–43; Psalm 118:1–2,14–24
1 Corinthians 15:19–26; Luke 24:1–12

O send out your light and your truth; let them lead me to your dwelling. Psalm 43:3

It was a strange and dreadful strife   367
when life and death contended;
the victory remained with life:
the reign of death was ended.
Stripped of pow'r, no more it reigns,
an empty form alone remains;
death's sting is lost forever!
Alleluia!

Now Christ is risen from the dead, and has become the firstfruits of those who have fallen asleep. 1 Corinthians 15:20 (NKJV)

We know that Christ is raised and dies no more.   366
Embraced by death he broke its fearful hold;
and our despair he turned to blazing joy.
Alleluia!

We give praise to you, powerful God, for breaking the bonds of death and driving away fear and hopelessness with the resurrection of your son, Jesus. Even as he lives, so may we become alive in the Spirit and on fire with your truth and love. In Christ we pray. Amen.

Easter Monday

Monday, March 28 — Psalm 40:1–8
Exodus 32:30–33:23 Matthew 26:47–58

Give us life, and we will call on your name.
Psalm 80:18

> Praise to the Lord!   530
>   O, let all that is in me adore him!
> All that has life and breath,
>   come now with praises before him!
> Let the amen sound from his people again.
> Gladly forever adore him!

Christ Jesus abolished death and brought life
and immortality to light through the gospel.
2 Timothy 1:10

> He has arisen, Alleluia!   357*
> Rejoice and praise him; Alleluia!
> For our Redeemer burst from the tomb,
>   even from death, dispelling its gloom.
> Let us sing praise to him with endless joy.
> Death's fearful sting he has come to destroy.
> Our sins forgiving, alleluia!
> Jesus is living, alleluia!

O God of majesty, we want to live as Easter people,
filled with the hope and power of the resurrection.
Let the praise and joy in our hearts be the evidence
that Christ is resurrected in us. In his Spirit we pray.
Amen.

*   © by Lutheran World Federation

Tuesday, March 29 — Psalm 40:9–17
Exodus 34; Matthew 26:59–75

In the shadow of your wings I will take refuge, until the destroying storms pass by. Psalm 57:1

See the Lord, your keeper, stand   729
omnipotently near.
Now he holds you by the hand,
and banishes your fear;
shadows with his wings your head,
guards from all impending harms;
round you and beneath are spread
the everlasting arms.

When it was evening on that day, the first day of the week, and the doors of the house where the disciples had met were locked, Jesus came and stood among them and said, "Peace be with you." John 20:19

That night the apostles met in fear;   369
among them came their Master dear
and said, "My peace be with you here."
Alleluia!

O great Creator, there are times when the conflicts and struggles of life leave us shaken and uncertain. Enable us to actively listen for your words of peace and in hearing be lifted up and renewed in spirit. Amen.

Wednesday, March 30 — Psalm 41
Exodus 35; Matthew 27:1–10

Lord, you are righteous, but this day we are covered with shame. Daniel 9:7 (NIV)

His righteous government and power   320
shall over all extend;
on judgment and on justice based,
his reign shall have no end.

A man had two sons; he went to the first and said, "Son, go and work in the vineyard today." He answered, "I will not;" but later he changed his mind and went. Matthew 21:28–29

You're our strength and motivation,   622*
Christ, you send us out to serve.
We hold back, but your salvation
gives us energy and nerve.
You still fill us with your Spirit;
lift us up on eagles' wings.
Give your call, we gladly hear it;
in your work our spirit sings.

We ask, ever-present God, for the courage to launch
new ministries where needs become visible, the
perseverance to follow through with ministries that
we have started, and the inspiration to celebrate
what we have accomplished in your precious name.
Amen.

*   © Darryl Bell

Thursday, March 31 — Psalm 42
Exodus 36; Matthew 27:11–31

Lord, do not let my heart be drawn to what is evil. Psalm 141:4 (NIV)

Save us from weak resignation   751*
to the evils we deplore;
let the gift of your salvation
be our glory evermore.
Grant us wisdom, grant us courage
serving you whom we adore,
serving you whom we adore.

Anyone, then, who knows the right thing to do and fails to do it, commits sin. James 4:17

Come as a shepherd; guard and keep   432
your fold from all that fosters sin,
and nourish lambs, and feed the sheep,
the wounded heal, the lost bring in.

Holy Father, you gave us the word. We confess that we use fragments of Scripture to support our biases; we justify sinful actions because we can't find it within ourselves to admit that we are wrong. Spirit of the living God, melt us, mold us, fill us, use us. In Jesus' name we pray. Amen.

* Used by permission of Elinor Fosdick Downs

Friday, April 1 — Psalm 43
Exodus 37; Matthew 27:32–44

I will exalt you, Lord, for you lifted me out of the depths. Psalm 30:1 (NIV)

> Out of the depths I cry to you;   761*
> O Father, hear me calling.
> Incline your ear to my distress
> in spite of my rebelling.
> Do not regard my sinful deeds.
> Send me the grace my spirit needs;
> without it I am nothing.

For just as the sufferings of Christ are abundant for us, so also our consolation is abundant through Christ. 2 Corinthians 1:5

> Who trusts in God, a strong abode,   p121
> in heav'n and earth possesses;
> who looks in love to Christ above,
> no fear the heart oppresses.
> In you alone, dear Lord, we own
> sweet hope and consolation,
> our shield from foes, our balm for woes,
> our great and sure salvation.

All-caring and merciful God, we are grateful that you do not ignore our suffering. We reach out to you from the depths of our troubles and give thanks that—through Christ—healing, salvation, and deliverance are ours. Amen.

Saturday, April 2 — Psalm 44:1–8
Exodus 38; Matthew 27:45–56

Be still, and know that I am God! Psalm 46:10

Be still and know our Lord is God,   20s*
whose love attends our prayers.
Each whispered word, each silent hope
finds comfort in God's care.

Jesus said to them, "Come away to a deserted place all by yourselves and rest a while." For many were coming and going, and they had no leisure even to eat. Mark 6:31

Lord, may I be at rest in you   569
and sweetly sleep the whole night through.
Refresh my strength, for your own sake,
so I may serve you when I wake.

God of the stillness, remind us to stop to refresh and renew our lives. May we wait patiently in the silence and truly listen to your voice and leading, rededicating ourselves in service to you and your children. Amen.

*   Willie Israel (2010). © 2013 by Interprovincial Board of Communication and Moravian Music Foundation.

Second Sunday of Easter

Watchword for the Week — Jesus says, "Peace be with you. As the Father has sent me, so I send you." John 20:21

Sunday, April 3 — Acts 5:27–32; Psalm 150
Revelation 1:4–8; John 20:19–31

The Lord is our judge, the Lord is our ruler, the Lord is our king; he will save us. Isaiah 33:22

> Blessed are they who show their mercy   595
> to the guilty and the poor,
> for to them, set free from judgment,
> shall be opened heaven's door.
> Blessed the sincere and truthful
> from the lie's deception free,
> for the God of truth and beauty
> they in joy will surely see.

The Lord is faithful; he will strengthen you and guard you from the evil one. 2 Thessalonians 3:3

> Under the shadow of your throne   461
> your saints have dwelt secure;
> sufficient is your arm alone,
> and our defense is sure.

Mighty God, thank you for the shelter of your love. Your grace surrounds us, keeping us safe, even though we know we don't deserve it. Help us to share your love and mercy with all we meet this day. Amen.

Monday, April 4 — Psalm 44:9–16
Exodus 39:1–31; Matthew 27:57–66

Just as I have watched over them to pluck up and break down, so I will watch over them to build and to plant, says the Lord. Jeremiah 31:28

We plow the fields, and scatter   453
the good seed on the land,
but it is fed and watered
by God's almighty hand;
he sends the snow in winter,
the warmth to swell the grain,
the breezes and the sunshine
and soft refreshing rain.
All good gifts around us
are sent from heav'n above;
then thank the Lord, O thank the Lord
for all his love.

Paul wrote: I planted, Apollos watered, but God gave the growth. So neither the one who plants nor the one who waters is anything, but only God who gives the growth. 1 Corinthians 3:6–7

Grant, Lord, that with thy direction,   673
"Love each other," we comply,
aiming with unfeigned affection
thy love to exemplify;
let our mutual love be glowing;
thus the world will plainly see
that we, as on one stem growing,
living branches are in thee.

Lord Jesus, you gave all glory to God. Help us to seek fields in need of planting and nurture, so that good fruit may grow! Let us be aware of you—the Vine on which we are all branches. Amen.

Tuesday, April 5 — Psalm 44:17–26
Exodus 39:32–40:23; Matthew 28:1–20

The Lord will save me, and we will sing to stringed instruments all the days of our lives at the house of the Lord. Isaiah 38:20

> Let ev'ry instrument be tuned for praise!   532*
> Let all rejoice who have a voice to raise!
> And may God give us faith to sing always
> alleluia!

Thanks be to God, who gives us the victory through our Lord Jesus Christ. 1 Corinthians 15:57

> Lead on, O King eternal: 753
> we follow, not with fears,
> for gladness breaks like morning
> where'er your face appears:
> your cross is lifted o'er us;
> we journey in its light;
> the crown awaits the conquest;
> lead on, O God of might!

Thanks to you, Lord Christ! Today we sing your praises, lifting our voices in joy and gratitude for all the many blessings that you have given to us and to those we love! Thank you for the assurance of salvation. Amen.

Wednesday, April 6 — Psalm 45:1–9
Exodus 40:24–Leviticus 1:17; Mark 1:1–8

The Lord has sent me to comfort all who mourn. Isaiah 61:1,2

O then what raptured greetings   394
on Canaan's happy shore;
what knitting severed friendships up,
where partings are no more!
Then eyes with joy shall sparkle
that brimmed with tears of late,
no orphans left without a home,
nor mourners desolate.

When Jesus rose early on the first day of the week, he appeared first to Mary Magdalene, out of whom he had driven seven demons. She went and told those who had been with him and who were mourning and weeping. Mark 16:9–10 (NIV)

Faith is a living power from heav'n   700
that grasps the promise God has giv'n,
a trust that can't be overthrown
fixed heartily on Christ alone.

God, the grief you must have endured in Jesus'
torment and death! Secure in the knowledge that
Jesus defeated death once and for all, we turn to
you in our times of sorrow to find comfort in your
arms. Heal our pain. Amen.

Thursday, April 7 — Psalm 45:10–17
Leviticus 2,3; Mark 1:9–20

In God we boast all day long, and praise your name forever. Psalm 44:8 (NKJV)

> Make it known to folks among us.   73s*
> Do it now, this very hour.
> Let us listen, love, and serve them,
> acting in the Spirit's pow'r.
> Make it known to those outside us,
> where the seed of faith is sown.
> We will pray and work together
> as we make the Lord's love known.

With gratitude in your hearts sing psalms, hymns, and spiritual songs to God. Colossians 3:16

> Our Lamb has conquered: let us follow him,   587
> with eagerness of heart and strength of limb,
> brave in endeavor, with your vision clear,
> and high thanksgiving for God's purpose here—
> Our Lamb has conquered: let us follow him.

Jesus, we could give thanks and praise all day
and night and never come close to expressing our
gratitude for all that you have done for us. Today
we pause to thank you for all our blessings, great
and small. Amen.

*   © 1993 by Darryl Bell

Friday, April 8 — Psalm 46
Leviticus 4; Mark 1:21–34

It is the Lord who goes before you. He will be with you; he will not fail you or forsake you. Do not fear or be dismayed. Deuteronomy 31:8

> Fear not, I am with you; O be not dismayed,   709
> for I am your God and will still give you aid;
> I'll strengthen you, help you, and cause you to stand
> upheld by my righteous, omnipotent hand.

I am convinced that neither death, nor life, nor angels, nor rulers, nor things present, nor things to come, nor powers, nor height, nor depth, nor anything else in all creation will be able to separate us from the love of God in Christ Jesus our Lord. Romans 8:38–39

> Nay, too closely am I bound   141r
> unto him by hope forever;
> faith's strong hand the rock has found,
> grasped it and will leave it never;
> not the ban of death can part
> from its Lord the trusting heart.

God—Father, Mother, Creator—what magnificent promises you make to us! You will never leave us. Nothing in all creation can separate us from your love in Christ Jesus our Lord. Let that assurance resonate in our hearts today! Amen.

Saturday, April 9 — Psalm 47
Leviticus 5:1–6:13; Mark 1:35–45

In the congregations I will bless the Lord. Psalm 26:12 (NKJV)

> Bless, O my soul, the God of grace;   p72
> his favors claim your highest praise;
> why should the wonders he has wrought
> be lost in silence and forgot?

Every day they continued to meet together in the temple courts. They broke bread in their homes and ate together with glad and sincere hearts, praising God. Acts 2:46–47 (NIV)

> With hearts in tune, with one accord,   438*
> we gather here to praise the Lord.
> A simple meal, a quiet time
> to celebrate a love divine;
> and as the ancient Christians fed,
> we, too, now share this lovefeast bread.

Come, Lord Jesus, and be our guest. As we eat alone, with family, or with friends, remind us not only of your presence, but also of how very blessed we are. Bless our food, our faith, and our fellowship together in you. Amen.

*   © 1985 by Lynn W. Hall. Used by permission.

Third Sunday of Easter

Watchword for the Week — Worthy is the Lamb that was slain to receive power and wealth and wisdom and might and honor and glory and blessing! Revelation 5:12

Sunday, April 10 — Acts 9:1–6,(7–20); Psalm 30
Revelation 5:11–14; John 21:1–19

Not one word has failed of all his good promise, which he spoke through his servant Moses. 1 Kings 8:56

> Sing, pray, and keep his ways unswerving,   712
> offer your service faithfully,
> and trust his word; though undeserving,
> you'll find his promise true to be.
> God never will forsake in need
> the soul that trusts in him indeed.

The one who calls you is faithful, and he will do this. 1 Thessalonians 5:24

> Have we trials and temptations?   743
> Is there trouble anywhere?
> We should never be discouraged;
> take it to the Lord in prayer!
> Can we find a friend so faithful
> who will all our sorrows share?
> Jesus knows our ev'ry weakness;
> take it to the Lord in prayer!

Brother Jesus, we forget that you've known everything we feel. We forget that you walk, hurt, and rejoice by our sides, faithful no matter what. Help us to acknowledge your presence alongside us as we go through this day. Amen.

Monday, April 11 — Psalm 48
Leviticus 6:14–7:21; Mark 2:1–12

Bring the full tithe, and thus put me to the test, says the Lord of hosts; see if I will not open the windows of heaven for you and pour down for you an overflowing blessing. Malachi 3:10

> We are called to faithful service   82s*
> for the blessings from your hand,
> to return the gifts you've granted,
> stewards in your perfect plan.
> Free us from our earthly treasure;
> us unite in heav'nly pleasure.
> May we sense from heav'n above
> how to live out boundless love.

The one who sows sparingly will also reap sparingly, and the one who sows bountifully will also reap bountifully. 2 Corinthians 9:6

> Where all is doubt, may we sow faith;   693**
> where all is gloom, may we sow hope;
> where all is night, may we sow light;
> where all is tears, may we sow joy.

Jesus, you teach that we are what we do. Let our words, actions, and hearts be generous. May we take all that you've given to us and be blessings to others—sowing joy, hope, and acceptance! Send us forth to love! Amen.

*   © 2007 by Nancy Sawtelle

**   © by James Quinn, S.J. Used by permission of Oregon Catholic Press.

Tuesday, April 12 — Psalm 49:1–12
Leviticus 7:22–8:17; Mark 2:13–28

For lo, the one who forms the mountains, creates the wind, and reveals his thoughts to mortals, the Lord, the God of hosts, is his name! Amos 4:13

God is love, let heav'n adore him;   463
God is love, let earth rejoice;
let creation sing before him
and exalt him with one voice.
God who laid the earth's foundation,
God who spread the heav'ns above,
God who breathes through all creation:
God is love, eternal love.

Jesus said, "You know how to interpret the appearance of the sky, but you cannot interpret the signs of the times." Matthew 16:3

But not for us alone this news   543
was brought by Christ our Lord.
'Twas meant for all the world to hear
and thus with one accord
with all God's children everywhere
his name and sign with pride we bear.
To us, to us, this task is giv'n:
to spread God's word. Amen.

God of power and might, we rejoice in your presence in all creation! We see many things plainly, but often, the simplest things escape us. May we pay attention to the signs around us pointing to you. In Jesus' name we pray. Amen.

Wednesday, April 13 — Psalm 49:13–20
Leviticus 8:18–9:11; Mark 3:1–12

Our heart is glad in the Lord, because we trust in his holy name. Psalm 33:21

Mortals join the mighty chorus,   544
which the morning stars began;
God's own love is reigning o'er us,
joining people hand in hand.
Ever singing, march we onward,
victors in the midst of strife;
joyful music leads us sunward
in the triumph song of life.

Set all your hope on the grace that Jesus Christ will bring you when he is revealed. 1 Peter 1:13

Jesus, yourself to us reveal.   p204
Grant that we may not only feel
some drawings of your grace,
but in communion with you live,
and daily from your death derive
the needful strength to run our race.

Jesus, we set our sights and hopes on your gift of
grace; a gift unearned. It is with great joy that we
await the revealing of this great mystery of love—
one day face-to-face with its Giver. Amen.

Thursday, April 14 — Psalm 50:1–6
Leviticus 9:12–10:20; Mark 3:13–19

These people draw near with their mouths and honor me with their lips, while their hearts are far from me. Isaiah 29:13

My heart is weak and poor   604
until it master find;
it has no spring of action sure,
it varies with the wind.
It cannot freely move
'til you have wrought its chain;
enslave it with your matchless love,
and deathless it shall reign

Jesus said, "Whoever does the will of God is my brother and sister and mother." Mark 3:35

Called by Christ to love each other,   627*
called by Christ to seek the lost,
may we each, as sister, brother,
follow Christ, not counting cost.
One in daring, one in sharing,
follow Christ, not counting cost.
One in daring, one in sharing,
follow Christ, not counting cost.

Lord of patience, our spirits are willing but our lives are so busy! We mean well, but forget. Remind us that in doing your will we become sisters and brothers in love. Slow us down to see what you require of us. Amen.

* © 1980 by Jane Parker Huber, from *A Singing Faith*.
  Used by permission of Westminster John Knox Press.

Friday, April 15 — Psalm 50:7–15
Leviticus 11:1–28; Mark 3:20–35

The Lord your God is gracious and merciful, and will not turn away his face from you, if you return to him. 2 Chronicles 30:9

> We want to love our God on high   58s*
> with heart and soul and might;
> we cannot pass our neighbor by,
> for love keeps both in sight.

Repent therefore, and turn to God so that your sins may be wiped out, so that times of refreshing may come from the presence of the Lord. Acts 3:19–20

> For he, my soul, has sent his Son   p72
> to die for wrongs which you have done;
> he paid the ransom, and forgives
> the hourly follies of our lives.

God, today we say more than a simple, "I'm sorry."
We ask forgiveness for all of the ways that we
fall short, resolving to truly repent and repair the
brokenness in our lives and in the world. Guide us
in Jesus' name. Amen.

*   William E. Gramley (1993). © 2013 by Interprovincial Board of Communication and
    Moravian Music Foundation.

Saturday, April 16 — Psalm 50:16–23
Leviticus 11:29–13:8; Mark 4:1–20

But you, O Lord, do not be far from me; O my Strength, hasten to help me! Psalm 22:19 (NKJV)

O God, be near in loneliness and need;   711*
from fear and doubting may our minds be freed.
When losses come, your consolation speed;
for strength and healing love, O Lord, we plead.

Bartimaeus, a blind beggar, began to shout out and say, "Jesus, Son of David, have mercy on me!" Many sternly ordered him to be quiet, but he cried out even more loudly, "Son of David, have mercy on me!" Mark 10:47–48

Bartimaeus was so blind   49s**
he was often left behind.
Even though his hopes were dim
he knew Christ could cure him.
In the darkness of our night
Jesus is our guiding light.
He's the hope for all of humankind.

Lord Jesus Christ, have mercy on our blindness!
Forgive our failure to see those who need our help
and our ignorance to the sufferings of those around
us. We cry out for strength and sight. Lord Jesus
Christ, have mercy on us! Amen.

Fourth Sunday of Easter

Watchword for the Week — Salvation belongs to our God who is seated on the throne, and to the Lamb! Revelation 7:10

Sunday, April 17 — Acts 9:36–43; Psalm 23
Revelation 7:9–17; John 10:22–30

I will sing aloud of your steadfast love in the morning. For you have been a fortress for me and a refuge in the day of my distress. Psalm 59:16

> While we your past dealings   770
> gratefully review,
> we're assured your mercies
> are each morning new;
> pardon our transgressions,
> hear our earnest cry;
> us in soul and body
> heal and sanctify.

Blessed be the God and Father of our Lord Jesus Christ, the Father of mercies and the God of all consolation. 2 Corinthians 1:3

> Most holy Lord and God,   p203
> holy, almighty God,
> holy and most merciful Savior,
> our eternal God!
> Grant that we may never lose
> the comforts from your death.
> Have mercy, O Lord.

Lord, thank you for the newness of each day and the mercies that come with each dawn. You are our refuge and shelter in all circumstances. You keep constant watch over us. Truly, we are blessed! Amen.

Monday, April 18 — Psalm 51:1–6
Leviticus 13:9–46; Mark 4:21–29

The God of heaven will set up a kingdom that shall never be destroyed. Daniel 2:44

Let ev'ry creature rise and bring   404
the highest honors to our King;
angels descend with songs again,
and earth repeat the loud Amen.

John wrote: Then I heard a loud voice in heaven, proclaiming, "Now have come the salvation and the power and the kingdom of our God and the authority of his Messiah." Revelation 12:10

O seed of Israel's chosen race,   403
now ransomed from the fall,
hail him who saves you by his grace,
and crown him Lord of all!
Hail him who saves you by his grace,
and crown him Lord of all!

Savior of our lives, we rejoice that your kingdom
is near. Let us work for peace and justice until it
comes. Find us ready to enter into your immediate
presence, having fulfilled your call to prepare the
way! Amen.

Tuesday, April 19 — Psalm 51:7–12
Leviticus 13:47–14:18; Mark 4:30–41

For the Lord is good; his steadfast love endures forever, and his faithfulness to all generations. Psalm 100:5

We now with a joyful mind   p19
praise you, Lord, for you are kind;
for your mercies shall endure,
ever faithful, ever sure.

God reconciled us to himself through Christ. 2 Corinthians 5:18

Hark! The herald angels sing: 295
"Glory to the newborn King!
Peace on earth and mercy mild,
God and sinners reconciled!"
Joyful, all you nations, rise,
join the triumph of the skies;
with th'angelic host proclaim:
"Christ is born in Bethlehem!"
Hark! The herald angels sing:
"Glory to the newborn king!"

Lord God, you amaze us by not rejecting your sinful children! Thank you for choosing to love us and to work wonders through us. Your love never ends and never fails! In Jesus' name, alleluia! Amen.

Wednesday, April 20 — Psalm 51:13–19
Leviticus 14:19–57; Mark 5:1–20

Return to me, says the Lord of hosts, and I will return to you. Zechariah 1:3

Come, Almighty to deliver,   474
let us all your life receive;
suddenly return, and never,
never more your temple leave.
You we would be always blessing,
serve you as your hosts above,
pray, and praise you without ceasing,
glory in your perfect love.

The Lord is not slow about his promise, as some think of slowness, but is patient with you, not wanting any to perish, but all to come to repentance. 2 Peter 3:9

Teach me your patience; share with me   735
a closer, dearer company.
In work that keeps faith sweet and strong,
in trust that triumphs over wrong,
in hope that sends a shining ray
far down the future's broad'ning way,
in peace that only you can give;
with you, O Master, let me live.

Merciful Lord, your patience is amazing! You wait
for us when we stray, search for us when we are
lost, and open your arms when we come running
back! Keep us close to your heart as we find our way
home. Amen.

Thursday, April 21 — Psalm 52
Leviticus 15:1–24; Mark 5:21–43

Listen to me, my people, and give heed to me, my nation; for a teaching will go out from me, and my justice for a light to the peoples. Isaiah 51:4

> Pray justice may come rolling down   696*
> as in a mighty stream,
> with righteousness in field and town
> to cleanse us and redeem.
> For God is longing to restore
> an earth where conflicts cease,
> a world that was created for
> a harmony of peace.

God our Savior desires everyone to be saved and to come to the knowledge of the truth. 1 Timothy 2:3–4

> I am trusting you, Lord Jesus,   542r
> trusting only you,
> trusting you for full salvation,
> great and free.

Jesus, let the knowledge of your love and sacrifice burn so brightly within us that all who meet us today will know that we are yours. Let the light of justice shine in our lives as we work for peace. Amen.

*   © 1989 by H. Kenn Carmichael

Friday, April 22 — Psalm 53
Leviticus 15:25–16:25; Mark 6:1–6

I—my hands—stretched out the heavens, and all their host I have commanded. Isaiah 45:12 (NKJV)

Wide as the world is your command,   455
vast as eternity your love;
firm as a rock your truth must stand,
when rolling years shall cease to move.

Great and amazing are your deeds, Lord God the Almighty! Revelation 15:3

O Lord of heaven and earth and sea,   406r
to you all praise and glory be!
How shall we show our love to you,
who gives us all?

Mighty God! Sometimes we forget your majesty. How blessed we are that you choose us as your family to share in all creation! Increase our awareness of your presence and of our stewardship over all entrusted to us. Amen.

Saturday, April 23 — Psalm 54
Leviticus 16:26–18:5; Mark 6:7–13

Hatred stirs up strife, but love covers all offenses. Proverbs 10:12

From sorrow, toil, and pain,   680
and sin we shall be free;
and perfect love and friendship reign
through all eternity.

Love is patient; love is kind; love is not envious or boastful or arrogant or rude. It does not insist on its own way; it is not irritable or resentful; it does not rejoice in wrongdoing, but rejoices in the truth. 1 Corinthians 13:4–6

Grant that we may love you truly;   p67
Lord, our thoughts and actions sway,
and to ev'ry heart more fully
your atoning pow'r display.

Lord Jesus, the love you inspire is the most powerful force in the world. Help us to do more than talk about it. Move us to love selflessly, sacrificially, and sincerely so that all will know your love. Amen.

Fifth Sunday of Easter

Watchword for the Week — Jesus says, "I am the Alpha and the Omega, the beginning and the end. To the thirsty I will give water as a gift from the spring of the water of life." Revelation 21:6

Sunday, April 24 — Acts 11:1–18; Psalm 148
Revelation 21:1–6; John 13:31–35

With weeping they shall come, and with consolations I will lead them back, I will let them walk by brooks of water, in a straight path in which they shall not stumble; for I have become a father to Israel. Jeremiah 31:9

> Lord, your body ne'er forsake,   p86
> ne'er your congregation leave;
> we in you our refuge take,
> of your fullness we receive:
> ev'ry other help be gone,
> you are our support alone;
> for on your supreme commands
> all the universe depends.

Now is your time of grief, but I will see you again and you will rejoice, and no one will take away your joy. John 16:22 (NIV)

> Then all grief is drowned;   594
> pure delight is found,
> joy and peace in his salvation,
> heav'nly bliss and consolation.
> Ev'ry grief is drowned
> where such bliss is found.

Lord, there are times when our pain seems too much to bear. In realizing that you have experienced the same pain and still choose to bear ours, we are comforted. Help us in our grief to find joy, healing, and renewed life. Amen.

Monday, April 25 — Psalm 55:1–8
Leviticus 18:6–19:11; Mark 6:14–29

Remember the former things of old; for I am God, and there is no other; I am God, and there is no one like me. Isaiah 46:9

> You are the truth; your word alone   661
> true wisdom can impart;
> you only can inform the mind
> and purify the heart.

For us there is one God, the Father, from whom are all things and for whom we exist, and one Lord, Jesus Christ, through whom are all things and through whom we exist. 1 Corinthians 8:6

> Join we all with one accord;   525
> praise we all our common Lord;
> for we all have heard his voice,
> all have made his will our choice.
> Join we with the saints of old,
> no more strangers in the fold,
> one the Shepherd who us sought,
> one the flock his blood has bought.

Lord—Father, Son, Spirit—you call us together as your people. You bless us with gifts and abilities to use in service to you and your children. Everything comes from you; today we pay special attention to that grace. Amen.

Tuesday, April 26 — Psalm 55:9–15
Leviticus 19:12–20:8; Mark 6:30–44

Does God not see my ways, and number all my steps? Job 31:4

> While life's dark maze I tread,   705
> and griefs around me spread,
> O, be my guide;
> make darkness turn to day,
> wipe sorrow's tears away,
> nor let me ever stray
> from you aside.

Nothing in all creation is hidden from God's sight. Everything is uncovered and laid bare before the eyes of him to whom we must give account. Hebrews 4:13 (NIV)

> O, send your Spirit, Lord,   502
> now unto me,
> that he may touch my eyes
> and make me see.
> Show me the truth concealed
> within your word,
> and in your book revealed
> I see my Lord.

Lord, if we came before you on our own merits, no one would stand. Thank you for the grace which redeems us through Jesus. We are grateful that you see what is unrevealed and redeemable in us. Amen.

Wednesday, April 27 — Psalm 55:16–19
Leviticus 20:9–21:12; Mark 6:45–56

For in many dreams and in many words there is emptiness. Rather, fear God. Ecclesiastes 5:7 (NASB)

> 'Twas grace that taught my heart to fear   783
> and grace my fears relieved;
> how precious did that grace appear
> the hour I first believed.

But avoid stupid controversies, genealogies, dissensions, and quarrels about the law, for they are unprofitable and worthless. Titus 3:9

> Build up each other in the faith,   60s*
> push evil thoughts aside;
> encourage others, as you do,
> thus we in Christ abide.

Father, we grieve you with our pettiness! People
know we are Christ's by the love we have for
each other. Remind us: in essentials, unity;
in non-essentials, liberty; and in everything, love.
Reconcile us to one another in you. Amen.

*   © 1996 by Barbara Jo Strauss

Thursday, April 28 — Psalm 55:20–23
Leviticus 21:13–22:16; Mark 7:1–8

I am poor and needy, but the Lord takes thought for me. Psalm 40:17

God is my strong salvation,   769
no enemy I fear;
he hears my supplication,
dispelling all my care;
if he, my head and master,
defend me from above,
what pain or what disaster
can part me from his love?

Jesus blessed and broke the loaves, and gave them to his disciples to set before the people; and he divided the two fish among them all. And all ate and were filled. Mark 6:41–42

Break now the bread of life,   502
dear Lord, to me,
as when you broke the loaves
beside the sea.
Beyond the sacred page
I seek you, Lord;
my spirit waits for you,
O living Word.

Jesus, you meet everyone at their points of need. In appreciation of that blessing from you to us, let us seek out the points where others need us and give them aid. As you bless and feed us, may we do the same for each other. Amen.

Friday, April 29 — Psalm 56:1–8
Leviticus 22:17–23:22; Mark 7:9–23

The Lord says, "I will not continually accuse, nor will I always be angry." Isaiah 57:16

> Enrich me always with your love;   733
> my kind protector ever prove;
> Lord, put your seal upon my heart,
> that I from you may not depart.

God saved us and called us with a holy calling, not according to our works but according to his own purpose and grace. This grace was given to us in Christ Jesus. 2 Timothy 1:9

> We have received Christ Jesus,   434*
> the Lord who sets us free
> as sisters and as brothers
> in one community,
> a people deeply rooted
> in Jesus' love and life.
> We know who we are called to be:
> Christ's body given melody
> to sing God's praise resoundingly.
> Alleluia!

Savior, your grace sustains and surprises us! You give us this gift freely, no strings attached. As a result, we feel your calling on our hearts—to follow where you lead—to serve. Thanks be to God! Amen.

*   © 1991 by John T. Hicks

Saturday, April 30 — Psalm 56:9–13
Leviticus 23:23–24:9; Mark 7:24–37

He guarded his people as the apple of his eye. Deuteronomy 32:10

> I love your church, O God!   513
> Her walls before you stand,
> dear as the apple of your eye,
> and graven on your hand.

We have known and believe the love that God has for us. 1 John 4:16

> Love will find you   57s*
> if you'll open up your heart
> and let it in, let it in;
> love will find you.
> Won't you open up your life
> so love comes in, love comes in?
> God is waiting for us all
> to wake up from our sleep.
> If we'd only hear the call
> such love we would receive.

God, how much we long for your love! We search
for it in many different places and ways, forgetting
sometimes that it is always near and available.
Wrap us in your arms and keep us close to your
heart. Amen.

*   © 1983 by Brad Bennett

Sixth Sunday of Easter

Watchword for the Week — Jesus says, "Peace I leave with you; my peace I give to you." John 14:27

Sunday, May 1 — Acts 16:9–15; Psalm 67
Revelation 21:10,22–22:5; John 14:23–29

I will give them a heart to know that I am the Lord. Jeremiah 24:7

I fully am persuaded   769
and joyfully declare
I'm never left unaided,
my Father hears my prayer;
his comforts never fail me,
he stands at my right hand;
when tempests fierce assail me,
they're calm at his command.

Remember Jesus Christ, raised from the dead. 2 Timothy 2:8

Christians, dismiss your fear;   p91
let hope and joy succeed;
the joyful news with gladness hear,
"The Lord is ris'n indeed!"
The promise is fulfilled
in Christ our only Head;
justice with mercy's reconciled,
he lives who once was dead.

Father, you constantly remind us that you will never leave us or forsake us. Help us give our hearts to you so that you may fill them with your grace and mercy. Amen.

Monday, May 2 — Psalm 57:1–6
Leviticus 24:10–25:17; Mark 8:1–13

He bore the sin of many, and made intercession for the transgressors. Isaiah 53:12

> Beneath the cross of Jesus 329
> I long to take my stand;
> the shadow of a mighty rock
> within a weary land,
> a home within a wilderness,
> a rest upon the way,
> from the burning of the noontide heat,
> and burdens of the day.

For our sake God made him to be sin who knew no sin, so that in him we might become the righteousness of God. 2 Corinthians 5:21

> O love, how deep, how broad, how high, 485
> beyond all thought and fantasy,
> that God, the Son of God, should take
> our mortal form for mortals' sake.

Father, in a world where there is so much sin, we humbly bow before your throne, beneath the cross of Jesus, to seek your forgiveness. Help us to forgive others as you forgive us in our times of need. Amen.

Tuesday, May 3 — Psalm 57:7–11
Leviticus 25:18–55; Mark 8:14–21

I will teach transgressors your ways, and sinners will return to you. Psalm 51:13

> Dear Lord and Father of mankind,   739
> forgive our foolish ways;
> reclothe us in our rightful mind;
> in purer lives thy service find,
> in deeper rev'rence, praise.

Jesus said, "The time is fulfilled, and the kingdom of God has come near; repent, and believe in the good news." Mark 1:15

> Good news! Our Christ has come!   630*
> Good news to all the world.
> He comes to preach good news,
> new life forevermore.
> God's Spirit dwells in all who care,
> in all who share 'til want is gone.

Have mercy on us, O God, have mercy. When we seek the good news of the kingdom, you always show us how to let the Holy Spirit lead. Help us to put our trust in you for all your promises. Amen.

*   © by Sharon M. Benson

Wednesday, May 4 — Psalm 58
Leviticus 26:1–35; Mark 8:22–38

There are glad songs of victory in the tents of the righteous: "The right hand of the Lord is exalted; the right hand of the Lord does valiantly." Psalm 118:15–16

Glorious Lord, yourself impart! 558
Light of light, from God proceeding,
open now our ears and heart,
help us by your Spirit's pleading;
hear the cry that we are raising;
hear, and bless our prayers and praising.

The righteous will shine like the sun in the kingdom of their Father. Matthew 13:43

His kingdom cannot fail; 372
he rules o'er earth and heav'n;
the keys of death and hell
to Christ the Lord are giv'n.
Lift up your heart, lift up your voice,
rejoice, again I say, rejoice!

We pray, O Father, for justice on the earth. When no justice can be found, help us to know that justice will ultimately triumph because you are a God who will judge with complete fairness. Thank you, God. Amen.

Ascension Day

Watchword for the Ascension — Christ says, "I, when I am lifted up from the earth, will draw all people to myself." John 12:32

Thursday, May 5 — Psalm 59:1–9
Leviticus 26:36–27:15; Mark 9:1–10

Ascension of the Lord — Acts 1:1–11; Psalm 47
Ephesians 1:15–23; Luke 24:44–53

God is our refuge and strength, a very present help in trouble. Therefore we will not fear. Psalm 46:1–2

Alleluia! Heav'nly High Priest,   373
here on earth our help, our stay;
alleluia! Hear the sinful cry
to you from day to day.
Intercessor, Friend of sinners,
earth's Redeemer, hear our plea,
where the songs of all the sinless
sweep across the crystal sea.

Jesus said, "All authority in heaven and on earth has been given to me." Matthew 28:18

We thank you then, O Father,   p162
for all things bright and good,
the seedtime and the harvest,
our life, our health, our food;
help us to show thanksgiving
for all you freely give;
to love you in our neighbor,
and by the way we live.
All good gifts around us
are sent from heav'n above;
then thank the Lord,
O thank the Lord for all his love.

With praise and thanksgiving in our hearts we thank you, God, for your saving grace and help. Your constant love continues to outpour on us each day. May we freely give to others as you give to us. Amen.

Friday, May 6 — Psalm 59:10–17
Leviticus 27:16–Numbers 1:16; Mark 9:11–29

A soft answer turns away wrath, but a harsh word stirs up anger. Proverbs 15:1

To avert from us God's wrath,   416*
Jesus suffered in our stead;
by an ignominious death
he a full atonement made;
and by his most precious blood
brought us, sinners, nigh to God.

The Lord's servant must not be quarrelsome but kindly to everyone, an apt teacher, patient, correcting opponents with gentleness. 2 Timothy 2:24–25

Let knowledge grow from more to more,   401r
but more of reverence in us dwell;
that mind and soul, according well,
may make one music as before.

In your unfailing love, O God, help us to never forget that you are our Fortress and Strength. Each day we will sing of your new mercies and the joy that you bring to us. Amen.

* © by Dirk French

Saturday, May 7 — Psalm 60
Numbers 1:17–54; Mark 9:30–37

Then you shall see the difference between the righteous and the wicked, between one who serves God and one who does not serve him.
Malachi 3:18

> O Jesus, I have promised   603
> to serve you to the end;
> be now and ever near me,
> my master and my friend.
> I shall not fear the battle
> if you are by my side,
> nor wander from the pathway
> if you will be my guide.

Not everyone who says to me, "Lord, Lord," will enter the kingdom of heaven, but only the one who does the will of my Father in heaven.
Matthew 7:21

> Be still, my soul: the Lord is on your side.   757
> Bear patiently the cross of grief or pain;
> leave to your God to order and provide;
> in ev'ry change God faithful will remain.
> Be still, my soul: your best, your heav'nly friend
> through thorny ways leads to a joyful end.

All-powerful God, real help comes from you alone when situations seem out of control. But we know that you can do mighty and great things when we leave it to you, our God, to order and provide. Help us, we pray, to still our souls and wait upon you. Amen.

Ascension Sunday
Seventh Sunday of Easter

Watchword for the Week — Rejoice in the Lord, O you righteous, and give thanks to his holy name! Psalm 97:12

Sunday, May 8 — Acts 16:16–34; Psalm 97
Revelation 22:12–14,16–17,20–21; John 17:20–26

Sing to the Lord! Give praise to the Lord! He rescues the life of the needy from the hands of the wicked. Jeremiah 20:13 (NIV)

All people that on earth do dwell,   539
sing to the Lord with cheerful voice;
serve him with joy, his praises tell,
come now before him and rejoice.

Be joyful in hope, patient in affliction, faithful in prayer. Romans 12:12 (NIV)

Give thanks in hope, rejoice, repent,   451*
and practice all you prayed;
true thanks can never be content
to foul the world God made.
Lord, teach us all an attitude
that thanks you all our days,
a love that shows our gratitude
through deeds that live our praise.

We rejoice in knowing that you, O Lord, are King above the earth. Give us the patience and courage to face the challenges that arise in our homes and family lives. Bless those in authority as parents and guardians to seek your direction and guidance in taking care of your children on earth. Amen.

* © 1990 by David G. Mehrtens

Monday, May 9 — Psalm 61
Numbers 2; Mark 9:38–50

I will establish my covenant with you, and you shall know that I am the Lord. Ezekiel 16:62

> We covenant in church and home   p121
> this peace to show each other,
> to represent your steadfast love
> as sister and as brother.
> O, may we through each other know
> your grace which fails us never,
> and find at last our true abode
> within your house forever.

You have heard of this hope before in the word of the truth, the gospel that has come to you. Just as it is bearing fruit and growing in the whole world, so it has been bearing fruit among yourselves from the day you heard it and truly comprehended the grace of God. Colossians 1:5–6

> Praise him for his grace and favor   529
> to his people in distress.
> Praise him, still the same forever,
> slow to chide, and swift to bless.
> Alleluia! Alleluia!
> Glorious in his faithfulness!

Heavenly Father, we are so grateful that we can trust you wherever we are in our lives. We know that your will is our answer when we cry for help. We give thanks for this assurance, in the name of Jesus. Amen.

Tuesday, May 10 — Psalm 62
Numbers 3:1–32; Mark 10:1–12

I will save you that you may become a blessing. Zechariah 8:13 (NASB)

> Come, thou Fount of ev'ry blessing,   782
> tune my heart to sing thy grace;
> streams of mercy, never ceasing,
> call for songs of loudest praise.
> Teach me some melodious sonnet,
> sung by flaming tongues above.
> Praise the mount—I'm fixed upon it—
> mount of God's redeeming love.

Paul wrote: Not that we are competent of ourselves to claim anything as coming from us; our competence is from God. 2 Corinthians 3:5

> Breathe on me, breath of God,   494
> fill me with life anew,
> that I may love the things you love
> and do what you would do.

Lord, you continue to breathe the breath of life within us. Purge our spirits so that your life anew in us will be pleasing in your sight when we recognize that all things come from and through you. Amen.

Wednesday, May 11 — Psalm 63
Numbers 3:33–4:14; Mark 10:13–31

I, the Lord, am your Savior and your Redeemer, the mighty One. Isaiah 60:16

> Guide me, O my great Redeemer,   790
> pilgrim through this barren land.
> I am weak, but you are mighty;
> hold me with your pow'rful hand.
> Bread of heaven, bread of heaven,
> feed me now and evermore,
> feed me now and evermore.

Jesus took her by the hand and said to her, "Talitha cum," which means, "Little girl, get up!" And immediately the girl got up and began to walk about. Mark 5:41–42

> Stretch forth your hand, our health restore,   267
> and make us rise to fall no more;
> O let your face upon us shine
> and fill the world with love divine.

Father in heaven, continue to help us to realize that you are our guide through a barren land. We thank you for restoring our faith in you as we trust you to feed us now and evermore on our life's journey. Amen.

Thursday, May 12 — Psalm 64
Numbers 4:15–49; Mark 10:32–45

Do not fear or be dismayed! Joshua 8:1

> In heav'nly love abiding,   732
> no change my heart shall fear;
> and safe is such confiding,
> for nothing changes here.
> The storm may roar around me,
> my heart may low be laid,
> but God is round about me,
> and can I be dismayed?

Fight the good fight of the faith. 1 Timothy 6:12

> Fight the good fight with all your might;   413r
> Christ is your strength, and Christ your right;
> lay hold on life, and it shall be
> your joy and crown eternally.

Gracious God, we give thanks, knowing that when
we are going through the storms of life you are
there. In all areas of our lives, help us to let go
and let you work in us. Let your glory be revealed.
Amen.

Friday, May 13 — Psalm 65:1–8
Numbers 5; Mark 10:46–52

There is forgiveness with you, so that you may be revered. Psalm 130:4

Pardon, Lord, and are there those   779
who my debtors are, or foes?
I, who by forgiveness live,
here their trespasses forgive.

If we walk in the light as he himself is in the light, we have fellowship with one another, and the blood of Jesus his Son cleanses us from all sin. 1 John 1:7

Be thou my vision, O Lord of my heart;   719
naught be all else to me save that thou art—
thou my best thought, by day or by night,
waking or sleeping, thy presence my light.

Thank you, O Father, for being our vision and
leading us in the paths of righteousness. Help us to
open our spiritual eyes to experience your greatness
and your divine presence. These things we ask in
Jesus' name. Amen.

Saturday, May 14 — Psalm 65:9–13
Numbers 6; Mark 11:1–11

You shall not covet your neighbor's wife. Deuteronomy 5:21 (NIV)

> Jesus calls us; o'er the tumult   600
> of our life's wild, restless sea,
> day by day his voice is sounding,
> saying, "Christian, follow me."

For this is the will of God, your sanctification: that you abstain from fornication. 1 Thessalonians 4:3

> Teach me to feel that you are always nigh,   490
> teach me the struggles of the soul to bear,
> to check the rising doubt, the rebel sigh;
> teach me the patience of unceasing prayer.

Heavenly Father, we thank you for the love with which you continue to fill our spirits and for helping us to be at peace with you. Teach us to wait on you for the answers to our unceasing prayers, so that we can truly see the glory of God shining through our lives. Amen.

Day of Pentecost

Watchword for the Week — For all who are led by the Spirit of God are children of God. Romans 8:14

Sunday, May 15 — Acts 2:1–21; Psalm 104:24–34,35b
Romans 8:14–17; John 14:8–17,(25–27)

With my whole heart I seek you; do not let me stray from your commandments. Psalm 119:10

> Spirit, working in creation,   p223*
> bringing order out of strife:
> come among God's gathered people,
> giving harmony and life.

It is well for the heart to be strengthened by grace. Hebrews 13:9

> Make me a captive, Lord,   604
> And then I shall be free;
> force me to render up my sword,
> and I shall conquer'r be.
> I sink in life's alarms
> when by myself I stand;
> imprison me within your arms,
> and strong shall be my hand.

The time is now, O God, when we need to reach out more to you in our faith. We continue to fight battles and you remind us that we fight for you and that the victory is ours. Free us from the forces that keep us from clinging to you and help us to press onward with your promises. Amen.

* © by John Richards

Monday, May 16 — Psalm 66:1–7
Numbers 7:1–35; Mark 11:12–26

I will say, "They are my people;" and they will say, "The Lord is our God." Zechariah 13:9

> Come now, O Lord, 742
> and teach us how to pray.
> Teach us to ask ourselves from day to day
> if we are yours and yours alone will be
> through earthly days and through eternity.

You were going astray like sheep, but now you have returned to the shepherd and guardian of your souls. 1 Peter 2:25

> Shepherd of souls, refresh and bless 411
> your chosen pilgrim flock
> with manna in the wilderness,
> with water from the rock.

Gracious God, we kneel before you to give thanks for the refreshment that only you can give. Pardon us for the mistakes that we have made and the results of those mistakes which sometimes cause pain and sorrow. We lean on you now as our Shepherd and Guardian. Amen.

Tuesday, May 17 — Psalm 66:8–15
Numbers 7:36–71; Mark 11:27–12:12

You shall be called priests of the Lord; you shall be named ministers of our God. Isaiah 61:6

> Ye who called, ye who called 636
> to Christ's service are,
> join together, join together
> both in work and prayer;
> venture all on him, our Lord,
> who assures us in his word,
> we are always, we are always
> objects of his care.

Paul wrote to Timothy: I remind you to rekindle the gift of God that is within you. 2 Timothy 1:6

> Spirit of God, who dwells within my heart, 490
> wean it from sin, through all its pulses move.
> Stoop to my weakness, mighty as you are,
> and make me love you as I ought to love.

We bow before you this day to honor, worship, and praise you, living God. The Psalmist reminds us that you are our light, strength, and salvation, and no good thing will you withhold from those who walk uprightly. Hear our prayer today at this time, and renew a right spirit within us. Amen.

Wednesday, May 18 — Psalm 66:16–20
Numbers 7:72–8:4; Mark 12:13–17

You shall be holy, for I the Lord your God am holy. Leviticus 19:2 (NASB)

Holy, holy, holy Lord God Almighty!   381
Early in the morning our song shall rise to thee;
holy, holy, holy, merciful and mighty!
God in three persons, blessed Trinity!

Clothe yourselves with the new self, created according to the likeness of God in true righteousness and holiness. Ephesians 4:24

New every morning is the love   510r
our wakening and uprising prove,
through sleep and darkness safely brought,
restored to life and power and thought.

We give thanks, dear Father, that you wake us to receive new mercies and blessings each day. We are so grateful that we can rise and know that you are always there to lead and guide us even when we become preoccupied. We love you, Father; in the name of Jesus we pray. Amen.

Thursday, May 19 — Psalm 67
Numbers 8:5–9:14; Mark 12:18–34

All people are grass, their constancy is like the flower of the field. The grass withers, the flower fades; but the word of our God will stand forever. Isaiah 40:6,8

O word of God incarnate, 505
O wisdom from on high,
O truth unchanged, unchanging,
O light of our dark sky:
we praise you for the radiance
that from the Scripture's page,
a lantern to our footsteps,
shines on from age to age.

Heaven and earth will pass away, but my words will not pass away. Mark 13:31

Beautiful Savior! 470
Lord of the nations!
Son of God and Son of man!
Glory and honor,
praise, adoration,
now and forevermore be thine!

We stand amazed at your goodness and greatness, gracious Savior, as we seek to walk closer in communion with you. Sin is so prevalent in our human societies. Give us a clear vision of who we are and remind us that we are your representation here on earth. Let us act justly and walk humbly before our God. Amen.

Friday, May 20 — Psalm 68:1–6
Numbers 9:15–10:36; Mark 12:35–44

You shall not join hands with the wicked to act as a malicious witness. Exodus 23:1

> How shall I follow him I serve?   191r
> How shall I copy him I love?
> Nor from those blessed footsteps swerve,
> which lead me to his seat above?

So then, putting away falsehood, let all of us speak the truth to our neighbors. Ephesians 4:25

> Lord, speak to me that I may speak   646
> in living echoes of your tone.
> As you have sought, so let me seek
> your erring children lost and lone.

We ask you, Gracious Savior, to calm our thoughts
and our spirits so that we may hear from you
when you need to speak to us. The still small voice
reminds us that you are never far away and we
only need to quiet ourselves before your throne.
Have mercy upon us we pray. Amen.

Saturday, May 21 — Psalm 68:7–18
Numbers 11; Mark 13:1–13

The Lord God is a sun and shield. Psalm 84:11

Lord of all being, throned afar, 464
your glory flames from sun and star;
center and soul of ev'ry sphere,
yet to each loving heart how near!

Therefore do not worry. Matthew 6:31

My Shepherd will supply my need; 730
the Lord God is his name.
In pastures fresh he makes me feed,
beside the living stream.
He brings my wand'ring spirit back
when I forsake his ways,
and leads me for his mercy's sake
in paths of truth and grace.

When we worry, Lord, it reminds us that we do
not trust you fully. We allow fear to override your
promises for us. Remind us that all things belong
to you and that you always have the final say. We
give you thanks. Amen.

Trinity Sunday

Watchword for the Week — Since we are justified by faith, we have peace with God through our Lord Jesus Christ. Romans 5:1

Sunday, May 22 — Proverbs 8:1–4,22–31; Psalm 8
Romans 5:1–5; John 16:12–15

Come, let us go to entreat the favor of the Lord, and to seek the Lord of hosts; I myself am going. Zechariah 8:21

> In the morning when I rise,   573
> in the morning when I rise,
> in the morning when I rise,
> give me Jesus.
> Give me Jesus, give me Jesus,
> you may have all this world,
> give me Jesus.

Through him we have access by one Spirit to the Father. Ephesians 2:18 (NKJV)

> Spirit of truth, and grace, and pow'r,   p99*
> blow through your church, we pray.
> Transform us from this very hour
> in all we do and say.

Thank you, God, that we have access to you and your Son Jesus Christ by the one Spirit. We behave at times as though we have no communication with you and need to fix all things on our own. Forgive us, gracious Father, and show us today that your promises never fail us when we stand on your word. Amen.

* © by Darryl Bell

Monday, May 23 — Psalm 68:19–27
Numbers 12:1–13:16 Mark 13:14–27

You shall rise up before the grayheaded and honor the aged. Leviticus 19:32 (NASB)

Grant us and all our children grace   496r
so here on earth to run our race
that we in heaven may meet and sing
eternal praise to you, our King.

Outdo one another in showing honor. Romans 12:10

Show God's mercy, show God's mercy   52s*
unto one and all;
without judging, without judging
as we heed our call;
this is how our church shall be:
filled with love and liberty,
in the Spirit, in the Spirit
of our Savior's law.

You have created us in your image to serve and to honor each other in Jesus Christ. Yet sometimes we behave as though we must choose whom we serve and care for. Teach us to respect and love each other so that our lives here on earth are blessings to others, as you always bless us. Amen.

* William E. Gramley (1993). © 2013 by Interprovincial Board of Communication and Moravian Music Foundation.

Tuesday, May 24 — Psalm 68:28–35
Numbers 13:17–33; Mark 13:28–37

Woe to those who make unjust laws to deprive the poor of their rights and withhold justice from the oppressed. Isaiah 10:1–2 (NIV)

Blessed are the poor in spirit,   595
claiming nothing as their own,
but as giv'n them by their Father
that his goodness may be shown.
Blessed are they who share the sorrow
of their God's unchanging love;
they shall know his presence with them
and his promised comfort prove.

What partnership is there between righteousness and lawlessness? Or what fellowship is there between light and darkness? 2 Corinthians 6:14

Still the earth in darkness lies.   276*
Up from death's dark vale arise
voices of a world in grief,
prayers of those who seek relief;
to our darkness bring new birth,
"Peace, good will to all on earth."

God of justice and mercy, guide the nations of the world into the way of justice and truth. Establish among them that peace which is the fruit of righteousness that they may become the kingdom of our Lord and Savior Jesus Christ. Amen.

* © by Eleanor R. Roller

Wednesday, May 25 — Psalm 69:1–12
Numbers 14; Mark 14:1–11

The Lord will command his angels concerning you to guard you in all your ways. On their hands they will bear you up, so that you will not dash your foot against a stone. Psalm 91:11–12

> Stand up, and bless the Lord,   531
> you people of his choice!
> Stand up and bless the Lord your God,
> with heart and soul and voice.

Paul wrote: The Lord stood by me and gave me strength. 2 Timothy 4:17

> The Lord's joy be our strength and stay   734
> in our employ from day to day;
> our thoughts and our activity
> through Jesus' merits hallowed be.

We forget that you, God, are our strength and stay, and even in our busyness we weary ourselves as we go about our day-to-day chores. In our hearts you are asking us to rest in you. Forgive us; bring us to the awareness that you alone give us true rest. In your name we pray. Amen.

Thursday, May 26 — Psalm 69:13–21
Numbers 15:1–31; Mark 14:12–31

Make known his deeds among the nations; proclaim that his name is exalted. Isaiah 12:4

We covenant with hand and heart   p209
to follow Christ our Lord;
with world, and sin, and self to part,
and to obey his word;
to love each other heartily,
in truth and with sincerity,
and under cross, reproach, and shame,
to glorify his name.

Jesus said to them, "Go into all the world and proclaim the good news to the whole creation." Mark 16:15

Go, go, go,   412*
into the world we must go;
go tell to others how Jesus loves them,
go to serve freely, thus, we may show them
God above gives all of us his love.

Heavenly Father, sometimes we are scared to go out and proclaim the good news to those we meet, as too often we prefer issues over people and selfishness over helping others. Forgive our foolish ways, dear Savior, and bring us to that saving knowledge that when we share the good news, we are also winning souls for your kingdom. Amen.

*   © by Albert H. Frank

Friday, May 27 — Psalm 69:22–29
Numbers 15:32–16:27; Mark 14:32–42

Lord, do not let the downtrodden be put to shame. Psalm 74:21

> So brothers, sisters, praise his name   781
> who died to set us free from sin,
> division, hate, and shame,
> from spite and enmity!

My grace is sufficient for you, for my power is made perfect in weakness. 2 Corinthians 12:9 (NIV)

> O majestic Being,   554
> may our souls and bodies
> at all times be at your service!
> Like the holy angels
> who bow down before you,
> may we ceaselessly adore you,
> and through grace, Jesus' grace,
> in our whole demeanor,
> offer praise and honor.

Heavenly Father, help us to receive the gift of grace that only you can give when we seek your salvation in our lives. Help us to remember that we toil unto you, and not unto ourselves, in your vineyard here on earth as we continue to seek your great salvation. Our thanks we lift to you. Amen.

Saturday, May 28 — Psalm 69:30–36
Numbers 16:28–17:13; Mark 14:43–52

He has redeemed my soul from going down to the pit, and my life shall see the light. Job 33:28

Refresh your people on their toilsome way;   p139
lead us from night to never-ending day;
fill all our lives with heav'n-born love and grace,
until at last we meet before your face.

God raised the Lord and will also raise us by his power. 1 Corinthians 6:14

Rise my soul, adore your Maker;   568
angels sing, praises bring,
with them be partaker.
Father, Lord of ev'ry spirit,
in your might, lead me right
through my Savior's merit.

God, we walk as though we have no hope in you.
Your word declares that nothing can separate
us from your love which is in Christ Jesus. Melt
us, mold us, fill us, use us in your ministry as we
journey on our toilsome way here on earth, for you
are our faithful God. Amen.

Second Sunday after Pentecost

Watchword for the Week — Declare God's glory among the nations, his marvelous works among all the peoples. Psalm 96:3

Sunday, May 29 — 1 Kings 8:22–23,41–43; Psalm 96:1–9
Galatians 1:1–12; Luke 7:1–10

I stretch out my hands to you; my soul thirsts for you like a parched land. Psalm 143:6

> I need thee ev'ry hour,   740
> most gracious Lord;
> no other voice but thine
> can peace afford.
> I need thee, O I need thee,
> ev'ry hour I need thee!
> O bless me now, my Savior—
> I come to thee.

Come to me, all you that are weary and are carrying heavy burdens, and I will give you rest. Matthew 11:28

> Help then, O Lord, our unbelief;   713
> and may our faith abound
> to call on you when you are near
> and seek where you are found.

We pause to say within our hearts that we need you, God. Troubles come our way, burdens are heavy, and we can no longer walk the path. We feel like giving up, but you remind us that you carried the cross to Calvary for us and took all of our burdens. Refresh our spirits, Lord, and have mercy on us. Amen.

Monday, May 30 — Psalm 70
Numbers 18:1–24; Mark 14:53–65

God said to Moses, "I am who I am." Exodus 3:14

Jerusalem the golden, 814
descending from above,
the city of God's presence,
the vision of God's love—
I know not, O I know not
what joys await us there,
what radiancy of glory,
what bliss beyond compare!

Jesus Christ says, "I am with you always, to the end of the age." Matthew 28:20

Lord God, Son, p35
the Savior of the world,
be gracious unto us.
Lord God, Holy Spirit,
abide with us forever.

Hear our prayer, O Lord, in the words of the hymn
writer. We are reminded of the great city Jerusalem,
descending from above and the joy that waits for
us there. We celebrate and rejoice in knowing and
tasting such sweet bliss beyond compare. Incline
your ear to us, and grant us your peace. Amen.

Tuesday, May 31 — Psalm 71:1–8
Numbers 18:25–19:22; Mark 14:66–72

Blessed are those who act justly, who always do what is right. Psalm 106:3 (NIV)

Jesus comes with clouds descending;   259
see the Lamb for sinners slain!
Thousand, thousand saints attending
Join to sing the glad refrain:
Alleluia! Alleluia!
Christ the Lord returns to reign!

This is my commandment, that you love one another as I have loved you. John 15:12

Love divine, all loves excelling,   474
joy of heav'n, to earth come down!
Fix in us your humble dwelling,
all your faithful mercies crown.
Jesus, you are all compassion,
pure, unbounded love impart!
Visit us with your salvation,
enter ev'ry trembling heart.

Fill our hearts today with the knowledge that we have a purpose to fulfill, as we come to your throne asking for the confidence and the courage to complete the tasks set before us. As we close another month in this year, help us to walk in your deep love with our brothers and sisters. Bless us we pray. Amen.

Wednesday, June 1 — Psalm 71:9–18a
Numbers 20:1–21:9; Mark 15:1–20

I gave them my statutes and showed them my ordinances, by whose observance everyone shall live. Ezekiel 20:11

> Then let us place ourselves   698*
> in God's creative hands,
> anchored in faith, but free
> to do what God commands:
> not pris'ners of our heritage
> but born to serve the present age.

Jesus answered, "Those who love me will keep my word, and my Father will love them, and we will come to them and make our home with them." John 14:23

> To you our vows with sweet accord,   677
> head of your church, we pay;
> we and our house will serve you, Lord;
> your word we will obey.
> Grant us and all our children grace
> in word and deed your name to praise,
> and in each family, your will
> and purpose to fulfill.

Lord, make your home in our hearts and guide us to live in your ways. Give us the strength to honor you through our words and actions, to praise you alone, and to shine your light in the world. Amen.

Thursday, June 2 — Psalm 71:18b–24
Numbers 21:10–22:6; Mark 15:21–32

Turn back from your evil ways; for why will you die? Ezekiel 33:11

Amazing grace! How sweet the sound   783
that saved a wretch like me!
I once was lost, but now am found,
was blind, but now I see.

There will be more joy in heaven over one sinner who repents than over ninety-nine righteous persons who need no repentance. Luke 15:7

For the herald's voice is crying   264
in the desert far and near,
calling us to true repentance,
since the Kingdom now is here.
O, that warning cry obey!
Now prepare for God a way!
Let the valleys rise to meet him,
and the hills bow down to greet him!

Faithful Father, thank you for the hope, peace,
joy, and love that knowing you brings to our lives.
Help us to take comfort in you in times of trial and
suffering, and to praise you with our whole beings
in times of joy and celebration. Amen.

Friday, June 3 — Psalm 72:1–11
Numbers 22:7–41; Mark 15:33–47

**Even the sparrow finds a home, and the swallow
a nest for herself, where she may lay her young,
at your altars, O Lord of hosts, my King and my
God. Psalm 84:3**

> The sure provisions of my God   730
> attend me all my days;
> O may your house be my abode
> and all my work be praise.
> There would I find a settled rest,
> while others go and come—
> no more a stranger or a guest,
> but like a child at home.

**So then you are no longer strangers and aliens,
but you are citizens with the saints and also
members of the household of God. Ephesians 2:19**

> By love's closest bonds united,   515
> as the Lord's own family,
> be to serve his name excited,
> be to him a fruitful tree.

Gracious, heavenly Father, teach all those
in positions of power about your justice and
righteousness. Be with those living in poverty and
oppression that they may find a life of abundance
through you. Empower us to do your mission, to be
your sheep, and to take the time to listen for you
each and every day. Amen.

Saturday, June 4 — Psalm 72:12–20
Numbers 23; Mark 16:1–13

**I will show love to Judah; and I will save them—
not by bow, sword or battle, or by horses and
horsemen, but I, the Lord their God, will save
them. Hosea 1:7 (NIV)**

Eternal Father, strong to save,   725
whose arm has bound the restless wave,
who bade the mighty ocean deep
its own appointed limits keep:
O hear us when we cry to thee
for those in peril on the sea.

**So it depends not on human will or exertion, but
on God who shows mercy. Romans 9:16**

Now to the ends of the earth   547*
see his salvation is shown;
and still he remembers
his mercy and truth,
unchanging in love to his own.

Heavenly Father, thank you for our many blessings,
gifts, and talents. Show us how to use these blessings
to glorify you. Give us true understanding of your
words of love, and give us trust in your ways that we
may better hear and see your will. Amen.

Third Sunday after Pentecost

Watchword for the Week — Sing praises to the Lord, O you his
faithful ones, and give thanks to his holy name. Psalm 30:4

Sunday, June 5 — 1 Kings 17:17–24; Psalm 30
Galatians 1:11–24; Luke 7:11–17

Moses said to the Lord, "If your presence does not go with us, do not send us up from here." Exodus 33:15 (NIV)

> Thanks we give and adoration   p145
> for the gospel's joyful sound;
> may the fruits of your salvation
> in our hearts and lives abound.
> May your presence, may your presence,
> with us, evermore, be found.

When the Spirit of truth comes, he will guide you into all the truth. John 16:13

> Thou, O Christ, art all I want;   724
> more than all in thee I find;
> raise the fallen, cheer the faint,
> heal the sick and lead the blind.
> Just and holy is thy name,
> I am all unrighteousness,
> false and full of sin I am,
> thou art full of truth and grace.

Loving God, thank you for your words that remind
us that your people will always have enough.
Thank you for our lives of abundance; help us to
share that abundance with those in need. Walk
with us each day, and help us to slow down to see
your love and works of wonder in the world around
us. Amen.

Monday, June 6 — Psalm 73:1–12
Numbers 24,25; Mark 16:14– Luke 1:4

Woe to you who join house to house, and add field to field, until there is room for no one but you, and you are left to live alone in the midst of the land! Isaiah 5:8

> For food in a world where many walk in hunger,   829
> for friends in a world where many walk alone,
> for faith in a world where many walk in fear,
> we give you thanks, O God.

Take care! Be on your guard against all kinds of greed; for one's life does not consist in the abundance of possessions. Luke 12:15

> Come, O Christ, and reign among us,   648
> King of love and Prince of peace;
> hush the storm of strife and passion,
> bid its cruel discords cease.
> By your patient years of toiling,
> by your silent hours of pain,
> quench our fevered thirst of pleasure;
> stem our selfish greed of gain.

Holy One, give us pure hearts and minds; help us to think and act with the love that you have taught us. Forgive us when we stray and think or act in jealousy, and remind us of our many blessings. Help us to proclaim your truth and love in all that we think and do. In Jesus' name we pray. Amen.

Tuesday, June 7 — Psalm 73:13–20
Numbers 26:1–24; Luke 1:5–25

You show me the path of life. Psalm 16:11

Wherever he may guide me,   732
no want shall turn me back;
my Shepherd is beside me,
and nothing can I lack.
His wisdom ever waking,
his sight is never dim,
he knows the way he's taking,
and I will walk with him.

The free gift of God is eternal life in Christ Jesus our Lord. Romans 6:23

Lord, you give beyond all measure: 82s*
gifts of beauty, gifts of grace,
gifts of earth and gifts of heaven,
gifts for all the human race;
sacred gift of Christ, most blessed,
freedom from our sins confessed:
all we have comes from above.
Thank you, Lord, for boundless love.

Teacher, light the path that you have laid for us to
follow so that we might see your plans for us and
know your will. Give us the strength and courage
to follow where you lead, trusting in you with our
whole selves. Amen.

* © 2007 by Nancy Sawtelle

Wednesday, June 8 — Psalm 73:21–28
Numbers 26:25–56; Luke 1:26–38

The Lord lifts up those who are bowed down.
Psalm 146:8

> This day is holy to the Lord;   821
> this day the Lord has made;
> we will rejoice with one accord
> and in his name be glad.
> Come, let us worship and bow down,
> with thanks appear before his throne;
> he to our songs of praise and prayer
> will lend a gracious ear.

Jesus said in a loud voice, "Let anyone who is thirsty come to me and drink." John 7:37 (NIV)

> Come, you thirsty, come and welcome,   765
> God's free bounty glorify;
> true belief and true repentance,
> ev'ry grace that brings you nigh.
> I will arise and go to Jesus;
> he will embrace me in his arms;
> in the arms of my dear Savior,
> O there are ten thousand charms.

Father, be with us when our minds and bodies are weak and we find it difficult to understand your ways. Help us to lay our burdens at your feet and take comfort and strength in you and your promise of eternity. Amen.

Thursday, June 9 — Psalm 74:1–9
Numbers 26:57–27:23; Luke 1:39–45

God will not take away a life; he will devise plans so as not to keep an outcast banished forever from his presence. 2 Samuel 14:14

> Good news is ours to tell! p160*
> Let no one fail to hear!
> God gives us life;
> God conquers death!
> What's left for us to fear?

The scribes said to Jesus' disciples, "Why does he eat with tax collectors and sinners?" When Jesus heard this, he said to them, "Those who are well have no need of a physician, but those who are sick." Mark 2:16–17

> Be welcome, Lord; be now our guest. 307
> By you poor sinners have been blessed.
> In nakedness and cold you lie.
> How can I thank you; how can I?

Lord, open our hearts to love all those we meet, our eyes to see all those in need, our hands to hold and help where we can, our minds to learn from others and to allow you to lead, and our ears to listen more than we speak and to hear your words. Amen.

Friday, June 10 — Psalm 74:10–17
Numbers 28:1–29:6; Luke 1:46–56

What god in heaven or on earth can perform deeds and mighty acts like yours! Deuteronomy 3:24

Lord of glory, God most high,   744
man exalted to the sky,
with your love my heart now fill;
prompt me to perform your will!
Then your glory I shall see;
blessed for all eternity.

Everyone then who hears these words of mine and acts on them will be like a wise man who built his house on rock. Matthew 7:24

What though my joys and comforts die?   701
The Lord my Savior's living.
What though the darkness gather round?
Songs in the night he's giving.
No storm can shake my inmost calm,
while to that Rock I'm clinging.
Since love is Lord of heaven and earth,
how can I keep from singing?

Gracious God, let our hearts be filled with gratitude,
let our voices rise to praise you, and let our hands
outstretch to serve you. Let us praise and honor you
with our gifts offered freely, for your blessings are
bountiful. Amen.

Saturday, June 11 — Psalm 74:18–23
Numbers 29:7–40; Luke 1:57–66

By the ordinances of the Lord is your servant warned. Psalm 19:11

Gather together, sing as one,   536*
raising up a joyful song
high and loud, into the air,
broadcast praises ev'rywhere.
Deep in our hearts we tend the flame,
and as your servants we remain.
By this, we will our voices unite,
bringing glory day and night.

Pay attention to how you listen. Luke 8:18

O let me hear you speaking   603
in accents clear and still,
above the storms of passion,
the murmurs of self-will.
O speak to reassure me,
to hasten or control;
and speak to make me listen,
O guardian of my soul.

Forgive us, God, when we fail to walk with you;
guide us back to you, and fill us with your love and
grace that we might better serve you. Amen.

Fourth Sunday after Pentecost

Watchword for the Week — We know that a person is justified not by the works of the law but through faith in Jesus Christ. Galatians 2:16

Sunday, June 12 — 2 Samuel 11:26–12:10,13–15; Psalm 32
Galatians 2:15–21; Luke 7:36–8:3

Teach me to do your will, for you are my God. Let your good spirit lead me on a level path. Psalm 143:10

> Be with me, Lord, where'er I go;   733
> teach me what you would have me do;
> suggest whate'er I think or say;
> direct me in the narrow way.

As you therefore have received Christ Jesus the Lord, continue to live your lives in him, rooted and built up in him and established in the faith. Colossians 2:6–7

> Blessed name! the rock on which we build,   487
> our shield and resting place,
> our never-failing comfort,
> filled with blessings of his grace.
> O Jesus, Shepherd, Guardian, Friend,
> our Prophet, Priest, and King,
> our Lord, our Life, our Way, our End,
> accept the praise we bring.

Thank you, God, for your gift of love and grace through your Son, Jesus Christ. Help us to live lives rooted deep in faith, acting in love toward all as Jesus taught. Amen.

Monday, June 13 — Psalm 75
Numbers 30:1–31:12; Luke 1:67–80

You shall be like a watered garden, like a spring of water, whose waters never fail. Isaiah 58:11

Living water, never ending   767*
quench the thirst and flood the soul.
Well-spring, source of life eternal,
drench our dryness, make us whole.

Those who drink of the water that I will give them will never be thirsty. The water that I will give will become in them a spring of water gushing up to eternal life. John 4:14

The cup of water giv'n for you   581
still holds the freshness of your grace;
yet long these multitudes to view
the strong compassion in your face.

God, we thank you for your promise of abundance.
Sustain us through difficult times and help us to
remain faithful to you. Bless all those who don't
have enough; teach us to be helping hands of
love and make us compassionate to those in need.
Amen.

*   © 1991 by G.I.A. Publications, Inc.

Tuesday, June 14 — Psalm 76
Numbers 31:13–47; Luke 2:1–20

Commit your way to the Lord; trust in him, and he will act. Psalm 37:5

If you but trust in God to guide you   712
and place your confidence in him,
you'll find him always there beside you
to give you hope and strength within;
for those who trust God's changeless love
build on the rock that will not move.

Through Jesus Christ we have obtained access to this grace in which we stand; and we boast in our hope of sharing the glory of God. Romans 5:2

Here may we gain from heav'n   517
the grace which we implore;
and may that grace, once giv'n,
be with us evermore,
until that day when all the blessed
to endless rest are called away!

Keep us humble and in wonder of your glory, God. Help us to trust in you, and to honor and praise you throughout our lives for the grace and hope that we share through the gift of your Son. Amen.

Wednesday, June 15 — Psalm 77:1–9
Numbers 31:48–32:27; Luke 2:21–32

Must I not take care to say what the Lord puts into my mouth? Numbers 23:12

Keep me from saying words   615
that later need recalling;
guard me, lest idle speech
may from my lips be falling;
but when, within my place,
I must and ought to speak,
then to my words give grace,
lest I offend the weak.

We cannot keep from speaking about what we have seen and heard. Acts 4:20

Together met, together bound,   415*
we'll go our different ways,
and as his people in the world,
we'll live and speak his praise.

Lord, be our comfort on stressful days and sleepless nights, when our minds are full of worry and anxiety. Shine in our hearts, ease our troubled minds, and give us the optimism, strength, and clarity of mind that we need to overcome our obstacles. Amen.

Thursday, June 16 — Psalm 77:10–15
Numbers 32:28–33:9; Luke 2:33–40

The Lord knows our thoughts, that they are but an empty breath. Psalm 94:11

> O that Jesus' love and merit   589
> filled our hearts both night and day!
> May the leading of his Spirit
> all our thoughts and actions sway!
> Then should we be ever ready
> cheerfully to testify
> how our spirit, soul, and body
> do in God our Savior joy.

Do not claim to be wiser than you are. Romans 12:16

> Be thou my wisdom, and thou my true word;   719
> I ever with thee and thou with me, Lord;
> thou my great Father, I thy true son;
> thou in me dwelling, and I with thee one.

Heavenly Father, guide our prayer and meditation to your wonder. Help our thoughts to remain positive and rooted in love. Let us speak only words of love and act with kindness and humility. Amen.

Friday, June 17 — Psalm 77:16–20
Numbers 33:10–56; Luke 2:41–52

Let the prophet who has a dream tell the dream, but let the one who has my word speak my word faithfully. What has straw in common with wheat? says the Lord. Jeremiah 23:28

My gracious master and my God,   548
assist me to proclaim,
to spread through all the earth abroad
the honors of your name.

Beloved, do not believe every spirit, but test the spirits. 1 John 4:1

So to our God we sing praises,   316*
who all our spirits upraises,
and we rejoice in the telling
of his dear grace in us dwelling.

Faithful Shepherd, lead us; through trial and injustice, lead us; through stress and business, lead us; through illness and loss, lead us. Carry us when we are weak and tired, find us when we are lost, heal us when we are sick; leave no one behind. Faithful Shepherd, lead your flock. Amen.

*   © Vernon H. Nelson

Saturday, June 18 — Psalm 78:1–8
Numbers 34; Luke 3:1–20

And Jerusalem shall be to me a name of joy, a praise and a glory before all the nations of the earth who shall hear of all the good that I do for them. Jeremiah 33:9

> In Christ now meet both east and west,   523
> in him meet south and north,
> all Christly souls are one in him
> throughout the whole wide earth.

Christ has become a servant of the circumcised on behalf of the truth of God in order that he might confirm the promises given to the patriarchs, and in order that the Gentiles might glorify God for his mercy. Romans 15:8–9

> Sing we now with joyfulness,   55s*
> our voices joined as one.
> Christ is our true happiness;
> all praise to God's dear Son.
> We lift our voices singing
> in grateful thanks and praise
> to Christ whose love surrounds us
> throughout our lifelong days.

God, in this time of greed and injustice where what we have is never enough, let us be reminded of what is truly important. Let our hearts and prayers be filled with gratitude. Help us to give to those with less, be fair and just with others, and listen to and live your teachings of love. Amen.

* © 2004 by Thom Stapleton

Fifth Sunday after Pentecost

Watchword for the Week — For dominion belongs to the Lord, and he rules over the nations. Psalm 22:28

Sunday, June 19 — Isaiah 65:1–9; Psalm 22:19–28
Galatians 3:23–29; Luke 8:26–39

Thus says the Lord: heaven is my throne and the earth is my footstool; what is the house that you would build for me? Isaiah 66:1

We are God's house of living stones,   512
built for his own habitation;
he fills our hearts, his humble thrones,
granting us life and salvation.
Yet to this place, an earthly frame,
we come with thanks to praise his name;
God grants his people true blessing.

If anyone says to you at that time, "Look! Here is the Messiah!" or "Look! There he is!"—do not believe it. Mark 13:21

Rejoice, rejoice, believers,   256
and let your lights appear;
the evening is advancing,
and darker night is near.
The bridegroom is arising
and soon is drawing nigh.
Up, pray and watch and wrestle;
at midnight comes the cry.

Heavenly Sustainer, as we gather for worship today, we pray for safety in our travels, and we thank you for our church fellowship. We ask that you strengthen and restore us. Let us be inspired by one another and by your words and our pastors' words. Strengthen us, restore us, and fill us with your peace and love to help us through the week ahead. Amen.

Monday, June 20 — Psalm 78:9–16
Numbers 35:1–30; Luke 3:21–38

Though the Lord is high, he regards the lowly; but the haughty he perceives from far away. Psalm 138:6

Humble, holy, all resigned   175r
to your will—your will be done!
Give me, Lord, the perfect mind
of your well-beloved Son.

God chose what is low and despised in the world. 1 Corinthians 1:28

Made to live at one with others,   91s*
we build human barriers high;
we make labels to divide us;
born to live, we choose to die.
Yet, among us God is loving;
may God's love through us be done.

Father, give us energy and serenity for the week ahead. Help us to feel fulfilled by the work that we do, and to be mindful that we do all things through you and for you. Be with us this week, lead our decisions, and calm our minds so that we may focus on you. Amen.

* Hermann I. Weinlick (1986). © 2013 by Interprovincial Board of Communication and Moravian Music Foundation.

Tuesday, June 21 — Psalm 78:17–31
Numbers 35:31–Deuteronomy 1:18; Luke 4:1–13

So acknowledge and take to heart this day that the Lord is God in heaven above and on the earth below. There is no other. Deuteronomy 4:39 (NIV)

> 'Tis a pleasant thing to see   670
> brothers in the Lord agree,
> sisters of a God of love
> live as they shall live above,
> acting each a Christian part,
> one in word and one in heart.

He is not far from each one of us. For "In him we live and move and have our being." Acts 17:27–28

> Proclaim to ev'ry people, tongue, and nation   618
> that God, in whom they live and move, is love;
> tell how he stooped to save his lost creation,
> and died on earth that we might live in love.
> Publish glad tidings, tidings of peace,
> tidings of Jesus, redemption, and release.

May our homes be a refuge from the stress and injustice in the world around us where we are safe, rejuvenated, and loved. May our schools inspire a love of learning where students and teachers feel safe, loved, and happy. Bless our homes and schools, that they may be places where we grow closer to you. Amen.

Wednesday, June 22 — Psalm 78:32–39
Deuteronomy 1:19–46; Luke 4:14–21

So now, O Israel, what does the Lord your God require of you? Only to fear the Lord your God, to walk in all his ways, to love him, to serve the Lord your God with all your heart and with all your soul. Deuteronomy 10:12

> Fairest Lord Jesus! King of creation!   470
> Son of God and Son of man!
> Truly I'd love thee, truly I'd serve thee,
> light of my soul, my joy, my crown.

Whoever obeys his word, truly in this person the love of God has reached perfection. By this we may be sure that we are in him. 1 John 2:5

> By faith your word has made us bold   p228
> to seize the gift of love retold;
> all that you are we here receive,
> and all we are to you we give.

Lord, hear the prayers of all those in need, of those who are sick, hungry, homeless, oppressed, and impoverished. For all those who carry a heavy burden, please lighten their load. Help them to find your light and love in the world. Amen.

Thursday, June 23 — Psalm 78:40–55
Deuteronomy 2; Luke 4:22–30

You have given me the shield of your salvation, and your right hand has supported me. Psalm 18:35

> Now God be with us, for the night is closing,   575
> the light and darkness are of his disposing;
> and 'neath his shadow here to rest
> we yield us, for he will shield us.

The kingdom of God does not consist in words but in power. 1 Corinthians 4:20 (NASB)

> Then let us adore and give him his right,   565
> all glory and pow'r and wisdom and might,
> all honor and blessing, with angels above,
> and thanks never ceasing for infinite love.

Guide our nation and world leaders, grant them wisdom, conviction, courage, and compassion. We pray for an end to hatred and war, for a world united in love and peace. We pray for the ecological healing of our world, that we may be conscious of our impact on your creation. Help us to be better stewards of the world we live in and all those who inhabit it. Amen.

Friday, June 24 — Psalm 78:56–64
Deuteronomy 3; Luke 4:31–44

O magnify the Lord with me, and let us exalt his name together. Psalm 34:3

Kindle within us and preserve that fire,   377
which will with holy love our hearts inspire,
and with an active zeal our soul inflame
to do your will and glorify your name.

There was a man sent from God, whose name was John. He came as a witness to testify to the light, so that all might believe through him. John 1:6–7

Teach us to love in truth,   801*
to give and to receive
with joyful and with open hearts,
with all that we believe;
to seek another's good,
to honor what is right,
to let our will and our desire
be held in holy light.

God, thank you for our church families where
we share and strengthen our faith. Empower and
inspire us to live your love in the world each and
every day. Amen.

Saturday, June 25 — Psalm 78:65–72
Deuteronomy 4:1–31; Luke 5:1–11

The steadfast love of the Lord is from everlasting to everlasting on those who fear him, and his righteousness to children's children, to those who keep his covenant. Psalm 103:17–18

Now let our souls be fed   p198
with manna from above,
and over us the banner spread
of everlasting love.

Jesus Christ is the same yesterday and today and forever. Hebrews 13:8

Bless the Lord, O my soul!   534*
All within me bless God's name!
Bless the Lord, who was, and is,
and shall ever be the same!
As a parent's love is endless,
so God's mercy follows us;
for the Lord who framed our being
well recalls that we are dust!

God, we pray for Christians, that we might hear your words and seek a deeper faith. Open our minds, hearts, and hands to love others so that we may share with them the good news of your grace. Amen.

Sixth Sunday after Pentecost

Watchword for the Week — If we live by the Spirit, let us also be guided by the Spirit. Galatians 5:25

Sunday, June 26 — 1 Kings 19:15–16,19–21; Psalm 16
Galatians 5:1,13–25; Luke 9:51–62

Do not be afraid, for I am with you and will bless you. Genesis 26:24

> Be present with your servants, Lord;   734
> we look to you with one accord;
> refresh and strengthen us anew,
> and bless what in your name we do.

When they saw the boldness of Peter and John and realized that they were uneducated and ordinary men, they were amazed and recognized them as companions of Jesus. Acts 4:13

> O Jesus, you have promised   603
> to all who follow you
> that where you are in glory
> your servants shall be too.
> And Jesus, I have promised
> to serve you to the end;
> O give me grace to follow,
> my master and my friend.

Lord our God, thank you for providing us with all that we need, for the many gifts that you have entrusted to us, and for your protection and presence throughout our lives. Guide our futures so that we may faithfully serve you. Amen.

Monday, June 27 — Psalm 79:1–8
Deuteronomy 4:32–5:21; Luke 5:12–26

Love the Lord, all you his saints. Psalm 31:23

To the great One in Three   555
eternal praises be
forevermore!
Your sov'reign majesty
may we in glory see
and to eternity
love and adore.

**The scribe said to Jesus, "You are right, Teacher;
you have truly said that 'He is one, and besides
him there is no other;' and 'to love him with all
the heart, and with all the understanding, and
with all the strength,' and 'to love one's neighbor
as oneself,'—this is much more important
than all whole burnt offerings and sacrifices."
Mark 12:32–33**

Lord, bless our homes   671
    with peace and love and laughter,
with understanding and with loyalty.
May we together follow Christ the Master
and know the blessing of his sov'reignty.

Teacher, help us to live in and be guided by the
Spirit. Help us to seek a true understanding of your
words, to be faithful and to love one another with
our whole selves, and to love you with all of our
hearts, minds, and souls. Amen.

Tuesday, June 28 — Psalm 79:9–13
Deuteronomy 5:22–6:25; Luke 5:27–39

You shall go out in joy, and be led back in peace. Isaiah 55:12

> The Lord is never far away,   p15
> but through all grief distressing,
> an ever-present help and stay,
> our peace, and joy, and blessing,
> as with a mother's tender hand,
> he leads his own, his chosen band.
> To God all praise and glory!

Peace I leave with you; my peace I give to you. I do not give to you as the world gives. Do not let your hearts be troubled, and do not let them be afraid. John 14:27

> He came singing peace   580*
> and he lived singing peace;
> he died, singing peace.
> He arose in silence.
> For the peace to go on
> we must make it our song;
> you and I be the singers.

Give us peaceful minds and loving hearts, O Lord, to share your love with all we connect with. Let us trust and take comfort in you when our hearts are troubled and we live in fear. Help us to feel your love shining in us always. Amen.

Wednesday, June 29 — Psalm 80:1–7
Deuteronomy 7; Luke 6:1–11

When you have eaten and are satisfied, praise the Lord your God. Deuteronomy 8:10 (NIV)

I, the Lord of wind and flame,   641*
I will tend the poor and lame.
I will set a feast for them,
my hand will save.
Finest bread I will provide
'til their hearts be satisfied.
I will give my life to them.
Whom shall I send?
Here I am, Lord. Is it I, Lord?
I have heard you calling in the night.
I will go, Lord, if you lead me.
I will hold your people in my heart.

God has not left himself without a witness in doing good—giving you rains from heaven and fruitful seasons, and filling you with food and your hearts with joy. Acts 14:17

Teacher, Creator, God,   801**
enfold us in your arms;
be with us as we try our wings,
and keep us safe from harm.
All good and perfect gifts
come to us from your hand.
O help us use them carefully
and live by love's command.

Let us praise you with joyous hearts for our many
blessings: for enough food to nourish our bodies; for
love and fellowship; for our warm and comfortable
homes; for the convenience technology brings to our
lives; for health, strength, and energy; and for the
beauty that we find in nature. Thank you. Amen.

Thursday, June 30 — Psalm 80:8–11
Deuteronomy 8:1–9:6; Luke 6:12–26

I have seen their ways, but I will heal them; I will lead them and repay them with comfort. Isaiah 57:18

> While we your past dealings   770
> gratefully review,
> we're assured your mercies
> are each morning new;
> pardon our transgressions,
> hear our earnest cry;
> us in soul and body
> heal and sanctify.

The Twelve went out and proclaimed that all should repent. They cast out many demons, and anointed with oil many who were sick and cured them. Mark 6:12–13

> One bread, one cup, one body we,   p228
> rejoicing in our unity,
> proclaim your love until you come
> to bring your scattered loved ones home.

Guide us, Lord, as we walk your path. Shine your light through us in the darkness and give us strength and courage for our journey. Live in our hearts, we pray. Amen.

Friday, July 1 — Psalm 80:12–19
Deuteronomy 9:7–10:22; Luke 6:27–38

But who am I, and who are my people, that we should be able to offer so willingly as this? For all things come from you, and of your own have we given you. 1 Chronicles 29:14 (NKJV)

Now thank we all our God 533
with heart and hands and voices,
who wondrous things has done,
in whom his world rejoices;
who, from our mother's arms,
has blessed us on our way
with countless gifts of love,
and still is ours today.

Paul wrote: At the present time your plenty will supply what they need, so that in turn their plenty will supply what you need. The goal is equality. 2 Corinthians 8:14 (NIV)

We give you but your own 657
in any gifts we bring;
all that we have is yours alone,
a trust from you, our King.

God of all creation, all we have is yours; we are but caretakers of your bounty. Open our hearts and our hands and make us willing to give back to you so that others will hear your good news! Amen.

Saturday, July 2 — Psalm 81:1–5
Deuteronomy 11; Luke 6:39–49

You, Lord, brought me up from the realm of the dead; you spared me from going down to the pit. Psalm 30:3 (NIV)

God, whose almighty word   380
chaos and darkness heard,
and took their flight:
hear us, we humbly pray.
And where the gospel day
sheds not its glorious ray,
let there be light!

He has rescued us from the power of darkness and transferred us into the kingdom of his beloved Son. Colossians 1:13

While life's dark maze I tread,   705
and griefs around me spread,
O, be my guide;
make darkness turn to day,
wipe sorrow's tears away,
nor let me ever stray
from you aside.

Gracious God, you rescued us from the depths of darkness. Help us to reach out to others and share your word with them so that they will not taste death, but will receive eternal life and live in your kingdom. Amen.

Seventh Sunday after Pentecost

Watchword for the Week — So let us not grow weary in doing what is right. Galatians 6:9

Sunday, July 3 — Isaiah 66:10–14; Psalm 66:1–9
Galatians 6:(1–6),7–16; Luke 10:1–11,16–20

Truly the day of the Lord is great; terrible indeed—who can endure it? Yet even now, says the Lord, return to me with all your heart. Joel 2:11–12

> Kindle our hearts to burn with your flame.   489
> Raise up your banners high in this hour.
> Stir us to build new worlds in your name.
> Spirit of God, O send us your pow'r!

The night is far gone, the day is near. Let us then lay aside the works of darkness and put on the armor of light. Romans 13:12

> "Wake, awake, for night is flying,"   258
> the watchmen on the heights are crying;
> "Awake, Jerusalem, arise!"
> Midnight hears the welcome voices
> and at the thrilling cry rejoices:
> "Where are the virgins, pure and wise?
> The bridegroom comes, awake!
> Your lamps with gladness take!
> Alleluia!
> With bridal care and faith's bold prayer,
> to meet the bridegroom, come, prepare!"

Savior of the world, the time of your return is drawing nigh; bring your light into our hearts and rekindle our spirits as we await your return. Equip us to endure the darkness that surrounds us. Amen.

Monday, July 4 — Psalm 81:6–10
Deuteronomy 12; Luke 7:1–17

I will sing to the Lord as long as I live; I will sing praise to my God while I have being. Psalm 104:33

> We thank you, our Creator,   453
> for all things bright and good,
> the seedtime and harvest,
> our life, our health, our food;
> accept the gifts we offer
> for all your love imparts,
> and what you most would treasure—
> our humble, thankful hearts.
> All good gifts around us
> are sent from heav'n above;
> then thank the Lord, O thank the Lord
> for all his love.

Sing psalms and hymns and spiritual songs among yourselves, singing and making melody to the Lord in your hearts. Ephesians 5:19

> Sing with humble hearts your praises   560
> for our Savior's boundless grace;
> pay due homage to Christ Jesus,
> come with thanks before his face.
> Praise him for his death and bleeding,
> all of our happiness lies there;
> praise him for his gracious leading,
> praise your faithful Shepherd's care.

Good Shepherd, we praise you for your abounding love and goodness. We thank you for your boundless and sacrificial gift of grace for us when we were lost to sin, and for the gift of eternal life! Amen.

Tuesday, July 5 — Psalm 81:11–16
Deuteronomy 13:1–14:21; Luke 7:18–30

Your hands have made and fashioned me; give me understanding that I may learn your commandments. Psalm 119:73

> I need thee ev'ry hour;   740
> teach me thy will,
> and thy rich promises
> in me fulfill.
> I need thee, O I need thee,
> ev'ry hour I need thee!
> O bless me now, my Savior—
> I come to thee!

I give thanks to my God always for you because of the grace of God that has been given you in Christ Jesus, for in every way you have been enriched in him, in speech and knowledge of every kind. 1 Corinthians 1:4–5

> Christian hearts, in love united,   673
> seek alone in Jesus rest;
> has he not your love excited?
> Then let love inspire each breast.
> Members—on our Head depending,
> lights—reflecting him, our Sun,
> brethren—his commands attending,
> we in him, our Lord, are one.

Lord Jesus, it pleases you for your people to be united as one. Grant us direction, Lord, so that we may remain united in love and service. Let your light shine in us, as we love and serve you and others. Amen.

Wednesday, July 6 — Psalm 82:1–4
Deuteronomy 14:22–15:18; Luke 7:31–38

John Hus Festival† — Isaiah 49:1–7; Psalm 135:1–13
1 Corinthians 1:18–24; Mark 8:34–38

The king of Israel, the Lord, is in your midst; you shall fear disaster no more. Zephaniah 3:15

Come now, almighty King,　　　　　　　555
help us your name to sing,
help us to praise.
Father all glorious,
ever victorious,
come and reign over us,
Ancient of Days.

Keep alert, stand firm in your faith, be courageous, be strong. 1 Corinthians 16:13

Stand up, stand up for Jesus,　　　　　752
as soldiers of the cross:
lift high his royal banner,
it must not suffer loss.
From vict'ry unto vict'ry
his army he shall lead,
'til ev'ry foe is vanquished
and Christ is Lord indeed.

King of kings and Lord of lords, empower us to stand firm as we continue to await your return. Give us renewed strength. Keep us alert and equip us for standing up against the evils of this dark world! Amen.

† On July 6, 1415, John Hus was martyred at the Council of Constance.

Thursday, July 7 — Psalm 82:5–8
Deuteronomy 15:19–17:7; Luke 7:39–50

**Do not say, "I am too young." You must go
to everyone I send you to and say whatever I
command you. Jeremiah 1:7 (NIV)**

> God made from one blood   678*
>   all the families of earth,
> the circles of nurture that raised us from birth,
> companions who join us to walk through each stage
> of childhood and youth and adulthood and age.

**The Lord said to Paul, "Do not be afraid, but
speak and do not be silent; for I am with you."
Acts 18:9–10**

> Lord Jesus Christ, be present now;   561
> our hearts in true devotion bow.
> Your Spirit send with light divine,
> and let your truth within us shine.

Lord, speak to us; graciously reveal your wisdom
and strength as we continue to let your light shine
in and through us in the world. Let us not be afraid,
but in boldness proclaim you as our Lord. Amen.

*   © 1988 by Oxford University Press, Inc. Used by permission.

Friday, July 8 — Psalm 83:1–8
Deuteronomy 17:8–18:22; Luke 8:1–15

The mighty one, God the Lord, speaks and summons the earth from the rising of the sun to its setting. Psalm 50:1

> Come now, Incarnate Word,   555
> our just and mighty Lord,
> our prayer attend.
> Come and your people bless
> and give your word success;
> strengthen your righteousness,
> Savior and Friend!

In the past God spoke to our ancestors through the prophets at many times and in various ways, but in these last days he has spoken to us by his Son. Hebrews 1:1–2 (NIV)

> At the name of Jesus   480
> ev'ry knee shall bow,
> ev'ry tongue confess him
> King of glory now;
> 'tis the Father's pleasure
> we should call him Lord,
> who from the beginning
> was the mighty Word.

King of glory, it is the Father's pleasure that you alone be honored, glorified, and praised, for you alone are worthy to have every knee bow and every tongue confess. You are Lord of all. Amen.

Saturday, July 9 — Psalm 83:9–12
Deuteronomy 19:1–20:9; Luke 8:16–25

Ah Lord God! It is you who made the heavens and the earth by your great power and by your outstretched arm! Nothing is too hard for you. Jeremiah 32:17

Great Father of glory, pure Father of light,   457
your angels adore you, all veiling their sight;
all praise we would render, O lead us to see
the light of your splendor, your love's majesty.

We rely not on ourselves but on God who raises the dead. He who rescued us from so deadly a peril will continue to rescue us; on him we have set our hope that he will rescue us again. 2 Corinthians 1:9–10

You make us rejoice in serving,   622*
giving strength where we had none;
certain tasks had seemed unnerving,
but you've proven you're the one
who gives gifts of love and power,
confidence and self-control.
Fill us now, this very hour;
help us reach your kingdom's goal.

Great Father of glory, nothing is too difficult for you. You render unto us the same strength and power that raised Jesus from the dead. It is you who equips and strengthens us to serve your kingdom. Amen.

*   © by Darryl Bell

Eighth Sunday after Pentecost

Watchword for the Week — Make me to know your ways, O Lord; teach me your paths. Psalm 25:4

Sunday, July 10 — Deuteronomy 30:9–14; Psalm 25:1–10 Colossians 1:1–14; Luke 10:25–37

You shall be a crown of beauty in the hand of the Lord, and a royal diadem in the hand of your God. Isaiah 62:3

You, Creator God, have written   685*
your great name on humankind;
for our growing in your likeness,
bring the life of Christ to mind;
that by our response and service
earth its destiny may find.

I saw the holy city, the new Jerusalem, coming down out of heaven from God, prepared as a bride adorned for her husband. Revelation 21:2

Open now the crystal fountain   790
where the healing waters flow;
let the fire and cloudy pillar
lead me all my journey through.
Strong deliv'rer, strong deliv'rer,
ever be my strength and shield;
ever be my strength and shield.

Strong Deliverer, shower us with your healing strength; be our Shield as we move as pilgrims in this land. Be our Pillar of fire that leads us on our journey. Be our Guide and Redeemer as we await your approaching return. Amen.

Monday, July 11 — Psalm 83:13–18
Deuteronomy 20:10–21:23; Luke 8:26–39

Amos cried out, "O Lord God, forgive, I beg you! How can Jacob stand? He is so small!" The Lord relented concerning this; "It shall not be," said the Lord. Amos 7:2–3

> God, when I stand, no path before me clear,   755*
> when ev'ry prayer seems pris'ner of my pain;
> come with a gentleness which calms my fear,
> Lord of my helplessness, my vict'ry gain.

Pray in the Spirit at all times in every prayer and supplication. To that end keep alert and always persevere in supplication for all the saints. Ephesians 6:18

> Come now, O Lord, and as in days of old   742
> to us your Spirit gracefully unfold;
> pour forth your love and all-abounding grace
> 'til we in spirit see you face to face.

God of hope, pour out your Spirit upon us; let us feel the warmth of your abounding love and your merciful grace. Let us feel surrounded by your calmness and gentleness as we daily gain our victory over sin. Amen.

* © 1980 by T. Herbert O'Driscoll

Tuesday, July 12 — Psalm 84:1–7
Deuteronomy 22; Luke 8:40–56

Seek good and not evil, that you may live.
Amos 5:14

> If dangers gather round,   615
> still keep me calm and fearless;
> help me to bear the cross
> when life is bleak and cheerless,
> to overcome my foes
> with words and actions kind;
> O God, your will disclose,
> your counsel let me find.

Let all that you do be done in love.
1 Corinthians 16:14

> My faith looks trustingly   705
> to Christ of Calvary,
> my Savior true!
> Lord, hear me while I pray,
> take all my guilt away,
> strengthen in ev'ry way
> my love for you!

Lover of our souls, we look trustingly and with hope toward the cross of Calvary, for you alone are our true salvation. You alone hear our prayers and fill our hearts with abounding love and forgiveness. Amen.

Wednesday, July 13 — Psalm 84:8–12
Deuteronomy 23:1–24:13; Luke 9:1–11

I said, "I will guard my ways that I may not sin with my tongue." Psalm 39:1

Praise to God, immortal praise,   p119
for the love that crowns our days!
Bounteous source of ev'ry joy,
let your praise our tongues employ;
all to you, our God, we owe,
source from which all blessings flow.

Let no evil talk come out of your mouths, but only what is useful for building up, as there is need, so that your words may give grace to those who hear. Ephesians 4:29

Forgive the hurts our selfishness inflicted   671
on those we love and those who love us best.
Christ, heal the scars, and draw us all together
in him whose will is peace and joy and rest.

Redeeming Lord, give to us your Spirit of grace and love so that evil will not prevail in our lives. Use us to build up and encourage those around us, both in our homes and in our communities. Amen.

Thursday, July 14 — Psalm 85:1–7
Deuteronomy 24:14–25:19; Luke 9:12–27

You who love the Lord, hate evil!
Psalm 97:10 (NKJV)

> He clothes us with his love,   546
> upholds us with his truth;
> and like the eagle he renews
> the vigor of our youth.

For it is God's will that by doing right you should silence the ignorance of the foolish. As servants of God, live as free people, yet do not use your freedom as a pretext for evil. 1 Peter 2:15–16

> Jesus, Master, I am yours;   614
> keep me faithful, keep me near;
> as your radiance through me pours
> all my homeward way to cheer.
> Jesus, at your feet I fall.
> O be now my all in all!

Jesus, Master, whom we serve, we are wholly yours: bodies, minds, and souls. We desire to do your perfect will in our lives; we desire to serve you and others faithfully all the days of our lives. Amen.

Friday, July 15 — Psalm 85:8–13
Deuteronomy 26:1–27:13; Luke 9:28–36

You shall not commit adultery. Exodus 20:14

No more let sin and sorrow grow,   294
nor thorns infest the ground;
he comes to make his blessings flow
far as the curse is found,
far as the curse is found,
far as, far as the curse is found.

Let marriage be held in honor. Hebrews 13:4

Mortals join the mighty chorus,   544
which the morning stars began;
God's own love is reigning o'er us,
joining people hand in hand.
Ever singing, march we onward,
victors in the midst of strife;
joyful music leads us sunward
in the triumph song of life.

Merciful God, how grateful we are for your
covenant love that reigns over us and within us.
May your love continue to unite all people, as we
strive to be living examples of your love to others.
Amen.

Saturday, July 16 — Psalm 86:1–10
Deuteronomy 27:14–28:24; Luke 9:37–50

O Lord, my strength and my stronghold, my refuge on the day of trouble. Jeremiah 16:19

> Ye servants of God, your Master proclaim,   565
> and publish abroad his wonderful name;
> the name all victorious of Jesus extol;
> his kingdom is glorious, he rules over all.

Jairus came and, when he saw Jesus, fell at his feet and begged him repeatedly, "My little daughter is at the point of death. Come and lay your hands on her, so that she may be made well, and live." So he went with him. Mark 5:22–24

> What a friend we have in Jesus,   743
> all our sins and griefs to bear!
> What a privilege to carry
> ev'rything to God in prayer!
> O what peace we often forfeit,
> O what needless pain we bear,
> all because we do not carry
> ev'rything to God in prayer.

Precious Savior and Friend, in our times of desperate need, when we bear great personal griefs, our hope is built on you alone. In you we find hope for healing, hope for the future, and hope for all eternity. Amen.

Ninth Sunday after Pentecost

Watchword for the Week — Is anything too wonderful for the Lord?
Genesis 18:14

Sunday, July 17 — Genesis 18:1–10a; Psalm 15
Colossians 1:15–28; Luke 10:38–42

He sent redemption to his people; he has commanded his covenant forever. Psalm 111:9

> The cov'nant is made   608
> with you as my Head.
> Lord, grant my request,
> to love and to serve you
> 'til with you I rest.

The crowd was amazed when they saw the mute speaking, the maimed whole, the lame walking, and the blind seeing. And they praised the God of Israel. Matthew 15:31

> What heights, what depths, of love divine   p73
> in your blessed incarnation shine!
> Let heav'n and earth unite their praise,
> to magnify your boundless grace.

Savior of the world, you died and rose to save and redeem a lost world. So wondrous is your gift of eternal salvation; you heal all the broken places of our bodies, minds, and souls. Amen.

Monday, July 18 — Psalm 86:11–17
Deuteronomy 28:25–57; Luke 9:51–62

The Lord's mercies never come to an end; they are new every morning; great is your faithfulness. Lamentations 3:22–23

We come to you, our Father,   433
with thoughts of thanks and praise,
for your abundant mercy,
and all your love and grace;
we praise you for your goodness
and for your loving care,
for daily show'rs of blessing,
for answers to our prayers.

So we do not lose heart. Even though our outer nature is wasting away, our inner nature is being renewed day by day. 2 Corinthians 4:16

O Breath of love, come breathe within us,   p47
renewing thought and will and heart.
Come, love of Christ, afresh to win us;
revive your church in ev'ry part.

Prince of Peace, we rejoice in our hearts knowing that we are not alone, for you neither sleep nor slumber. Despite our physical deterioration, you continue to renew our inner beings, as we await your return. Amen.

Tuesday, July 19 — Psalm 87
Deuteronomy 28:58–29:21; Luke 10:1–16

My thoughts are not your thoughts, nor are your ways my ways, says the Lord. Isaiah 55:8

"For my thoughts are not like your thoughts,"   780*
says the Lord, "nor your ways mine.
Farther still than earth from heaven
are things human from divine."

John said to Jesus, "Teacher, we saw someone casting out demons in your name, and we tried to stop him, because he was not following us." But Jesus said, "Do not stop him. Whoever is not against us is for us." Mark 9:38–39a,40

What brought us together,   675
     what joined our hearts?
The pardon which Jesus, our High Priest, imparts;
'tis this which cements the disciples of Christ,
who are into one by the Spirit baptized.

Master, whom we serve, give us the mind of Christ
as we seek to faithfully obey your precepts. Give us
the strength of Christ as we strive to serve others
and be Christ-like examples to them. Amen.

Wednesday, July 20 — Psalm 88:1–5
Deuteronomy 29:22–31:8; Luke 10:17–24

All shall give as they are able, according to the blessing of the Lord your God that he has given you. Deuteronomy 16:17

> As you, Lord, have lived for others,   648
> so may we for others live;
> freely have your gifts been granted;
> freely may your servants give.
> Yours the gold and yours the silver,
> yours the wealth of land and sea;
> we but stewards of your bounty
> held in solemn trust will be.

Like good stewards of the manifold grace of God, serve one another with whatever gift each of you has received. 1 Peter 4:10

> God is gracious, God is caring,   73s*
> God has shown us how to live.
> We find joy and satisfaction
> when, like Christ, we learn to give.
> We have boldness, strength for action,
> when the Spirit's pow'r is shown,
> reaching out to others through us,
> freely making God's love known.

Chief Elder of our heart, kindle in us your abounding love and heartfelt compassion for others; use the gifts, talents, and resources you have blessed each of us with to serve all of humanity. Amen.

*   © 1993 by Darryl Bell

Thursday, July 21 — Psalm 88:6–12
Deuteronomy 31:9–32:9; Luke 10:25–42

I the Lord will speak the word that I speak, and it will be fulfilled. Ezekiel 12:25

> Let the earth now praise the Lord, 261
> who has truly kept his word
> and at last to us did send
> Christ, the sinner's help and friend.

May the Lord direct your hearts to the love of God and to the steadfastness of Christ. 2 Thessalonians 3:5

> See the Lord, your keeper, 729
> stand omnipotently near.
> Now he holds you by the hand,
> and banishes your fear;
> shadows with his wings your head,
> guards from all impending harms;
> round you and beneath are spread
> the everlasting arms.

Jesus, Master and Friend, keep our tongues pure and holy; fill our mouths with your words. Set our hearts and minds on the heavenly things above. Set our feet on your firm and strong foundation. Amen.

Friday, July 22 — Psalm 88:13–18
Deuteronomy 32:10–43; Luke 11:1–13

Lord, your decrees are my delight, they are my counselors. Psalm 119:24

O blessed Lord, teach me your law,   510
your righteous judgments I declare;
your testimonies make me glad,
for they are wealth beyond compare.

Jesus' parents found him in the temple, sitting among the teachers, listening to them and asking them questions. Luke 2:46

Within the Father's house   318
the Son has found his home,
and to his temple suddenly
the Lord of life has come.

Most gracious and loving Father, Jesus was found
in the temple listening and asking questions; let us,
O Lord, also be found daily seeking your rich words
of wisdom and truth as proclaimed in Scripture.
Amen.

Saturday, July 23 — Psalm 89:1–8
Deuteronomy 32:44–33:17; Luke 11:14–28

Do not fear the reproach of others, and do not be dismayed when they revile you. Isaiah 51:7

The peace of Christ makes fresh my heart,   701
a fountain ever springing!
All things are mine since I am his!
How can I keep from singing?
No storm can shake my inmost calm,
while to that Rock I'm clinging.
Since love is Lord of heaven and earth,
how can I keep from singing?

Woe to you when all speak well of you. Luke 6:26

Prayer is the contrite sinner's voice   749
returning from his ways,
while angels in their songs rejoice,
and cry, "Behold he prays!"

Lord over all, help us to remember that we are all sinners, saved only by your merciful grace. Help us to resolve in our own individual hearts a sincere desire and need to come before you in prayer. Amen.

Tenth Sunday after Pentecost

Watchword for the Week — Lord, teach us to pray. Luke 11:1

Sunday, July 24 — Genesis 18:20–32; Psalm 138
Colossians 2:6–15,(16–19); Luke 11:1–13

The Lord frustrates the plans of the peoples.
Psalm 33:10

> O may I never do my will,   733
> but yours, and only yours fulfill;
> let all my time and all my ways
> be spent and ended to your praise.

God raised Jesus from the dead and seated him
at his right hand in the heavenly places, far
above all rule and authority and power and
dominion, and above every name that is named.
Ephesians 1:20–21

> How good the name of Jesus sounds   487
> to all believing ears!
> It soothes our sorrows, heals our wounds,
> and drives away our fears.
> It makes the wounded spirit whole,
> and calms the troubled mind;
> his manna for each hungry soul,
> the lost and weary find.

Savior of the world, how comforting it is to know that you are our Savior at all times. Your name, Jesus, is worthy to be praised above all creation, for you, Lord, offered up yourself for the sins of all the world! Amen.

Monday, July 25 — Psalm 89:9–18
Deuteronomy 33:18–34:12; Luke 11:29–36

By the word of the Lord the heavens were made, and all their host by the breath of his mouth. Psalm 33:6

> For the beauty of the earth,   538
> for the glory of the skies,
> for the love which from our birth
> over and around us lies,
> Lord of all, to you we raise
> this our hymn of grateful praise.

God is not served by human hands, as if he needed anything. Rather, he himself gives everyone life and breath and everything else. Acts 17:25 (NIV)

> Lord of all life, below,   464
> above, whose light is truth,
> whose warmth is love,
> before your ever-blazing throne
> we ask no luster of our own.

Creator God, Lord of all the living, fill our hearts with the abundant warmth of your abounding love. Light up our contrite hearts so that we will remain faithful and ablaze for you until your return! Amen.

Tuesday, July 26 — Psalm 89:19–29
Joshua 1,2; Luke 11:37–54

The Lord God helps me; therefore I have not been disgraced. Isaiah 50:7

> Other refuge have I none   724
> hangs my helpless soul on thee;
> leave, ah, leave me not alone,
> still support and comfort me.
> All my trust on thee is stayed,
> all my help from thee I bring;
> cover my defenseless head
> with the shadow of thy wing.

On him we have set our hope that he will rescue us again, as you also join in helping us by your prayers. 2 Corinthians 1:10–11

> Thus may we, as your anointed,   716
> walk with you in truth and grace
> in the path you have appointed,
> 'til we reach your dwelling-place.

Lord Jesus, your word reminds us that no servant of yours will ever be put to shame. Help us to be mindful of your anointing upon us as we journey our pathways of life in this dark world. Amen.

Wednesday, July 27 — Psalm 89:30–37
Joshua 3,4; Luke 12:1–12

Rise up, O Lord! Do not let mortals prevail. Psalm 9:19

Let all mortal flesh keep silence,   271
and with fear and trembling stand,
ponder nothing earthly minded,
for with blessing in his hand
Christ our God to earth descended
our full homage to demand.

And will not God grant justice to his chosen ones who cry to him day and night? Luke 18:7

Now we bring ourselves to you;   741
cleanse us, Lord, we humbly pray;
undeserving though we be,
draw us closer ev'ry day.
Lord, our refuge, hope, and strength!
Keep, O keep us safe from harm,
shield us through our earthly life
by your everlasting arm.

Redeeming Savior, Lord of all hope, we come before
you with contrite hearts; hear our cries for healing
and cleansing. Be our safe and secure Refuge;
restore us to the wealth of our eternal salvation.
Amen.

Thursday, July 28 — Psalm 89:38–45
Joshua 5,6; Luke 12:13–21

Return to your God, hold fast to love and justice, and wait continually for your God. Hosea 12:6

Here I find my greatest treasure;   782
hither by thy help I've come;
and I hope, by thy good pleasure,
safely to arrive at home.
Jesus sought me when a stranger,
wand'ring from the fold of God;
he, to rescue me from danger,
bought me with his precious blood.

As God's chosen ones, holy and beloved, clothe yourselves with compassion, kindness, humility, meekness, and patience. Colossians 3:12

May the mind of Christ my Savior   585
live in me from day to day,
By his love and pow'r controlling
all I do and say.

Mighty God, as your chosen people, let the mind
of Christ richly dwell in us. Grant us the power
to surrender ourselves to your leading as we look
beyond this earthly home toward our heavenly
home. Amen.

Friday, July 29 — Psalm 89:46–52
Joshua 7; Luke 12:22–34

Consider then and realize how evil and bitter it is for you when you forsake the Lord your God and have no awe of me. Jeremiah 2:19 (NIV)

O that such may be our union   673
as thine with the Father is,
and not one of our communion
e'er forsake the path of bliss;
may our light break forth with brightness,
from thy light reflected shine;
thus the world will bear us witness
that we, Lord, are truly thine.

Hold fast to what you have, so that no one may seize your crown. Revelation 3:11

Plow up the trodden way,   501*
and clear the stone away;
tear out the weed, and sow the seed.
Prepare our hearts your word to heed,
that we good soil may be.
Begin, O Lord, with me!

Gracious Savior, teach us your ways so that we will never forget your greatness or go astray. Plant seeds of your holiness and righteousness within us so that we will yield good fruit for your kingdom. Amen.

* © 1976 by Norman P. Olson

Saturday, July 30 — Psalm 90
Joshua 8:1–29; Luke 12:35–48

**He has told you, O mortal, what is good; and
what does the Lord require of you but to do
justice, and to love kindness, and to walk
humbly with your God? Micah 6:8**

> How shall our life fulfill God's law   695*
>   so hard and high?
> Let Christ endure our will with grace to fortify.
> Then justly, in mercy, we'll humbly walk with God.

**Jesus says, "For I have set you an example,
that you also should do as I have done to you."
John 13:15**

> O Master, let me walk with you   735
> in lowly paths of service true;
> tell me your secret; help me bear
> the strain of toil, the fret of care.

Master of our souls, be present with us, your feeble
servants; lead us on your pathway. Refresh and
renew our hearts and minds in service to you.
We reach out to all those in the world around us!
Amen.

Eleventh Sunday after Pentecost

Watchword for the Week — Set your minds on things that are above, not on things that are on earth. Colossians 3:2

Sunday, July 31 — Ecclesiastes 1:2,12–14;2:18–23; Psalm 49:1–12 Colossians 3:1–11; Luke 12:13–21

You shall not revile the deaf or put a stumbling-block before the blind; you shall fear your God. Leviticus 19:14

God reveals his presence;   554
let us now adore him
and with awe appear before him.
God is in his temple;
all in us keep silence
and before him bow with reverence.
Him alone God we own;
he's our Lord and Savior.
Praise his name forever.

When you give a banquet, invite the poor, the crippled, the lame, and the blind. And you will be blessed, because they cannot repay you. Luke 14:13–14

Church, rejoice! Raise your voice,   631
sing Jehovah's worthy praise;
extol his name forever;
laud him, our God and Savior;
proclaim to ev'ry nation
the tidings of salvation;
bear the witness to his greatness;
spread the story of his glory
to the earth's remotest bounds.

Gracious God, your boundless love for us and your gifts of abundance far exceed our needs. Lord, make us servants of your bounty so that we will sow seeds of faith, hope, and love in the world around us! Amen.

Monday, August 1 — Psalm 91:1–8
Joshua 8:30–9:27; Luke 12:49–59

The Lord executes justice for the orphan and the widow, and loves the strangers, providing them food and clothing. You shall also love the stranger. Deuteronomy 10:18–19

> The sure provisions of my God   730
> attend me all my days;
> O may your house be my abode
> and all my work be praise.
> There would I find a settled rest,
> while others go and come—
> no more a stranger or a guest,
> but like a child at home.

**I was a stranger and you welcomed me.
Matthew 25:35**

> To comfort and to bless,   657
> to find a balm for woe,
> to tend those lost in loneliness
> is angels' work below.

Holy Father, thank you for our many blessings. Help us, Lord, to share our gifts and our talents with the world around us. Give us strength to use our hands and feet to show the love of Christ to our friends, neighbors, and coworkers. Amen.

Tuesday, August 2 — Psalm 91:9–16
Joshua 10:1–28; Luke 13:1–17

One generation shall laud your works to another, and shall declare your mighty acts. Psalm 145:4

Before the hills in order stood, 461
or earth received its frame,
from everlasting you are God,
to endless years the same.

Every tongue should confess that Jesus Christ is Lord, to the glory of God the Father. Philippians 2:11

A thousand ages in your sight 461
are like an evening gone,
short as the watch that ends the night
before the rising sun.

Gracious Savior, you have given us the blessings of minds to think and hearts to love. Lord, please forgive us our shortcomings, and strengthen us to do your will. Help us to remember to forgive, as we are forgiven. Amen.

Wednesday, August 3 — Psalm 92:1–8
Joshua 10:29–11:23; Luke 13:18–30

He does what he wills with the host of heaven and the inhabitants of the earth. There is no one who can stay his hand or say to him, "What are you doing?" Daniel 4:35

> Holy Spirit, pow'r divine,   p223
> fortify this will of mine;
> bend it to your own pure will,
> all my life with graces fill.

The kingdom of the world has become the kingdom of our Lord and of his Messiah, and he will reign forever and ever. Revelation 11:15

> For all the saints who from their labors rest,   390
> who to the world by faith their Lord confessed,
> your name, O Jesus, be forever blessed.
> Alleluia! Alleluia!

Dear Lord, Provider of our every need, help us to be grateful for all of your many gifts and remind us that we must also give back to you. Make us cheerful givers, Lord, generous with our gifts, sharing with those in need. Amen.

Thursday, August 4 — Psalm 92:9–15
Joshua 12:1–13:7; Luke 13:31–14:6

Seek the Lord while he may be found, call upon him while he is near. Isaiah 55:6

O let us know you always near,   p204
as is the light that shines so clear,
or as the air we breathe;
in all our thoughts, our words, and ways,
thus may our lives show forth your praise,
our hearts be freed from things beneath.

See, now is the acceptable time; see, now is the day of salvation! 2 Corinthians 6:2

Save us from weak resignation   751*
to the evils we deplore;
let the gift of your salvation
be our glory evermore.
Grant us wisdom, grant us courage
serving you whom we adore,
serving you whom we adore.

Dear Jesus, Friend to all, help us to mirror your ways. Lord, help us to understand that our actions, no matter how small, affect others. Jesus, we ask that you guide our ways and help us to follow your example to love others. Amen.

* Used by permission of Elinor Fosdick Downs

Friday, August 5 — Psalm 93
Joshua 13:8–14:5; Luke 14:7–24

The Lord gives strength to his people.
Psalm 29:11 (NKJV)

> I fully am persuaded   769
> and joyfully declare
> I'm never left unaided,
> my Father hears my prayer;
> his comforts never fail me,
> he stands at my right hand;
> when tempests fierce assail me,
> they're calm at his command.

May the God of peace make you complete in everything good so that you may do his will. Hebrews 13:20–21

> We are yours; in love befriend us,   731
> be the guardian of our way;
> keep your flock, from sin defend us,
> seek us when we go astray.
> Blessed Jesus, blessed Jesus,
> hear your children when we pray.
> Blessed Jesus, blessed Jesus,
> hear your children when we pray.

Holy Redeemer, we call to you in times of trouble and praise you in times of joy. Lord, help us to always be in your service, to stand fast to those in our lives. Lord, strengthen our congregations so that we may grow your kingdom on earth. Amen.

Saturday, August 6 — Psalm 94:1–11
Joshua 14:6–15:19; Luke 14:25–32

Steadfast love surrounds those who trust in the Lord. Psalm 32:10

> Give us faith to be more faithful,   398*
> give us hope to be more true,
> give us love to go on learning:
> God! Encourage and renew!

Ask and you will receive, so that your joy may be complete. John 16:24

> Ask and it shall be given unto you,   605
> seek and you shall find,
> knock and the door shall be opened unto you—
> Allelu, alleluia!

Gracious Lord, you have given all for our sins. The world needs you; and we, your humble servants, are tasked with sharing your love and grace. Lord, help us not only to be grateful, but also to share your love with those we encounter. Amen.

Twelfth Sunday after Pentecost

Watchword for the Week — Jesus says, "Do not be afraid, little flock, for it is your Father's good pleasure to give you the kingdom." Luke 12:32

Sunday, August 7 — Genesis 15:1–6; Psalm 33:12–22
Hebrews 11:1–3,8–16; Luke 12:32–40

But where are your gods that you made for yourself? Let them come, if they can save you, in your time of trouble. Jeremiah 2:28

> Lord, forgive me, day by day, 779
> debts I cannot hope to pay,
> duties I have left undone,
> evils I have failed to shun.

You have one instructor, the Messiah. Matthew 23:10

> Much forgiven, may I learn 779
> love for hatred to return;
> then my heart assured shall be
> you, my God, have pardoned me.

O merciful Savior, thank you for your grace. Dear Lord, help us to live in joyful praise of all your mighty works. Help us to see your trustworthy hand at work in our lives, in our church, and in the world. Amen.

Monday, August 8 — Psalm 94:12–23
Joshua 15:20–63; Luke 15:1–10

A king is not saved by his great army; a warrior is not delivered by his great strength. Psalm 33:16

His sov'reign pow'r without our aid 455
formed us of clay and gave us breath;
and when like wand'ring sheep we strayed,
he saved us from the pow'r of death.

Now, that you have come to know God, or rather to be known by God, how can you turn back again to the weak and beggarly elemental spirits? Galatians 4:9

Through all the passing years, O Lord, 512
grant that, when church bells are ringing,
many may come to hear God's word
where he this promise is bringing:
"I know my own, my own know me,
you, not the world, my face shall see;
my peace I leave with you." Amen.

God, our Sustainer, help us to run the race you
have set before us. Help us to live each day anew
and look for new opportunities to share your truth
with those in our lives who may not have heard the
good news. Amen.

Tuesday, August 9 — Psalm 95
Joshua 16,17; Luke 15:11–32

Thus says the Lord, "How long will you refuse to humble yourself before me?" Exodus 10:3

> Praise to the Father for his loving kindness,   383
> tenderly caring for his erring children;
> praise him, all angels; praise him in the heavens;
> praise to the Father!

You say, "I am rich, I have prospered, and I need nothing." You do not realize that you are wretched, pitiable, poor, blind, and naked. Revelation 3:17

> Come, O long-expected Jesus,   262
> born to set your people free;
> from our fears and sins release us;
> O, in you our rest shall be.
> Israel's strength and consolation,
> hope to all the earth impart,
> dear desire of ev'ry nation,
> joy of ev'ry longing heart.

Ruler of all creatures here below, let us see miracles in our common lives. You have provided food, shelter, warmth, health, friendship, and so much more. Help us to always remain humble in the sight of your glory. Amen.

Wednesday, August 10 — Psalm 96:1–9
Joshua 18:1–19:9; Luke 16:1–15

May all who seek you rejoice and be glad in you. Psalm 40:16

All people that on earth do dwell,   539
sing to the Lord with cheerful voice;
serve him with joy, his praises tell,
come now before him and rejoice.

Jesus said, "Zacchaeus, hurry and come down; for I must stay at your house today." So he hurried down and was happy to welcome him. Luke 19:5–6

O enter then his gates with joy;   539
within his courts his praise proclaim.
Let thankful songs your tongues employ;
O bless and magnify his name.

Welcoming Savior, you will never leave us or
forsake us. Lord, help us to be loyal and faithful to
those in our lives who are in need. Help us never to
be separated from your love. Amen.

Thursday, August 11 — Psalm 96:10–13
Joshua 19:10–39; Luke 16:16–31

**Restore us, O Lord God of hosts; let your face
shine, that we may be saved. Psalm 80:19**

> O my God, be ever near me;   568
> for your rest, for your feast,
> more and more prepare me.
> Still assure me of my calling;
> keep me near, in your care,
> saved from final falling.

**When the Lord saw the widow, he had
compassion for her and said to her, "Do not
weep." Then he came forward and touched the
bier, and the bearers stood still. And he said,
"Young man, I say to you, rise!" Luke 7:13–14**

> May we go out from here sharing God's love.   540*
> Help us in coming days our faith to prove.
> All together, joyfully sing!

Loving Redeemer, you will never leave our side—
we are never alone. You are our dear friend, Jesus.
Lord, help us to be better friends to those who are
suffering in our world. Amen.

Friday, August 12 — Psalm 97:1–6
Joshua 19:40–21:8; Luke 17:1–10

May the Lord our God incline our hearts to him, to walk in all his ways. 1 Kings 8:58

Help me the slow of heart to move 735
by some clear, winning word of love;
teach me the wayward feet to stay,
and guide them in the homeward way.

His divine power has given us everything needed for life and godliness. 2 Peter 1:3

Not your merit brings God near, 275*
but God's great compassion
for the creature he fashioned.
He will prove his faithfulness to you
and in holy ways he will lead you.
So to God give praise which is his due.

Kind Shepherd, you lead us to life-giving water,
to paths of righteousness, and to everlasting life.
Strengthen us so that we may bring others into the
fold. Amen.

* © 1994 by Brian Henkelmann

Saturday, August 13 — Psalm 97:7–12
Joshua 21:9–45; Luke 17:11–19

August Thirteenth Festival† — Joshua 24:16–24; Psalm 133
1 John 4:1–13; John 17:1–2,6–19

Who knows? God may relent and change his mind; he may turn from his fierce anger, so that we do not perish. Jonah 3:9

Father, now your sinful child   779
through your love is reconciled.
By your pard'ning grace I live;
daily still I cry, forgive.

If we confess our sins, he who is faithful and just will forgive us our sins and cleanse us from all unrighteousness. 1 John 1:9

Since we, though unworthy,   746
through electing grace,
'mid your ransomed people
have obtained a place,
Lord, may we be faithful
to our cov'nant found,
to you, as our shepherd,
and your flock fast bound.

God of fire and flame, ignite in us a renewed spirit. Give us loud voices to sing your praise. Cleanse our hearts so that we may love deeply and forgive, as you have forgiven us. Amen.

† At the conclusion of a Holy Communion service in the church at Berthelsdorf, Germany, on August 13, 1727, the residents of Herrnhut were united into the Renewed Brethren's Church through the Spirit of God.

Thirteenth Sunday after Pentecost

Watchword for the Week — Let us run with perseverance the race that is set before us, looking to Jesus the pioneer and perfecter of our faith. Hebrews 12:1–2

Sunday, August 14 — Jeremiah 23:23–29; Psalm 82
Hebrews 11:29–12:2; Luke 12:49–56

All the earth worships you; they sing praises to you, sing praises to your name. Psalm 66:4

From all that dwell below the skies 551
let the Creator's praise arise;
let the Redeemer's name be sung
through every land, by every tongue.

The name of our Lord Jesus may be glorified in you. 2 Thessalonians 1:12

Your lofty themes, all mortals, bring; 551
in songs of praise divinely sing;
the great salvation loud proclaim,
and shout for joy the Savior's name.

God, our Creator, mighty are your works. You breathed the universe to life, formed us in the womb, and have made a place for us at your right hand. Help us to delight in the knowledge that we are your children. Lord, help us to live in fellowship with one another, lifting each other up. Amen.

Monday, August 15 — Psalm 98
Joshua 22; Luke 17:20–25

The eyes of the Lord are in every place, keeping watch on the evil and the good. Proverbs 15:3

Take my hands and let them move   610
at the impulse of your love.
Take my feet and lead their way;
never let them go astray,
never let them go astray.

The kingdom of heaven is like a net that was thrown into the sea and caught fish of every kind. Matthew 13:47

Riches I heed not nor man's empty praise,   719
thou mine inheritance now and always;
thou and thou only first in my heart,
high King of heaven, my treasure thou art.

All-seeing Lord, you know all of our transgressions, and yet you still love us. God, forgive us our sins and draw us closer to you and give us strength. Guide us as we strive to love our neighbors, and do not let us yield to our weaknesses. Amen.

Tuesday, August 16 — Psalm 99
Joshua 23:1–24:13; Luke 17:26–37

Then I myself will gather the remnant of my flock out of all the lands where I have driven them, and I will bring them back to their fold, and they shall be fruitful and multiply. Jeremiah 23:3

> Long before our proclamation   684
> you announced God's liberty,
> seeding hope in ev'ry nation
> of unending jubilee.
> Thus the Kingdom spreads its branches,
> grows in all humanity.

Jesus said, "I have other sheep that do not belong to this fold. I must bring them also, and they will listen to my voice. So there will be one flock, one shepherd." John 10:16

> Jesus makes my heart rejoice,   662
> I'm his sheep and know his voice;
> he's a Shepherd, kind and gracious,
> and his pastures are delicious;
> constant love to me he shows,
> yea, my very name he knows.

Loving Father, you are so good to us. You comfort us during times of loss, pain, and sickness. You freely give your grace even though we are so undeserving. Lord, help us to accept your love, and to share it with those in our lives. Amen.

Wednesday, August 17 — Psalm 100
Joshua 24:14–Judges 1:16; Luke 18:1–17

When the poor and needy seek water, and there is none, and their tongue is parched with thirst, I the Lord will answer them. Isaiah 41:17

O Lord, hear my prayer,   745
O Lord, hear my prayer:
when I call answer me.
O Lord, hear my prayer,
O Lord, hear my prayer,
Come and listen to me.

Let everyone who is thirsty come. Let anyone who wishes take the water of life as a gift. Revelation 22:17

I heard the voice of Jesus say,   606
"Behold, I freely give
the living water; thirsty one,
stoop down and drink and live."
I came to Jesus, and I drank
of that life-giving stream;
my thirst was quenched,
my soul revived,
and now I live in him.

Trusted Rock, faithful Savior, thank you for offering shelter to our weary souls. Thank you for healing our brokenness. You have called us by name. We hear your voice, and we will follow you. Amen.

Thursday, August 18 — Psalm 101
Judges 1:17–2:23; Luke 18:18–30

I will extol you, O Lord, among the nations, and sing praises to your name. Psalm 18:49

A charge to keep I have,   645
a God to glorify,
a never-dying soul to save
and fit it for the sky.

Paul proclaimed the kingdom of God and taught about the Lord Jesus Christ—with all boldness and without hindrance! Acts 28:31 (NIV)

"The soul that on Jesus still leans for repose,   709
I will not, I will not desert to its foes;
that soul, though all hell should endeavor to shake,
I'll never, no, never, no, never forsake!"

Light of the world, you are our beacon in the
darkness. Lord, teach us to discern your will for
our lives. Strengthen us to show others your truth.
Guide us, Jesus, to love as you have loved. Amen.

Friday, August 19 — Psalm 102:1–11
Judges 3; Luke 18:31–43

Thus says the Lord, "Just as I have brought all this great disaster upon this people, so I will bring upon them all the good fortune that I now promise them." Jeremiah 32:42

Pass me not, O gentle Savior,   772
hear my humble cry;
while on others thou art smiling,
do not pass me by.
Savior, Savior, hear my humble cry;
while on others thou art calling;
do not pass me by.

Paul wrote: Our hope for you is unshaken; for we know that as you share in our sufferings, so also you share in our consolation. 2 Corinthians 1:7

Let me at thy throne of mercy   772
find a sweet relief;
kneeling there in deep contrition,
help my unbelief.
Savior, Savior, hear my humble cry;
while on others thou art calling,
do not pass me by.

Faithful Lord, we know you will not forsake us in times of trouble. We are crying. We are suffering. We are in need of your salvation. Let us remember to always seek you out. Come by here, Lord. Thanks be to God for his saving hand. Amen.

Saturday, August 20 — Psalm 102:12–22
Judges 4; Luke 19:1–10

Remember the wonderful works he has done, his miracles, and the judgments he has uttered. Psalm 105:5

> Remember thee, and all thy pains,   422
> and all thy love to me?
> Yea, while a breath, a pulse remains
> will I remember thee.

See what love the Father has given us, that we should be called children of God. 1 John 3:1

> Perfect submission, all is at rest,   714
> I in my Savior am happy and blessed,
> watching and waiting, looking above,
> filled with his goodness, lost in his love.
> This is my story, this is my song,
> praising my Savior all the day long.
> This is my story, this is my song,
> praising my Savior all the day long.

Holy Spirit, please come upon us—fill our lives with your peace. We are redeemed by your sacrifice. We are saved from our sins because of your love. God, help us to be all that you created us to be. Amen.

Fourteenth Sunday after Pentecost

Watchword for the Week — The steadfast love of the Lord is from everlasting to everlasting on those who fear him. Psalm 103:17

Sunday, August 21† — Isaiah 58:9b–14; Psalm 103:1–8
Hebrews 12:18–29; Luke 13:10–17

How can a man be in the right before God? If one wished to dispute with him, he could not answer him once in a thousand times. Job 9:2–3 (NASB)

As we ask that you stay with us,   798*
and we watch what you are doing,
then our eyes begin to open,
for we see you in the breaking of the bread.

By this we will know that we are from the truth and will reassure our hearts before him whenever our hearts condemn us; for God is greater than our hearts, and he knows everything. 1 John 3:19–20

Great things he has taught us,   550
    great things he has done,
and great our rejoicing through Jesus the Son:
but purer, and higher, and greater will be
our wonder, our transport when Jesus we see.
Praise the Lord, praise the Lord,
let the earth hear his voice!
Praise the Lord, praise the Lord,
let the people rejoice!
O come to the Father through Jesus the Son,
and give him the glory—great things he has done!

Lord of sea and sky, hear our prayers. Forgive us as we stumble in our humanity. We turn away from you in our conceit. We suffer from our pride. Yet, with each heartbreak you are waiting for us. Thank you for never giving up on us. Amen.

† On this day in 1732, the first missionaries departed from Herrnhut bound for St. Thomas.

Monday, August 22 — Psalm 102:23–28
Judges 5; Luke 19:11–27

Indeed, you are my lamp, O Lord, the Lord lightens my darkness. 2 Samuel 22:29

O word of God incarnate,   505
O wisdom from on high,
O truth unchanged, unchanging,
O light of our dark sky:
we praise you for the radiance
that from the Scripture's page,
a lantern to our footsteps,
shines on from age to age.

Christ says, "I have come as light into the world, so that everyone who believes in me should not remain in the darkness." John 12:46

The church from you, dear Master,   p23
received this gift divine,
and still that light is lifted
o'er all the earth to shine.
It is the chart and compass
that all life's voyage through,
'mid mists and rocks and quicksands,
still guides, O Christ, to you.

Provider of wholeness, give our souls peace. Light our hearts' flames yet again. You are the giver of all good and wonderful gifts. Let us never forget to use those blessings to glorify you. Amen.

Tuesday, August 23 — Psalm 103:1–5
Judges 6; Luke 19:28–44

**Six days you shall labor and do all your work.
But the seventh day is a sabbath to the Lord your
God; you shall not do any work. Exodus 20:9–10**

> Now all the woods are sleeping,   572
> through fields the shadows creeping,
> and cities sink to rest;
> let us as night is falling,
> on God our Maker calling,
> give thanks to him, who loves us best.

**The sabbath was made for humankind.
Mark 2:27**

> O Sabbath rest by Galilee!   739
> O calm of hills above,
> where Jesus knelt to share with thee
> the silence of eternity,
> interpreted by love!

Star of the morning, you have written on our hearts
your divine salvation. You are the Lord of the ages;
your love never ends. Your grace is perfectly eternal.
Only you can grant us true rest. Let us be ever
humbled by this amazing gift. Amen.

Wednesday, August 24 — Psalm 103:6–18
Judges 7; Luke 19:45–20:8

Sow with a view to righteousness, reap in accordance with kindness. Hosea 10:12 (NASB)

> The God of harvest praise;   452
> hands, hearts, and voices raise
> with sweet accord;
> from field to store the grain
> bearing your sheaves again,
> and in your glad refrain
> now bless the Lord.

Admonish the idlers, encourage the fainthearted, help the weak, be patient with all of them. See that none of you repays evil for evil, but always seek to do good to one another and to all. 1 Thessalonians 5:14–15

> Have we trials and temptations?   743
> Is there trouble anywhere?
> We should never be discouraged;
> take it to the Lord in prayer!
> Can we find a friend so faithful
> who will all our sorrows share?
> Jesus knows our ev'ry weakness;
> take it to the Lord in prayer!

Merciful Redeemer, you always pick us up, no matter how far we fall. Jesus, you are worthy of our love and praises. Even though we continue to fail you, you never give up on us. Lord, help us to love others as deeply as you love us. Amen.

Thursday, August 25 — Psalm 103:19–22
Judges 8; Luke 20:9–19

My lips will shout for joy when I sing praises to you; my soul also, which you have rescued. Psalm 71:23

New songs of celebration render   545*
to God who has great wonders done;
awed by his love his foes surrender
and fall before the Mighty One.
He has made known his great salvation
which all his friends with joy confess;
he has revealed to ev'ry nation
his everlasting righteousness.

Rejoice that your names are written in heaven. Luke 10:20

He blesses me so sensibly   596
that, though I'm poor and lowly,
yet in him I can rejoice
as my Savior holy.

Precious Lamb of God, let us never grow tired of singing your praises! You have set our feet upon your firm foundation. We are so blessed. Lord, open new ways to share your love to all those whom we touch, both near and far. In Jesus' name, we pray. Amen.

Friday, August 26 — Psalm 104:1–9
Judges 9:1–33; Luke 20:20–26

Daniel was taken up out of the den, and no kind of harm was found on him, because he had trusted in his God. Daniel 6:23

God is my strong salvation,   769
no enemy I fear;
he hears my supplication,
dispelling all my care;
if he, my head and master,
defend me from above,
what pain or what disaster
can part me from his love?

Do not abandon that confidence of yours; it brings a great reward. Hebrews 10:35

While we, deeply humbled,   746
own we're oft to blame,
this remains our comfort,
you are still the same.
In you all the needy
have a friend most dear,
whose love and forbearance
unexampled are.

Constant Sustainer, your love is ever-present. It is always enough. Lord, guide us to live life from your fullness of grace, rather than from the emptiness the world offers. Alone, we are weak; together, we are strong. With you, nothing is impossible. Amen.

Saturday, August 27 — Psalm 104:10–18
Judges 9:34–10:18; Luke 20:27–40

Many of those who sleep in the dust of the earth shall awake, some to everlasting life, and some to shame and everlasting contempt. Daniel 12:2

> Then let us praise the Father   391
> and worship God the Son
> and sing to God the Spirit,
> eternal Three in One,
> 'til all the ransomed number
> who stand before the throne
> ascribe all pow'r and glory
> and praise to God alone.

God, through Jesus Christ, will judge the secret thoughts of all. Romans 2:16

> His righteous government and power   320
> shall over all extend;
> on judgment and on justice based,
> his reign shall have no end.

Jesus, dear friend, you have provided a perfect example for us to follow. God, grant us strong hands, quick feet, and full hearts to carry your message to the ends of the earth. Amen.

Fifteenth Sunday after Pentecost

Watchword for the Week — Let mutual love continue. Hebrews 13:1

Sunday, August 28 — Proverbs 25:6–7; Psalm 112
Hebrews 13:1–8,15–16; Luke 14:1,7–14

The Lord is my stronghold and my refuge, my Savior; you save me from violence. 2 Samuel 22:3

> Sometimes 'mid scenes of deepest gloom,   787
> sometimes where Eden's bowers bloom,
> by waters calm, o'er troubled sea,
> still 'tis his hand that leadeth me.
> He leadeth me, he leadeth me;
> by his own hand he leadeth me,
> his faithful foll'wer I would be,
> for by his hand he leadeth me.

We are afflicted in every way, but not crushed; perplexed, but not driven to despair; persecuted, but not forsaken; struck down, but not destroyed. 2 Corinthians 4:8–9

> I heard the voice of Jesus say,   606
> "Come unto me and rest;
> lay down, O weary one, lay down
> your head upon my breast."
> I came to Jesus as I was,
> so weary, worn, and sad,
> I found in him a resting-place,
> and he has made me glad.

Brothers and sisters, abandon your fears and be joyful in the promise of the Lord! He has redeemed us, despite our unworthiness. This is such an amazing gift. God, help us to share this good news with the lost among us. Amen.

Monday, August 29 — Psalm 104:19–23
Judges 11:1–27; Luke 20:41–21:4

You shall not be partial to the poor or defer to the great. Leviticus 19:15

Take my life that it may be   610
all your purpose, Lord, for me.
Take my moments and my days;
let them sing your ceaseless praise,
let them sing your ceaseless praise.

Believers in our glorious Lord Jesus Christ must not show favoritism. James 2:1 (NIV)

So brothers, sisters, praise his name   781
who died to set us free
from sin, division, hate, and shame,
from spite and enmity!

O Great Provider, your love is a never-ending river.
We pray that we are washed with your grace and
that we never forget the blood you shed for us.
As your children, teach us to walk in your ways.
Amen.

Tuesday, August 30 — Psalm 104:24–30
Judges 11:28–12:15; Luke 21:5–28

**Out of the ground the Lord God formed every
animal of the field and every bird of the air, and
brought them to the man. The man gave names
to all. Genesis 2:19,20**

> All things bright and beautiful,   467
> all creatures great and small,
> all things wise and wonderful—
> the Lord God made them all.
> Each little flow'r that opens,
> each little bird that sings—
> God made their glowing colors,
> God made their tiny wings.

**Are not five sparrows sold for two pennies?
Yet not one of them is forgotten in God's sight.
Luke 12:6**

> All things bright and beautiful,   467
> all creatures great and small,
> all things wise and wonderful—
> the Lord God made them all.
> God gave us eyes to see them,
> and lips that we might tell
> how great is God Almighty,
> who has made all things well.

Father, you have provided us with loving families.
We are so grateful for these special people in our
lives. Lord, please help us to reach out to those who
are lonely and without family. Amen.

Wednesday, August 31 — Psalm 104:31–35
Judges 13; Luke 21:29–38

Out of the mouths of babes and infants you have founded a bulwark. Psalm 8:2

> Little children, welcome!   679*
> Earth is yours to live in;
> arms of love protect you,
> little children, welcome!

Let the little children come to me; do not stop them; for it is to such as these that the kingdom of God belongs. Mark 10:14

> Jesus loves me! This I know,   726
> for the Bible tells me so.
> Little ones to him belong;
> they are weak but he is strong.
> Yes, Jesus loves me, yes, Jesus loves me,
> yes, Jesus loves me, the Bible tell me so.

Blessed Jesus, thank you for all the children in our lives. Give us strength to serve as models for them. Lord, present us with opportunities to teach them about your love and sacrifice. Amen.

Thursday, September 1 — Psalm 105:1–7
Judges 14,15; Luke 22:1–13

The Lord made us, and we are his; we are his people, and the sheep of his pasture. Psalm 100:3

Gracious God, I come before you;   12r
come you also down to me;
where we find you and adore you,
there a heaven on earth must be.
To my heart, O enter Thou;
let it be your temple now.

Once you were not a people, but now you are God's people. 1 Peter 2:10

We are called to be God's people,   635*
showing by our lives his grace,
one in heart and one in spirit,
sign of hope for all the race.
Let us show how he has changed us,
and remade us as his own,
let us share our life together
as we shall around his throne.

Good and gentle Shepherd, you claim us as your
own. Even more, you call us by name. When we
are rebellious and stray from the paths you've set
before us, you seek us out and bring us back to the
safety of the fold. Amen.

*   © 2012 by LifeWay Worship. Used by permission.

Friday, September 2 — Psalm 105:8–15
Judges 16,17; Luke 22:14–23

Give generously to your needy brother and do so without a grudging heart. Deuteronomy 15:10 (NIV)

> As you, Lord, have lived for others,   648
> so may we for others live;
> freely have your gifts been granted;
> freely may your servants give.
> Yours the gold and yours the silver,
> yours the wealth of land and sea;
> we but stewards of your bounty
> held in solemn trust will be.

If anyone gives even a cup of cold water to one of these little ones who is my disciple, truly I tell you, that person will certainly not lose their reward. Matthew 10:42 (NIV)

> Bind us all as one together   407r
> in your Church's sacred fold,
> weak and healthy, poor and wealthy,
> sad and joyful, young and old.
> Is there want, or pain, or sorrow?
> Make us all the burden share.
> Are there spirits crushed and broken?
> Teach us, Lord, to soothe their care.

O Lord, give us compassion for the poor and powerless. Warm our cold hearts to reflect in them your love for all people. Teach us humility and forgive our feelings of self-importance. Remind us that all we have—even our next breath—comes from you. Amen.

Saturday, September 3 — Psalm 105:16–22
Judges 18; Luke 22:24–38

You let people ride over our heads; we went through fire and through water; yet you have brought us out to a spacious place. Psalm 66:12

> Holy God of all creation,   84s*
> give us vision, love, and nerve
> to respond to our first calling
> on this earth to care and serve.
> Show the world by our example
> how to live each waking hour,
> as we strive to humbly follow,
> sharing your creative power.

Be alert at all times, praying that you may have the strength. Luke 21:36

> Savior, now for strength we plead,   417r
> in your love together banded,
> to advance where you do lead
> doing what you have commanded.
> Heart and hand we pledge you here;
> give us grace to persevere.

O God, our Deliverer, rescue us from bondage that comes from our unwillingness to resist the world. Save us! Bring us out of the noisiness and clutter of our lives and into the quiet grace—the spacious place—of your peace. Amen

*   Rick Beck. © 2013 by Interprovincial Board of Communication and Moravian Music Foundation.

Sixteenth Sunday after Pentecost

Watchword for the Week — Choose life so that you and your descendants may live, loving the Lord your God, obeying him, and holding fast to him. Deuteronomy 30:19,20

Sunday, September 4 — Deuteronomy 30:15–20; Psalm 1
Philemon 1–21; Luke 14:25–33

Our God is a God who saves; from the Sovereign Lord comes escape from death. Psalm 68:20 (NIV)

Give to our God immortal praise;   171r
mercy and truth are all his ways;
wonders of grace to God belong,
repeat his mercies in your song.

That evening, at sunset, they brought to Jesus all who were sick or possessed with demons. Mark 1:32

O Master, from the mountain side   581
make haste to heal these hearts of pain;
among these restless throngs abide;
O tread the city's streets again.

Father, in our weakness, strengthen us. In our despair, comfort us. In our infirmity, heal us. Amen.

Monday, September 5 — Psalm 105:23–36
Judges 19; Luke 22:39–51

Now there was a great wind, so strong that it was splitting mountains and breaking rocks in pieces before the Lord, but the Lord was not in the wind; and after the wind an earthquake, but the Lord was not in the earthquake; and after the earthquake a fire, but the Lord was not in the fire; and after the fire a sound of sheer silence. 1 Kings 19:11–12

> Your blessed unction from above   226r
> is comfort, life, and fire of love.
> Enable with perpetual light
> the dullness of our blinded sight.

The Lord is the Spirit, and where the Spirit of the Lord is, there is freedom. 2 Corinthians 3:17

> Grant us your truth, your freedom give,   464
> that hearts for you might solely live
> 'til all your living altars claim
> one holy light, one heav'nly flame!

Spirit of the living God, fall afresh on us! Open our eyes to the needs of the poor; open our ears to the cries of the suffering; open our hearts to the pain of the lonely. On this day, God, make us blessings to your people. Amen.

Tuesday, September 6 — Psalm 105:37–45
Judges 20:1–31; Luke 22:52–62

For a brief moment I abandoned you, but with great compassion I will gather you. Isaiah 54:7

God is love; and love enfolds us,   463
all the world in one embrace;
with unfailing grasp God holds us,
ev'ry child of ev'ry race.
And when human hearts are breaking
under sorrow's iron rod,
then we find that self-same aching
deep within the heart of God.

God, who is rich in mercy, out of the great love with which he loved us even when we were dead through our trespasses, made us alive together with Christ. Ephesians 2:4–5

As sure as I prove your mercy and love,   608
as life you did gain
for me, and my comfort does ever remain,
so may I prove true, devoted to you,
and cheerfully stand,
prepared to comply with your ev'ry command.

Loving God, we are afflicted with the human condition: what we shouldn't do, we do anyway; what we know is right, we neglect. The weight of our sin is suffocating. Yet, you still love us. We acknowledge that your love is unmerited; that we are unworthy; and that your grace is a gift. We accept this gift with gladness and praise! Amen.

Wednesday, September 7 — Psalm 106:1–5
Judges 20:32–21:25; Luke 22:63–71

By his bruises we are healed. Isaiah 53:5

> Rock of Ages, cleft for me,   333r
> let me hide myself in thee;
> let the water and the blood,
> from your riven side which flowed,
> be of sin the double cure,
> cleanse me from its guilt and power.

Christ himself bore our sins in his body on the cross. 1 Peter 2:24

> My sin, O, the bliss of this glorious thought!   754
> My sin—not in part, but the whole—
> is nailed to his cross and I bear it no more,
> praise the Lord, praise the Lord, O my soul.
> It is well with my soul,
> it is well, it is well with my soul.

O Christ, you became vulnerable like us when you walked the lonely road to Calvary. Our sins became yours when you were raised upon the tree, and in your death we are redeemed. It is too awesome for us to understand, but may we persevere as we seek a deeper relationship with you. Amen.

Thursday, September 8 — Psalm 106:6–12
Ruth 1; Luke 23:1–12

Proclaim, give praise, and say, "Save, O Lord, your people." Jeremiah 31:7

> God whom we serve, our God can save,   p106
> can damp the scorching flame,
> can build an ark, can smooth a wave,
> for such as love his name.

Jesus said to him, "Go home to your friends, and tell them how much the Lord has done for you, and what mercy he has shown you." Mark 5:19

> Stand up, and bless the Lord,   531
> you people of his choice!
> Stand up and bless the Lord your God,
> with heart and soul and voice.

Precious Savior, your mercy is never-ending.
Your blessings never cease. May our praises and
testimonies to your goodness bring glory to your
name and inspire in others a desire to know you, O
giver of life. Amen.

Friday, September 9 — Psalm 106:13–23
Ruth 2,3; Luke 23:13–31

When you pass through the waters, I will be with you; and through the rivers, they shall not overwhelm you; when you walk through fire you shall not be burned, and the flame shall not consume you. Isaiah 43:2

O Trinity of love and pow'r,   725
all trav'lers guard in danger's hour;
from rock and tempest, fire and foe
protect them wheresoe'er they go;
thus evermore shall rise to thee
glad hymns of praise from land and sea.

Jesus woke up and rebuked the wind, and said to the sea, "Peace! Be still!" Then the wind ceased, and there was a dead calm. He said to them, "Why are you afraid?" Mark 4:39–40

When ends life's transient dream,   705
when death's cold, sullen stream
rolls over me,
blessed Savior, then, in love,
fear and distrust remove;
O bear me safe above,
redeemed and free!

Ever-present God, there is great comfort in knowing that when life is darkest, you are a light in the darkness with us. We forget that there is no detail of our lives that is too insignificant for you. May we be reminded that you care about all of our struggles; that what matters to us, matters to you. Amen.

Saturday, September 10 — Psalm 106:24–31
Ruth 4; Luke 23:32–43

When deeds of iniquity overwhelm us, you forgive our transgressions. Psalm 65:3

> God forgives all your transgressions,   458
> all diseases gently heals,
> God redeems you from destruction,
> and with you so kindly deals.

But the tax collector, standing far off, would not even look up to heaven, but was beating his breast and saying, "God, be merciful to me, a sinner!" Luke 18:13

> Faithful soul, pray, always pray,   729
> and still in God confide;
> he your stumbling steps shall stay,
> and shall not let you slide;
> safe from known or secret foes,
> free from sin and Satan's hold,
> when the flesh, earth, hell oppose,
> he'll keep you in his fold.

Jesus, our righteous Judge, we know our sins and we are ashamed. Yet, you do not hold sin against us; rather, you accept our burdens as your own. Thank you for reaching into the pits of our sin and despair and for bringing us into your marvelous light. Amen.

Seventeenth Sunday after Pentecost

Watchword for the Week — The sacrifice acceptable to God is a broken spirit; a broken and contrite heart, O God, you will not despise. Psalm 51:17

Sunday, September 11 — Exodus 32:7–14; Psalm 51:1–10
1 Timothy 1:12–17; Luke 15:1–10

You have been my help. Do not cast me off, do not forsake me, O God of my salvation! Psalm 27:9

O, to grace how great a debtor   782
daily I'm constrained to be!
Let that grace, Lord, like a fetter,
bind my wand'ring heart to thee.
Prone to wander, Lord, I feel it,
prone to leave the God I love,
Here's my heart, O take and seal it;
seal it for thy courts above.

Jesus said, "This is the will of him who sent me, that I should lose nothing of all that he has given me." John 6:39

Lamb of God, you shall remain forever   346
of our songs the only theme;
for your boundless love, your grace and favor,
we will praise your saving name;
that for our transgressions you were wounded
shall by us in nobler strains be sounded,
when we, perfected in love,
once shall join the church above.

Everlasting Father, we know that nothing can separate us from your love. As that love abides in us, may we abide in you so that we might bear fruit as your disciples. Amen.

Monday, September 12 — Psalm 106:32–39
1 Samuel 1:1–2:11; Luke 23:44–56

I, the Lord, am the vineyard's keeper; every moment I water it. I guard it night and day so that no one can harm it. Isaiah 27:3

> We come to you, our Father,   433
> with thoughts of thanks and praise,
> for your abundant mercy,
> and all your love and grace;
> we praise you for your goodness
> and for your loving care,
> for daily show'rs of blessing,
> for answers to our prayers.

My Father is glorified by this, that you bear much fruit and become my disciples. John 15:8

> Since, O Lord, you have demanded   401*
> that our lives your love should show,
> so we wait to be commanded
> forth into your world to go.
> Kindle in us love's compassion
> so that ev'ryone may see
> in our faith and hope the promise
> of a new humanity.

Jesus, you call us to labor in your vineyard, the church. May we discern the tasks you have for us. Strengthen us for that work and use us in building your kingdom. In all things, may we glorify you. Amen.

* © 1983 by Walter Klaassen

Tuesday, September 13 — Psalm 106:40–48
1 Samuel 2:12–36; Luke 24:1–12

Many are saying to me, "There is no help for you in God." But you, O Lord, are a shield around me, my glory, and the one who lifts up my head. Psalm 3:2–3

I fear no foe with you at hand to bless,   807
though ills have weight, and tears their bitterness.
Where is death's sting? Where, grave, your victory?
I triumph still, if you abide with me.

A leper came to Jesus begging him, and kneeling he said to him, "If you choose, you can make me clean." Moved with pity, Jesus stretched out his hand and touched him, and said to him, "I do choose. Be made clean!" Mark 1:40–41

Your hands, O Lord, in days of old   736*
were strong to heal and save;
they triumphed over pain and death,
fought darkness and the grave.
To you they went, the blind, the mute,
the palsied and the lame,
the leper set apart and shunned,
the sick and those in shame.

Healer, faithful Friend, have mercy upon us! You see us in all of our frailty; you know all of the ways that we are "unclean." We acknowledge you as the Great Physician of our bodies and our souls. Hear our humble petition: Stretch out your hand and touch us! Amen.

Wednesday, September 14 — Psalm 107:1–9
1 Samuel 3,4; Luke 24:13–27

But the Lord is the true God; he is the living God and the everlasting King. Jeremiah 10:10

Praise, my soul, the King of heaven,   529
to his feet your tribute bring.
Ransomed, healed, restored, forgiven,
evermore his praises sing.
Alleluia! Alleluia!
Praise the everlasting King.

It is the King of kings and Lord of lords alone who has immortality and dwells in unapproachable light, whom no one has ever seen or can see; to him be honor and eternal dominion. 1 Timothy 6:15–16

Look, O look, the sight is glorious,   406
see the man of sorrows now;
from the fight returned victorious,
ev'ry knee to him shall bow.
Crown him! Crown him!
Crown him! Crown him!
Crowns become the victor's brow.

Eternal King, we call you both Father and Friend;
yet, you are beyond our imaginations in power and
grandeur. We recognize you as the source of every
blessing in our lives; nonetheless, we sometimes
find ourselves saying, "I believe, but help me in my
unbelief!" In our uncertainty, lead us to stronger
faith. Remove our doubt and comfort us with your
almighty hand. Amen.

Thursday, September 15 — Psalm 107:10–16
1 Samuel 5:1–7:1; Luke 24:28–35

I will make an everlasting covenant with them, never to draw back from doing good to them. Jeremiah 32:40

Wonder of wonders, here revealed;   410*
God's covenant with us is sealed.
And long before we know or pray,
God's love enfolds us ev'ry day.

Having been justified by the grace of Jesus Christ, we might become heirs according to the hope of eternal life. Titus 3:7

Hail, all hail, victorious Lord and Savior,   p82
you have burst the bonds of death,
grant us, as to Mary, the great favor
to embrace your feet in faith:
you have in our stead the curse endured,
and for us eternal life procured;
joyful, we with one accord
hail you as our risen Lord.

Lamb of God, as you conquered sin and death, empower us to reject the temptations and culture of materialism that are rampant in our world. Thank you for your covenant of grace and the ultimate inheritance that awaits us. Amen.

Ministers' Covenant Day†

Friday, September 16 — Psalm 107:17–22
1 Samuel 7:2–8:22; Luke 24:36–53

They shall be my people and I will be their God, in faithfulness and in righteousness.
Zechariah 8:8

Come now, Incarnate Word,   555
our just and mighty Lord,
our prayer attend.
Come and your people bless
and give your word success;
strengthen your righteousness,
Savior and Friend!

He is the head of the body, the church; he is the beginning, the firstborn from the dead.
Colossians 1:18

The church's one foundation   511
is Jesus Christ, her Lord;
she is his new creation
by water and the word;
from heav'n he came and sought her
to be his holy bride;
with his own blood he bought her,
and for her life he died.

Alpha and Omega, beginning and end, you have purchased us for yourself, as your church and as your bride. Help us, Lord, to live more righteously that we might become worthy of your favor and grace. Amen.

† During a synodal conference in London, Jesus Christ was recognized as chief elder of the Brethren's Church. The day is observed as a covenanting day for servants of the church.

Saturday, September 17 — Psalm 107:23–32
1 Samuel 9; John 1:1–13

You who fear the Lord, trust in the Lord! Psalm 115:11

> If you but trust in God to guide you   712
> and place your confidence in him,
> you'll find him always there beside you
> to give you hope and strength within;
> for those who trust God's changeless love
> build on the rock that will not move.

Hope does not disappoint us, because God's love has been poured into our hearts through the Holy Spirit that has been given to us. Romans 5:5

> Spirit of God, who dwells within my heart,   490
> wean it from sin, through all its pulses move.
> Stoop to my weakness, mighty as you are,
> and make me love you as I ought to love.

Eternal Father, we thank you for giving us your
Holy Spirit: for the comfort it brings; for its guidance
as we seek your truth; for its enlightenment as
we read your word; for the changes in heart that
it provokes. As we persevere in the course that
you have set for us, we ask that you continue to
pour out your Spirit that we might grow in our
discipleship. Amen.

Eighteenth Sunday after Pentecost

Watchword for the Week — From the rising of the sun to its setting the name of the Lord is to be praised. Psalm 113:3

Sunday, September 18 — Amos 8:4–7; Psalm 113
1 Timothy 2:1–7; Luke 16:1–13

The Lord said, "Do not be afraid, Abram. I am your shield, your very great reward." Genesis 15:1 (NIV)

> Now God be with us, for the night is closing,   575
> the light and darkness are of his disposing;
> and 'neath his shadow here to rest we yield us,
> for he will shield us.

Abraham, having patiently endured, obtained the promise. Hebrews 6:15

> You have promised to receive us,   731
> poor and sinful though we be;
> you have mercy to relieve us,
> grace to cleanse and pow'r to free.
> Blessed Jesus, blessed Jesus,
> early let us turn to you.
> Blessed Jesus, blessed Jesus,
> early let us turn to you.

Sustainer of life, teach us to slow down; remind us that we can only live one day at a time. Teach us the value of walking a sure and steady course with you. Help us to draw nearer to you through the challenges we face and the struggles we endure. Amen.

Monday, September 19 — Psalm 107:33–43
1 Samuel 10; John 1:14–28

My tongue shall tell of your righteousness and of your praise all day long. Psalm 35:28

> O for a thousand tongues to sing   548
> my great Redeemer's praise,
> the glories of my God and King,
> the triumphs of his grace!

Anna worshiped with fasting and prayer night and day. At that moment she came, and began to praise God and to speak about the child to all who were looking for the redemption of Jerusalem. Luke 2:37–38

> Praise to the Lord, the almighty,   530
>   the King of creation!
> O my soul, praise him, for he is your health and
>   salvation!
> Let all who hear now to his temple draw near,
> joining in glad adoration.

Blessed Redeemer, shore up our courage so that we can better share our faith. Give us confidence to tell your story. Provide the words to describe your grace. Increase our love as we live in your service. Amen.

Tuesday, September 20 — Psalm 108:1–5
1 Samuel 11,12; John 1:29–42

You prepare a table before me in the presence of my enemies; you anoint my head with oil; my cup overflows. Psalm 23:5

> When I walk through the shades of death,   730
> your presence is my stay;
> one word of your supporting breath
> drives all my fears away.
> Your hand, in sight of all my foes,
> shall still my table spread;
> my cup with blessings overflows;
> your oil anoints my head.

While Jesus was at Bethany in the house of Simon the leper, as he sat at the table, a woman came with an alabaster jar of very costly ointment of nard, and she broke open the jar and poured the ointment on his head. But some were there who said to one another in anger, "Why was the ointment wasted in this way?" But Jesus said, "Let her alone; why do you trouble her? She has performed a good service for me." Mark 14:3–4,6

> Take my life, O Lord, renew,   647
> consecrate my heart to you;
> take my moments and my days;
> let me sing your ceaseless praise.

Loving Shepherd, you care for us in more ways than we can acknowledge; yet, our thanks is sometimes paltry. Lord, lead us to desire you more deeply, give to you more generously, and sacrifice more willingly. Amen.

Wednesday, September 21 — Psalm 108:6–13
1 Samuel 13; John 1:43–51

When my spirit grows faint within me, it is you who watch over my way. Psalm 142:3 (NIV)

> The Lord is never far away,   537
> but through all grief distressing,
> an ever-present help and stay,
> our peace, and joy, and blessing.
> As with a mother's tender hand,
> he leads his own, his chosen band.
> To God all praise and glory!

Blessed be the God who consoles us in all our affliction, so that we may be able to console those who are in any affliction with the consolation with which we ourselves are consoled by God. 2 Corinthians 1:3–4

> Jesus' name, Jesus' name,   324
> source of life and happiness!
> In this name true consolation
> mourning sinners may possess;
> here is found complete salvation.
> Blessed Jesus, we your name will praise
> all our days, all our days.

Omnipotent God, why do we wait so long to turn to you? Remind us that you are watching when we suffer physical weakness. You are aware of our spiritual struggles. You see our failures and know our disappointments and our sadness. But when we lean on your strong shoulders, you both console us and equip us to offer that same loving care to others. Amen.

Thursday, September 22 — Psalm 109:1–7
1 Samuel 14:1–40; John 2:1–11

Am I my brother's keeper? Genesis 4:9

In loving service may our lives be spent,   587
in other's gladness finding sweet content,
striving to show God's fellowship to all.
To show God's loving work—the servants' call.
In loving service may our lives be spent.

Let each of you look not to your own interests, but to the interests of others. Philippians 2:4

Let us each for others care,   672
each another's burden bear,
to your church a pattern give,
showing how believers live.

Heavenly Father, you call us to love our neighbors and to serve them. It is not always easy. Help us focus, Father, on our common ground rather than on the ways in which we are different. Remind us that we all are created in your image and that you made us to live in community. Amen.

Friday, September 23 — Psalm 109:8–20
1 Samuel 14:41–15:23; John 2:12–25

**If only you had paid attention to my commands,
your peace would have been like a river,
your well-being like the waves of the sea.
Isaiah 48:18 (NIV)**

> Blessed are the brave and peaceful,   595
> bringing peace where'er they live,
> God shall own them as his children
> and through them his peace will give.
> All for love and truth who suffer,
> in your God rejoice and sing;
> he, the end of all your striving,
> he, your Father, Lord, and King.

**The kingdom of God is not food and drink
but righteousness and peace and joy in the
Holy Spirit. The one who thus serves Christ is
acceptable to God and has human approval.
Romans 14:17–18**

> Rejoice, rejoice, the kingdom comes;   260*
> be glad, for it is near.
> It comes with joy surprising us;
> it triumphs o'er our fears.
> Give thanks, for as the kingdom comes
> it brings God's own shalom,
> a state of peace and justice
> where all with God are one.

Jesus, you have shown us the example of a
suffering servant; yet, we admit to self-absorption.
We are embarrassed by our fascination with the
superficial and temporal. Guide us, Jesus, beyond
our own needs and desires. Teach us that peace and
joy come through service in your name and that
our truest identities are found in you. Amen.

---

* © 1987 by M. Lynnette Delbridge

Saturday, September 24 — Psalm 109:21–31
1 Samuel 15:24–16:13; John 3:1–15

Know then in your heart that as a parent disciplines a child so the Lord your God disciplines you. Deuteronomy 8:5

Lead me, guide me, along the way,   728*
for if you lead me, I cannot stray.
Lord, let me walk each day with you,
lead me my whole life through.
I am lost if you take your hand from me,
I am blind without your light to see.
Lord, forever may I your servant be.
Lead me, O Lord, lead me.

Grow in the grace and knowledge of our Lord and Savior Jesus Christ. 2 Peter 3:18

Each day unto my heart   737
new life and grace impart.
Do now my needs supply
lest I should droop and die.
Continually I've need
by faith on you to feed.

Merciful God, it is never easy to give up control; we are rebellious and think that we know a better way. Lord, help us to learn that only when we put our trust in you, rather than in ourselves, can we grow in you and fulfill your will for our lives. Amen.

Nineteenth Sunday after Pentecost

Watchword for the Week — There is great gain in godliness combined with contentment. 1 Timothy 6:6

Sunday, September 25 — Amos 6:1a,4–7; Psalm 146
1 Timothy 6:6–19; Luke 16:19–31

I will cleanse them from all the guilt of their sin against me, and I will forgive. Jeremiah 33:8

Far as east from west is distant,   458
God has put away our sin;
like the pity of a father
has the Lord's compassion been.

Our Savior Jesus Christ gave himself for us that he might redeem us from all iniquity and purify for himself a people of his own who are zealous for good deeds. Titus 2:13–14

You have cancelled my transgressions,   p202
Jesus, by your precious blood;
may I find therein salvation,
happiness, and peace with God;
and since you, for sinners suff'ring
on the cross were made an off'ring,
from all sin deliver me,
that I wholly yours may be.

Forgiving Savior, what solace we find in knowing that our scarlet sins are washed white as snow; in knowing that you not only forgive but that you also forget. The weight of our sin is great; yet, you have taken it from us with your own life so that we might live. We praise you and thank you for this greatest of all gifts! Amen.

Monday, September 26 — Psalm 110
1 Samuel 16:14–17:31; John 3:16–26

All that the Lord has spoken we will do, and we will be obedient. Exodus 24:7

You have kindly led us   p205
through our joys and tears;
now accept our praises
and remove our fears.
Grant us all with gladness
to obey your voice;
let your will and pleasure
be our only choice.

Do not lag in zeal, be ardent in spirit, serve the Lord. Romans 12:11

The task your wisdom has assigned   638
here let me cheerfully fulfill,
In all my work your presence find
and prove your good and perfect will.

Glorious Lord, thank you for opportunities
to serve. Renew our strength that we might
work energetically and with gladness. May our
faithfulness be a testimony to your goodness and
grace. Amen.

Tuesday, September 27 — Psalm 111
1 Samuel 17:32–58; John 3:27–36

The Lord said, "My presence will go with you, and I will give you rest." Exodus 33:14

I need your presence every passing hour.   807
What but your grace can foil the tempter's pow'r?
Who like yourself my guide and strength can be?
Through cloud and sunshine, O abide with me.

Since, then, we have such a hope, we act with great boldness. 2 Corinthians 3:12

Nay, too closely am I bound   p215
unto him by hope forever;
faith's strong hand the rock has found,
grasped it and will leave it never;
not the ban of death can part
from the Lord the trusting heart.

Father, your word is consistent in proclaiming
your abiding presence and faithfulness. We believe
this but sometimes we are hesitant, tentative in
our actions. On this day, may we feel your hand
gently pushing us, moving us to greater confidence
in letting our light shine as we serve you and our
world. Amen.

Wednesday, September 28 — Psalm 112
1 Samuel 18:1–19:7; John 4:1–26

His dominion is an everlasting dominion that will not pass away, and his kingdom is one that will never be destroyed. Daniel 7:14 (NIV)

> Life-giving Creator of both great and small;   457
> of all life the maker, the true life of all;
> we blossom, then wither like leaves on the tree,
> but you live forever who was and will be.

God was pleased to have all his fullness dwell in Christ, and through him to reconcile to himself all things, whether things on earth or things in heaven, by making peace through his blood, shed on the cross. Colossians 1:19–20 (NIV)

> And can it be that I should gain   773
> an int'rest in the Savior's blood?
> Died he for me, who caused his pain—
> for me, who caused his bitter death?
> Amazing love! How can it be
> that you, my Lord, should die for me?
> Amazing love! How can it be
> that you, my Lord, should die for me?

Sovereign God, you have shown us your face through the life of your Son. Through his sacrifice, you have reconciled us from sin and back into your favor. Thank you, Gracious Father, for your marvelous plan of hope and salvation. Amen.

Thursday, September 29 — Psalm 113
1 Samuel 19:8–20:17; John 4:27–38

**The Lord says, "Why do you spend your money
for that which is not bread, and your labor for
that which does not satisfy? Listen carefully to
me, and eat what is good." Isaiah 55:2**

Guide me, O my great Redeemer,   790
pilgrim through this barren land.
I am weak, but you are mighty;
hold me with your pow'rful hand.
Bread of heaven, bread of heaven,
feed me now and evermore,
feed me now and evermore.

**Do not work for the food that perishes, but for
the food that endures for eternal life, which the
Son of Man will give you. John 6:27**

You are the bread of life,   502
O Lord, to me.
Your holy word the truth
that rescues me.
Give me to eat and live
with you above;
teach me to love your truth,
for you are love.

Bread of life and living Water, we feed on your word
and the life it reveals. Fill us, complete us, save us!
Amen.

Friday, September 30 — Psalm 114
1 Samuel 20:18–21:9; John 4:39–42

O Lord, do not rebuke me in your anger, or discipline me in your wrath. Psalm 6:1

He will not always chide; 546
he will with patience wait;
his wrath is ever slow to rise
and ready to abate.

Who is to condemn? It is Christ Jesus, who died, yes, who was raised, who is at the right hand of God, who indeed intercedes for us. Romans 8:34

Who can condemn, since Christ was dead, 364
and ever lives to God?
Now our whole debt is fully paid;
he saves us by his blood.
The ransomed hosts in earth and heav'n
through countless choirs proclaim,
"He has redeemed us; praise be giv'n
to God and to the Lamb."

O Christ our Intercessor, have mercy on us! You see beyond our selfish and childish ways. With all of our faults and imperfections, you still love us. May we be as forgiving and merciful to others as you are to us. Amen.

Saturday, October 1 — Psalm 115:1–8
1 Samuel 21:10–22:23; John 4:43–54

I hold my life in my hand continually, but I do not forget your law. Psalm 119:109

> O God, in whom our trust we place,   p161
> we thank you for your word of grace;
> help us its precepts to obey
> 'til we shall live in endless day.

Lord, to whom can we go? You have the words of eternal life. John 6:68

> Eternal Source, whence all did spring,   279
> almighty and all-glorious King,
> the whole creation's Head and Lord,
> by all in heav'n and earth adored;
> Lord, whom high heav'n cannot contain,
> you as a lowly infant came,
> and left your throne in heav'n above,
> O myst'ry deep, O boundless love.

Christ, living Word made flesh, we profess that in your word we find truth, and your truth we will not forget. O Word of life eternal, only in you can we truly live. Come O Christ, come O Life, and fill our souls again! Amen.

Twentieth Sunday after Pentecost

Watchword for the Week — Commit your way to the Lord; trust in him, and he will act. Psalm 37:5

Sunday, October 2 — Habbakuk 1:1–4,2:1–4; Psalm 37:1–9
2 Timothy 1:1–14; Luke 17:5–10

All the ends of the earth have seen the salvation of our God. Psalm 98:3 (NIV)

Blessings abound where'er he reigns,   404
the pris'ners leap to lose their chains,
the weary find eternal rest,
and all who suffer want are blessed.

Jesus said, "Is a lamp brought to be put under a basket or under a bed? Is it not to be set on a lampstand?" Mark 4:21 (NKJV)

Savior, you came to give   380
those who in darkness live
healing and sight,
health to the sick in mind,
sight to the inward blind:
now to all humankind
let there be light!

Your salvation, O Lord, stretches as far as the east is to the west, and the north is to the south. There is no corner, depth, or height where you will not go to seek us out. Mighty God, to you be all glory forever. Amen.

Monday, October 3 — Psalm 115:9–18
1 Samuel 23; John 5:1–15

Cast your burden on the Lord, and he will sustain you. Psalm 55:22

His oath, his covenant, his blood   771
sustain me in the raging flood;
when all supports are washed away,
he then is all my hope and stay.
On Christ the solid rock, I stand;
all other ground is sinking sand,
all other ground is sinking sand.

Do not worry about anything, but in everything by prayer and supplication with thanksgiving let your requests be made known to God. Philippians 4:6

My Shepherd will supply my need;   730
the Lord God is his name.
In pastures fresh he makes me feed,
beside the living stream.
He brings my wand'ring spirit back
when I forsake his ways,
and leads me for his mercy's sake
in paths of truth and grace.

Sustainer, today we cling to the everlasting hope found in you. Whatever may come our way, we will boldly profess that we serve a God who provides exceedingly and abundantly, above all that we could ever hope for or imagine. Amen.

Tuesday, October 4 — Psalm 116:1–7
1 Samuel 24:1–25:17; John 5:16–30

In God's hand are the depths of the earth; the heights of the mountains are his also. Psalm 95:4

It is God who holds the nations   p140*
in the hollow of his hand;
it is God whose light is shining
in the darkness of the land;
it is God who builds his city
on the rock and not the sand:
the living God be praised!

The God who made the world and everything in it, he who is Lord of heaven and earth, does not live in shrines made by human hands. Acts 17:24

Lord of all being, throned afar,   464
your glory flames from sun and star;
center and soul of ev'ry sphere,
yet to each loving heart how near!

Creator, not made or dependent upon human
hands, how blessed are we that you considered
us more than the dust that we are? Father of the
universe, how marvelous are the works of your
hand; we are awestruck by the limitlessness of your
love. Hallelujah! Amen.

Wednesday, October 5 — Psalm 116:8–14
1 Samuel 25:18–44; John 5:31–47

If anyone secretly entices you—even if it is your brother, your father's son or your mother's son, or your own son or daughter, or the wife you embrace, or your most intimate friend— saying, "Let us go worship other gods," you must not yield to or heed any such persons. Deuteronomy 13:6,8

To you, most holy Lord, 633
we sing with hearts and voices;
in you, with one accord,
your church on earth rejoices!
We bend before your throne
and humbly chant your praise;
we worship you alone,
whose love has crowned our days.

If anyone is detected in a transgression, you who have received the Spirit should restore such a one in a spirit of gentleness. Take care that you yourselves are not tempted. Galatians 6:1

O let me feel you near me; 603
the world is ever near:
I see the sights that dazzle,
the tempting sounds I hear.
My foes are ever near me,
around me and within;
but, Jesus, draw still nearer
and shield my soul from sin!

You, O Lord, are the only living God, the only sovereign Lord. Rule our hearts, minds, and souls. In us, through us, wherever we may go, command our souls forevermore. Amen.

Thursday, October 6 — Psalm 116:15–19
1 Samuel 26,27; John 6:1–15

All deeds are right in the sight of the doer, but the Lord weighs the heart. Proverbs 21:2

> Breathe on me, breath of God,   494
> until my heart is pure,
> until with you I will one will
> to do or to endure.

"All things are lawful for me," but not all things are beneficial. "All things are lawful for me," but I will not be dominated by anything. 1 Corinthians 6:12

> O give me Samuel's ear!   609
> The open ear, O Lord,
> alive and quick to hear
> each whisper of thy word;
> like him to answer at thy call,
> and to obey thee first of all.

Hearken our ears, Elohim, to hear you calling us and to know and live your will—not the will of the world and not of our flesh. Search and purify our hearts, dear Emmanuel. You are the only living God, and we serve only you. Amen.

Friday, October 7 — Psalm 117
1 Samuel 28,29; John 6:16–24

After that whole generation had been gathered to their ancestors, another generation grew up, who knew neither the Lord nor what he had done for Israel. Judges 2:10 (NIV)

> Lord, enter now our souls   318
> and teach us by your grace
> each dim revealing of yourself
> with loving awe to trace.

Simeon prayed: "My eyes have seen your salvation, which you have prepared in the presence of all peoples, a light for revelation to the Gentiles and for glory to your people Israel." Luke 2:30–32

> We've a story to tell to the nations,   621
> that shall turn their hearts to the right,
> a story of truth and mercy,
> a story of peace and light,
> a story of peace and light.
> For the darkness shall turn to dawning,
> and the dawning to noon-day bright;
> and Christ's great kingdom shall come on earth,
> the kingdom of love and light.

Peel the scales from our eyes, remove the blockages from our ears and hearts, O Lord, so that we may receive you. Let not this day pass without us drawing nigh unto you, our Savior, Redeemer, and Sustainer. Amen.

Saturday, October 8 — Psalm 118:1–9
1 Samuel 30,31; John 6:25–42

The unfolding of your words gives light; it imparts understanding to the simple. Psalm 119:130

When the sacred vow is made,   426
when the hands are on them laid,
come in this most solemn hour
with your strength'ning gift of pow'r.
Give them light, your truth to see;
give them life, your own to be;
daily pow'r to conquer sin;
patient faith, the crown to win.

Whatever was written in former days was written for our instruction, so that by steadfastness and by the encouragement of the Scriptures we might have hope. Romans 15:4

To God who gave the Scriptures   508*
we lift our souls in prayer,
for eyes the Spirit opens
to find the treasures there;
that as we read and ponder
one voice alone is heard,
the Christ of all the Scriptures,
the true and living Word.

Word of life, Word made flesh, today we declare
that, indeed, you are a lamp unto our feet and
a light unto our path. In you, living Word, is the
blueprint for all aspects of life's journey. Order our
steps in your word today. Amen.

Twenty-First Sunday after Pentecost

Watchword for the Week — If we have died with him, we will also live with him. 2 Timothy 2:11

Sunday, October 9 — 2 Kings 5:1–3,7–15c; Psalm 111
2 Timothy 2:8–15; Luke 17:11–19

The Lord said, "I do forgive, just as you have asked." Numbers 14:20

> I come with joy to meet my Lord,   p222*
> forgiven, loved, and free;
> in awe and wonder to recall
> his life laid down for me.

Just as the Lord has forgiven you, so you also must forgive. Colossians 3:13

> Pardon, Lord, and are there those   779
> who my debtors are, or foes?
> I, who by forgiveness live,
> here their trespasses forgive.

Seventy times seven you said, Lord; yet, you forgive us our sins beyond this measure daily. The praise and thanksgiving we offer you cannot cover your depth of forgiveness. Thus, O Lord, let us go and do for others as you have done for us. Amen.

Monday, October 10 — Psalm 118:10–14
2 Samuel 1; John 6:43–51

The Lord is righteous. He loves righteousness. Psalm 11:7 (NASB)

Wind of God, O earth-stirring Spirit,   **499***
yours the passion we need this day.
Yours the thirst for peace and for justice,
yours the yearning, the will, the way.
Source of righteousness, source of power,
source of light in the world's dark hour,
the poor, the lonely know you as friend.
Stir us to action, O holy wind.

Live as children of light—for the fruit of the light is found in all that is good and right and true. Ephesians 5:8–9

I heard the voice of Jesus say,   **606**
"I am the dark world's Light;
look unto me, your morn shall rise,
and all your day be bright."
I looked to Jesus, and I found
in him my Star, my Sun;
and in that Light of life I'll walk,
'til trav'ling days are done.

Good and Righteous God, lead us to walk, talk, and
be within your righteous goodness. Let your light so
shine in and through us as a testimony to who you
are; the true and living God! Amen.

Tuesday, October 11 — Psalm 118:15–21
2 Samuel 2; John 6:52–59

I will recount the gracious deeds of the Lord, the praiseworthy acts of the Lord, because of all that the Lord has done for us. Isaiah 63:7

> Ev'ry day will be the brighter   310
> when your gracious face we view;
> ev'ry burden will be lighter
> when we know it comes from you.
> Spread your love's broad banner o'er us;
> give us strength to serve and wait,
> 'til the glory breaks before us
> through the city's open gate.

Indeed you have tasted that the Lord is good. 1 Peter 2:3

> O, may this grace be ours: 312
> in you always to live
> and drink of those refreshing streams
> which you alone can give.

Alleluia, alleluia, the highest of praise be to you, Christ Jesus, King of kings and Lord of lords! Because of your blood shed and body broken for our sake, we have a foretaste of the goodness of your kingdom. Amen.

Wednesday, October 12 — Psalm 118:22–29
2 Samuel 3:1–34; John 6:60–71

I myself will search for my sheep and look after them. Ezekiel 34:11 (NIV)

> How great the bliss to be a sheep of Jesus,   593
> and to be guided by his shepherd staff!
> Earth's greatest honors, howsoe'er they please us,
> compared to this are vain and empty chaff.
> Yea, what this world can never give,
> may, through the Shepherd's grace,
> each needy sheep receive.

As Jesus passed along the Sea of Galilee, he saw Simon and his brother Andrew casting a net into the sea—for they were fishermen. And Jesus said to them, "Follow me." Mark 1:16–17

> Should not I for gladness leap,   662
> led by Jesus as his sheep?
> For when these blessed days are over
> to the arms of my dear Savior
> I shall be conveyed to rest.
> Amen, yea, my lot is blessed.

Christ, the Good Shepherd, tune our ears to discern your voice amongst so many wolves masquerading as you. Help us to hear your voice beckoning us to follow you, and grant us courage in faith to drop our nets and go wherever you lead. Amen.

Thursday, October 13 — Psalm 119:1–8
2 Samuel 3:35–5:16; John 7:1–13

I am the Lord, that is my name; my glory I give to no other, nor my praise to idols. Isaiah 42:8

> Hail, First and Last, the great I Am,   703
> in whom we live and move;
> increase our little spark of faith,
> and fill our hearts with love.

Even though there may be so-called gods—for us there is one God, the Father, from whom are all things and for whom we exist, and one Lord, Jesus Christ, through whom are all things and through whom we exist. 1 Corinthians 8:5–6

> O Christ, our hope, our heart's desire,   374
> redemption's only spring;
> creator of the world are you,
> its Savior and its King,
> its Savior and its King.

We declare and decree that you, O Lord Jesus Christ, are the great I Am. You are the Alpha and the Omega, the beginning and the end. You are the Creator, the source and sustenance of life and the only God we praise! Amen.

Friday, October 14 — Psalm 119:9–16
2 Samuel 5:17–6:23; John 7:14–24

My people have committed two evils: they have forsaken me, the fountain of living water, and dug out cisterns for themselves, cracked cisterns that can hold no water. Jeremiah 2:13

> Grateful that God dared to rescue   19s*
> me from dusty, deep despair,
> joyful I go where God leads me,
> bold good news and call to share.
> God has sought us! God has found us!
> Live God's love, a gift so rare.

The woman said to him, "Sir, you have no bucket, and the well is deep. Where do you get that living water?" John 4:11

> Trusting his mild staff always,   662
> I go in and out in peace;
> he will feed me with the treasure
> of his grace in richest measure;
> when athirst to him I cry,
> living water he'll supply.

Like the woman at the well, we seldom realize that our souls are utterly dry, deprived of your living water, so wallowed in the sins that squeeze your breath from our mortal beings, cisterns become normal. Purge us, Lord, and fill us with your living water! Amen.

Saturday, October 15 — Psalm 119:17–24
2 Samuel 7; John 7:25–44

In your days I will speak the word and fulfill it, says the Lord God. Ezekiel 12:25

> Father in heav'n, fulfill your word; 519
> grant us the Spirit of our Lord,
> that through your truth, which cannot fail,
> we may o'er ev'ry ill prevail.

Peter wrote: We did not follow cleverly devised myths when we made known to you the power and coming of our Lord Jesus Christ, but we had been eyewitnesses of his majesty. 2 Peter 1:16

> Child of our destiny, 407*
> God from eternity,
> love of the Father
> on sinners outpoured;
> see now what God has done
> sending his only Son,
> Christ the beloved one—
> Jesus is Lord!

We realize that the time of your return draws near, O Lord. While there is still time, however, we pray that your Holy Spirit will prepare our hearts. We pray also that, as you lead, we will continue to bring your good news to all people. Amen.

Twenty-Second Sunday after Pentecost

Watchword for the Week — Proclaim the message; be persistent whether the time is favorable or unfavorable; convince, rebuke, and encourage, with the utmost patience in teaching. 2 Timothy 4:2

Sunday, October 16 — Genesis 32:22–31; Psalm 121
2 Timothy 3:14–4:5; Luke 18:1–8

Fools say in their hearts, "There is no God." Psalm 14:1

> Savior, now with contrite hearts   741
> we approach your throne of love,
> asking pardon for our sins,
> peace and comfort from above.
> You once suffered on the cross
> to atone for sinners' guilt;
> may we never, Lord, forget
> that for us your blood was spilled.

This is eternal life, that they may know you, the only true God, and Jesus Christ whom you have sent. John 17:3

> God sent his Son, they called him Jesus,   706
> he came to love, heal, and forgive;
> he lived and died to buy my pardon,
> an empty grave is there to prove my Savior lives.
> Because he lives I can face tomorrow,
> because he lives all fear is gone;
> because I know he holds the future,
> and life is worth the living just because he lives.

Wise Jehovah, time and time again you remind us that even your foolishness is wiser than our wisdom. Though in our humanity we cannot fully comprehend all that you are and all that you do, when we gaze upon creation we know that you alone are God Almighty. Amen.

Monday, October 17 — Psalm 119:25–32
2 Samuel 8,9; John 7:45–52

His greatness will reach to the ends of the earth. Micah 5:4 (NIV)

> Gracious and holy Three,   380
> glorious Trinity,
> wisdom, love, might:
> boundless as ocean's tide
> rolling in fullest pride,
> through the world far and wide,
> let there be light!

Your kingdom come. Matthew 6:10

> We've a Savior to show to the nations,   621
> who the path of sorrow has trod,
> that all of the world's great peoples
> might come to the truth of God,
> might come to the truth of God.
> For darkness shall turn to dawning,
> and dawning to noonday bright;
> and Christ's great kingdom shall come on earth,
> the kingdom of love and light.

Father, let your holy will be done on earth as it is in heaven. May your will for our lives manifest so that in all that we do and say we bring glory to your name. Amen.

Tuesday, October 18 — Psalm 119:33–40
2 Samuel 10,11; John 8:1–11

You are my witnesses, says the Lord. Isaiah 43:10

While with her sweetest flowers 269
thy waiting Zion strews thy way,
I'll raise with all my powers,
Savior, to thee a grateful lay;
to thee, the King of glory,
my heart will tune a song divine
and make thy love's bright story
through me in living witness shine.

We do not proclaim ourselves; we proclaim Jesus Christ as Lord. 2 Corinthians 4:5

Christ for the world we sing! 640
The world to Christ we bring
with joyful song,
the newborn souls, whose days,
reclaimed from error's ways,
inspired with hope and praise
to Christ belong.

Let your light in us shine before all people, so that they may see our good works and glorify you, the living God. You are worthy of all praise. Out of love, you gave your life for us. We will proclaim you to the world. Amen.

Wednesday, October 19 — Psalm 119:41–48
2 Samuel 12; John 8:12–30

Your steadfast love, O Lord, endures forever. Do not forsake the work of your hands. Psalm 138:8

> Be still and know our Lord is God,   20s*
> whose love attends our prayers.
> Each whispered word, each silent hope
> finds comfort in God's care.

For we are what he has made us, created in Christ Jesus for good works, which God prepared beforehand to be our way of life. Ephesians 2:10

> O dearly, dearly has he loved,   353
> and we must love him too,
> and trust in his redeeming blood,
> and try his works to do.

Christ you are the Vine and we are the branches; apart from you we cannot bear good fruit. Source of goodness, help us to stay connected to you, bearing fruit that testifies to righteousness. Amen.

* Willie Israel (2010). © 2013 by Interprovincial Board of Communication and Moravian Music Foundation.

Thursday, October 20 — Psalm 119:49–56
2 Samuel 13:1–33; John 8:31–41

Be silent before the Lord God! For the day of the Lord is at hand. Zephaniah 1:7

In all the world around me 792
I see his loving care,
and though my heart grows weary,
I never will despair;
I know that he is leading
through all the stormy blast,
the day of his appearing
will come at last.

Be serious and discipline yourselves for the sake of your prayers. Above all, maintain constant love for one another. 1 Peter 4:7–8

Grant, Lord, that with thy direction, 673
"Love each other," we comply,
aiming with unfeigned affection
thy love to exemplify;
let our mutual love be glowing;
thus the world will plainly see
that we, as on one stem growing,
living branches are in thee.

Let us take off our shoes in the presence of your holiness. Let us sit in silence and listen to your voice. Let us bask in your glory as we are being refilled to be your loving hands and feet until you return. Amen!

Friday, October 21 — Psalm 119:57–64
2 Samuel 13:34–14:33; John 8:42–59

The Lord says, "I will look with favor upon you and make you fruitful and multiply you; and I will maintain my covenant with you." Leviticus 26:9

> Our children, Lord, in faith and prayer,　　409
> we baptize in your name.
> Let them your cov'nant mercies share
> as we our faith proclaim.

You are God's field, God's building. 1 Corinthians 3:9

> Christ is our cornerstone,　　517
> on him alone we build;
> with his true saints alone
> the courts of heav'n are filled;
> on his great love our hopes we place
> of present grace and joys above.

We are the clay and you are the Potter. We are the beauty of the works of your hand, fearfully and wonderfully made in your image. Continue to refine us to courageously share your good news with all the world. Amen.

Saturday, October 22 — Psalm 119:65–72
2 Samuel 15:1–29; John 9:1–12

"From the rising of the sun to its setting my name is great among the nations," says the Lord. Malachi 1:11

When morning gilds the skies,   552
my heart awaking cries:
may Jesus Christ be praised!
In all my work and prayer
I ask his loving care:
may Jesus Christ be praised!

Many will come from the east and the west, and will take their places at the feast with Abraham, Isaac, and Jacob in the kingdom of heaven. Matthew 8:11 (NIV)

Come, let us eat, for now the feast is spread.   423
Come, let us eat, for now the feast is spread.
Our Lord's body let us take together.
Our Lord's body let us take together.

Wonderful Counselor, the mighty God, the everlasting Father, the Prince of peace, O what a foretaste you have given us of your heavenly feast. 'Til we shall recline at your great banquet table, continue to nourish our souls with your living bread and wine. Amen.

Twenty-Third Sunday after Pentecost

Watchword for the Week — Jesus says, "All who exalt themselves will be humbled, but all who humble themselves will be exalted." Luke 18:14

Sunday, October 23 — Jeremiah 14:7–10;19–22; Psalm 84:1–7
2 Timothy 4:6–8,16–18; Luke 18:9–14

O that you would tear open the heavens and come down! Isaiah 64:1

Immauel, to you we sing,   280
O prince of life, almighty King;
that you, expected ages past,
did come to visit us at last.

They will see "the Son of Man coming in clouds" with great power and glory. Mark 13:26

Come, you sinners, poor and needy,   765
weak and wounded, sick and sore,
Jesus, Son of God, will save you,
full of pity, love, and pow'r.
I will arise and go to Jesus;
he will embrace me in his arms;
in the arms of my dear Savior,
O there are ten thousand charms.

Holy of Holies are you, Lord. Though you are the Lord of all creation, you humbly assumed the lowliest of duties for our sake. We give you thanks for the ways you meet us each day; until we shall meet face-to-face. Amen.

Monday, October 24 — Psalm 119:73–80
2 Samuel 15:30–16:23; John 9:13–34

I will both lie down and sleep in peace; for you alone, O Lord, make me lie down in safety. Psalm 4:8

> Through the long night watches,   567
> may your angels spread
> their bright wings above me,
> watching round my bed.

He is our peace. Ephesians 2:14

> Alleluia, alleluia, alleluia, alleluia!   369
> That night the apostles met in fear;
> among them came their Master dear
> and said, "My peace be with you here."
> Alleluia!

We are grateful for your peace which surpasses all understanding. Peace of Christ, comfort us amidst the storms of life; intercede on our behalf, grant us wisdom, and lead us in all your truth. Alleluia to the Source of peace. Amen.

Tuesday, October 25 — Psalm 119:81–88
2 Samuel 17; John 9:35–41

See, the former things have come to pass, and new things I now declare; before they spring forth, I tell you of them. Isaiah 42:9

> Finish, then, your new creation,   p218
> pure and spotless, gracious Lord;
> let us see your great salvation
> perfectly in you restored.
> Changed from glory into glory,
> 'til in heav'n we take our place,
> 'til we sing before th'Almighty
> lost in wonder, love, and praise.

The mystery from which true godliness springs is great: he appeared in the flesh, was vindicated by the Spirit, was seen by angels, was preached among the nations, was believed on in the world, was taken up in glory. 1 Timothy 3:16 (NIV)

> O perfect redemption, the purchase of blood,   550
> to ev'ry believer the promise of God:
> the vilest offender who truly believes,
> that moment from Jesus a pardon receives.
> Praise the Lord, praise the Lord,
> let the earth hear his voice!
> Praise the Lord, praise the Lord,
> let the people rejoice!
> O come to the Father through Jesus the Son,
> and give him the glory—great things he has done!

Lord, we believe that you are excited to share your wonders with us, so that we, together, may marvel at your infinite power and the beauty of your hands. Help us to believe the unbelievable and to not be ashamed to be perceived as fools. Amen.

Wednesday, October 26 — Psalm 119:89–96
2 Samuel 18:1–30; John 10:1–10

Thus says the Lord, "I remember the devotion of your youth, your love as a bride, how you followed me in the wilderness, in a land not sown." Jeremiah 2:2

> And when these failing limbs grow numb,   422
> and mind and memory flee,
> when thou shalt in thy kingdom come,
> Jesus, remember me.

Let us hold fast to the confession of our hope without wavering, for he who has promised is faithful. Hebrews 10:23

> Remember thee, and all thy pains,   422
> and all thy love to me?
> Yea, while a breath, a pulse remains
> will I remember thee.

As the days and years edge on, help us, Lord, to not be weary and to not faint. Let our zeal for you never run dry. Daily renew us by the power of your Spirit. Let us by your power and strength finish the race. Amen.

Thursday, October 27 — Psalm 119:97–104
2 Samuel 18:31–19:30; John 10:11–21

Do not devise evil in your hearts against one another. Zechariah 7:10

Lord, as you have lived for others,   p41
so may we for others live;
freely have your gifts been granted;
freely may your servants give.
Yours the gold and yours the silver,
yours the wealth of land and sea,
we but stewards of your bounty
sharing all by your decree.

The eye cannot say to the hand, "I have no need of you," nor again the head to the feet, "I have no need of you." On the contrary, the members of the body that seem to be weaker are indispensable. 1 Corinthians 12:21–22

When a poor one who has nothing   689*
    shares with strangers,
when the thirsty water give unto us all,
when the crippled in their weakness
    strengthen others,
then we know that God still goes that road with us,
then we know that God still goes that road with us.

We command our beings to submit to your
authority, Lord Jesus. Where there is evil, blot it out
and fill those spaces with your Holy Spirit. Fill us
to be fruitful members of your body, and thereby
equip others to be likewise. Amen.

Friday, October 28 — Psalm 119:105–112
2 Samuel 19:31–20:26; John 10:22–33

Seek the Lord and his strength; seek his presence continually. Psalm 105:4

Break now the bread of life,   502
dear Lord, to me,
as when you broke the loaves
beside the sea.
Beyond the sacred page
I seek you, Lord;
my spirit waits for you,
O living Word.

Lord, teach us to pray. Luke 11:1

Lord, teach us how to pray aright,   750
with rev'rence and with fear;
though dust and ashes in your sight,
we may, we must draw near.

Humbly we come before your throne of grace, O
Lord, seeking all that you are, O God. For without
you we are but dust. Silence now our hearts and
minds in order that we might hear you even in
marrow. Amen.

Saturday, October 29 — Psalm 119:113–120
2 Samuel 21; John 10:34–42

Gideon said, "I will not rule over you; the Lord will rule over you." Judges 8:23

> Come, holy Comforter,   555
> your sacred witness bear
> in this glad hour.
> Your grace to us impart,
> now rule in ev'ry heart,
> never from us depart,
> Spirit of pow'r!

Jesus said, "You know that among the Gentiles those whom they recognize as their rulers lord it over them, and their great ones are tyrants over them. But it is not so among you; but whoever wishes to become great among you must be your servant." Mark 10:42–43

> May it in our walk be seen   586
> that we have with Jesus been,
> that as king o'er us he reigns
> and unrivaled pow'r maintains.

We have one Lord, who is the only true and living God, in Jesus Christ. We rebuke anything that seeks to take the place of Christ in our lives. Jesus, you are the solid rock on which we stand; all other ground is sinking sand. Amen.

Twenty-Fourth Sunday after Pentecost

Watchword for the Week — Jesus says, "For the Son of Man came to seek out and to save the lost." Luke 19:10

Sunday, October 30 — Isaiah 1:10–18; Psalm 32:1–7
2 Thessalonians 1:1–4,11–12; Luke 19:1–10

The hope of the righteous ends in gladness. Proverbs 10:28

No condemnation now I dread,   773
for Christ, and all in him, is mine!
Alive in him, my living Head,
and clothed in righteousness divine,
bold I approach the eternal throne
and claim the crown, through Christ, my own.

You also must be patient. Strengthen your hearts, for the coming of the Lord is near. James 5:8

Then when you will come again   261
as the glorious king to reign,
I with joy will see your face,
freely ransomed by your grace.

With each waking day, great I Am, purify and guard our hearts. Clothe us in your armor from the crowns of our heads to the soles of our feet. Until you return, may we be unshaken, unmoved by every false wind. In Jesus' name we pray. Amen.

Reformation Day

Monday, October 31 — Psalm 119:121–128
2 Samuel 22:1–25; John 11:1–16

Shout aloud and sing for joy, people of Zion, for great is the Holy One of Israel among you. Isaiah 12:6 (NIV)

Glorious things of you are spoken,   522
Zion, city of our God;
he whose word cannot be broken
formed you for his own abode;
on the rock of ages founded,
what can shake your sure repose?
With salvation's walls surrounded
you may smile at all your foes.

God did not withhold his own Son, but gave him up for all of us, will he not with him also give us everything else? Romans 8:32

Lord, be ever my protector;   568
with me stay, all the day,
ever my director.
Holy, holy, holy giver
of all good, life and food,
reign adored forever.

Hosanna, the love of God made flesh. Hosanna, God's agape, highest of praise, be unto you. May your praise never cease from our lips. May we glorify you in our going and our coming, in our good times and bad. Alleluia! Amen.

All Saints Day

Watchword for All Saints Day — Salvation belongs to our God who is seated on the throne, and to the Lamb! Revelation 7:10

Tuesday, November 1 — Psalm 119:129–136
2 Samuel 22:26–23:17; John 11:17–30

All Saints Day — Daniel 7:1–3,15–18; Psalm 149
Ephesians 1:11–23; Luke 6:20–31

He stands at the right hand of the needy, to save them from those who would condemn them to death. Psalm 109:31

> Apostles, prophets, martyrs,   p107
> and all the sacred throng
> who wear the spotless raiment,
> who raise the ceaseless song;
> for those passed on before us,
> our Savior, we adore,
> and walking in their footsteps,
> would serve you more and more.

Jesus is not ashamed to call them brothers and sisters. Hebrews 2:11

> Praise to the Lord, the Almighty,   p18
> the King of creation!
> O my soul, praise him,
> for he is your health and salvation!
> Come all who hear,
> brothers and sisters draw near;
> join now in glad adoration.

Loving God, we thank you for the saints in our lives, for those who have entered into your more immediate presence, and for those still with us. For all the saints we give you thanks, in Christ's name. Amen.

Wednesday, November 2 — Psalm 119:137–144
2 Samuel 23:18–24:25; John 11:31–44

By his knowledge my righteous servant will justify the many, and he will bear their iniquities. Isaiah 53:11 (NIV)

All our knowledge, sense, and sight   558
lie in deepest darkness shrouded,
'til your Spirit breaks our night
with the beams of truth unclouded;
you alone to God can win us;
you must work all good within us.

The Son of Man came not to be served but to serve, and to give his life a ransom for many. Mark 10:45

While a helpless infant still,   336*
he had to flee his foes,
and, in time, rejected by
the people whom God chose;
yet he came to seek and serve
the wayward and the lost,
faithful to his Father's will
and heedless of the cost.

Jesus, help us to have a spirit of service instead of one of being served. Guide us to help those who need you. Use us today as the hands and feet of your kingdom. Amen.

* Text by Jaroslav J. Vajda © 1983 Concordia Publishing House. Used with permission. www.cph.org.

Thursday, November 3 — Psalm 119:145–152
1 Kings 1:1–27; John 11:45–57

The Lord said to me, "You are my servant, Israel, in whom I will be glorified." Isaiah 49:3

> Servant of God, well done!   811
> Rest from your loved employ;
> the battle fought,
> the victory won,
> enter your Master's joy.

God has not rejected his people whom he foreknew. Romans 11:2

> Long my imprisoned spirit lay   773
> fast bound in sin and nature's night.
> Your sunrise turned that night to day;
> I woke—the dungeon flamed with light!
> My chains fell off, your voice I knew;
> was freed, I rose, and followed you.
> My chains fell off, your voice I knew;
> was freed, I rose, and followed you.

God of love, thank you for not rejecting us; thank you for loving us as we are, for being who you are, and for saving us from our transgressions. In Jesus' name we pray. Amen.

Friday, November 4 — Psalm 119:153–160
1 Kings 1:28–53; John 12:1–11

You who seek God, let your hearts revive. Psalm 69:32

Come, Almighty to deliver,   474
let us all your life receive;
suddenly return, and never,
never more your temple leave.
You we would be always blessing,
serve you as your hosts above,
pray, and praise you without ceasing,
glory in your perfect love.

Let us run with perseverance the race that is set before us, looking to Jesus the pioneer and perfecter of our faith. Hebrews 12:1–2

The congregation stand amazed,   393*
their joy beyond expressing.
The saints who died and now are raised
delight in endless blessing:
they see where Christ Jesus sits, crowned on the
    throne,
the equal of God our creator,
his kingdom, his power, his glory made known:
our king and great liberator.

Most holy God, keep us vigilant in seeking you.
Give us the strength and faith to trust wholly in you
and to keep our eyes fixed upon you as we run the
race that is perfect in your will. All glory is yours, O
Father. In Jesus' name we pray. Amen.

* © 1994 by Madeleine Forell Marshall

Saturday, November 5 — Psalm 119:161–168
1 Kings 2:1–38; John 12:12–19

God says, "O that my people would listen to me." Psalm 81:13

O let me hear you speaking   603
in accents clear and still,
above the storms of passion,
the murmurs of self-well.
O speak to reassure me,
to hasten or control;
and speak to make me listen,
O guardian of my soul.

Continue securely established and steadfast in the faith, without shifting from the hope promised by the gospel that you heard. Colossians 1:23

Church, go forth o'er the earth;   631
Christ, your head, has hallowed you,
a chosen bridge forever,
adorned now for our Savior;
be strong and be not cheerless,
and may your saints be fearless;
in all places, with all races,
may that story of his glory
be the hope of all the world.

Gracious Lord, as we go about this day we pray that you will be with us and help us to tell your story of glory in all that we do and say. In Jesus' name we pray. Amen.

Twenty-Fifth Sunday after Pentecost

Watchword for the Week — For I know that my Redeemer lives, and that at the last he will stand upon the earth. Job 19:25

Sunday, November 6 — Job 19:23–27a; Psalm 17:1–9
2 Thessalonians 2:1–5,13–17; Luke 20:27–38

For God will bring every deed into judgment, including every secret thing, whether good or evil. Ecclesiastes 12:14

> We entreat, we entreat,   528
> Lord, lift up your countenance
> on your ransomed congregations;
> grace to ev'ry soul dispense.
> May we in our situations
> daily in your great salvation share.
> Hear our prayer, hear our prayer.

When the Son of Man comes, will he find faith on earth? Luke 18:8

> Pass me not, O gentle Savior,   772
> hear my humble cry;
> while on others thou art smiling,
> do not pass me by.
> Savior, Savior, hear my humble cry;
> while on others thou art calling;
> do not pass me by.

Father, in all of our transgressions you show mercy; you know each of us as we are. We prepare for you until you return. Amen.

Monday, November 7 — Psalm 119:169–176
1 Kings 2:39–3:28; John 12:20–36

I am the Lord; I act with steadfast love, justice, and righteousness in the earth. Jeremiah 9:24

> We covenant in church and home   p121
> this peace to show each other,
> to represent your steadfast love
> as sister and as brother.
> O, may we through each other know
> your grace which fails us never,
> and find at last our true abode
> within your house forever.

Let everyone who calls on the name of the Lord turn away from wickedness. 2 Timothy 2:19

> Jesus calls us; o'er the tumult   600
> of our life's wild, restless sea,
> day by day his voice is sounding,
> saying, "Christian, follow me."

Great I Am, as we enter into this day we pray that you will keep us true in word, thought, and deed. Be with us and let us forever be reflections of your love. In Jesus' name we pray. Amen.

Tuesday, November 8 — Psalm 120
1 Kings 4:1–28; John 12:37–50

I heard the voice of the Lord saying, "Whom shall I send, and who will go for us?" And I said, "Here am I; send me!" Isaiah 6:8

I, the Lord of sea and sky,   641*
I have heard my people cry.
All who dwell in deepest sin
my hand will save.
I who made the stars of night,
I will make their darkness bright.
Who will bear my light to them?
Whom shall I send?
Here I am, Lord. Is it I, Lord?
I have heard you calling in the night.
I will go, Lord, if you lead me.
I will hold your people in my heart.

To each one the manifestation of the Spirit is given for the common good. 1 Corinthians 12:7 (NIV)

Breathe on me, breath of God,   494
fill me with life anew,
that I may love the things you love
and do what you would do.

Father, pour out your Spirit upon us so that we may be of you. Make our hearts holy, and send us to be your hands in this world. In your Spirit we pray. Amen.

Wednesday, November 9 — Psalm 121
1 Kings 4:29–5:18; John 13:1–17

When your judgments are in the earth, the inhabitants of the world learn righteousness. Isaiah 26:9

O God, our help in ages past,   461
our hope for years to come,
remain our guard while life shall last,
and our eternal home.

John wrote: I saw heaven opened, and there was a white horse! Its rider is called Faithful and True, and in righteousness he judges and makes war. Revelation 19:11

Crown him the Lord of years,   405
the risen Lord sublime,
Creator of the rolling spheres,
the Master of all time.
All hail, Redeemer, hail!
For you have died for me;
your praise and glory shall not fail
throughout eternity.

Lord, as we await your coming in sure and certain hope, keep us ever focused in faith and love until you return from above. In your name we pray. Amen.

Thursday, November 10 — Psalm 122
1 Kings 6; John 13:18–30

God, I think of you on my bed, and meditate on you in the watches of the night. Psalm 63:6

> All praise to you, my God, this night 569
> for all the blessings of the light.
> Keep me, O keep me, King of kings,
> beneath the shelter of your wings.

O the depth of the riches and wisdom and knowledge of God! How unsearchable are his judgments and how inscrutable his ways! Romans 11:33–34

> My faith looks trustingly 705
> to Christ of Calvary,
> my Savior true!
> Lord, hear me while I pray,
> take all my guilt away,
> strengthen in ev'ry way
> my love for you!

Father, our trust and rest lie in you. We look to you for guidance in what you would have us do. Be our guide, O Lord. Amen.

Friday, November 11 — Psalm 123
1 Kings 7:1–33; John 13:31–38

I delight in the way of your decrees as much as in all riches. Psalm 119:14

> O blessed Lord, teach me your law,   510
> your righteous judgments I declare;
> your testimonies make me glad,
> for they are wealth beyond compare.

The kingdom of heaven is like a merchant in search of fine pearls; on finding one pearl of great value, he went and sold all that he had and bought it. Matthew 13:45–46

> Earth's glory to inherit   484
> is not what I desire;
> to heav'n aspires my spirit,
> to glow with nobler fire;
> where Christ himself appearing,
> in bright majesty,
> for me a place preparing,
> there, there I long to be.

Lord, help us to know that your kingdom is worth more than all the riches of the earth. Let the material world around us not dissuade us from the ultimate treasure of your glory. Amen.

Saturday, November 12 — Psalm 124
1 Kings 7:34–8:16; John 14:1–14

In the midst of the congregation I will praise you. Psalm 22:22

Praise, my soul, the King of heaven,   529
to his feet your tribute bring.
Ransomed, healed, restored, forgiven,
evermore his praises sing.
Alleluia! Alleluia!
Praise the everlasting King!

May the God of steadfastness and encouragement grant you to live in harmony with one another, in accordance with Christ Jesus, so that together you may with one voice glorify the God and Father of our Lord Jesus Christ. Romans 15:5–6

O bless the Lord, my soul!   546
His grace to all proclaim!
And all that is within me join
to bless his holy name.

Father, we will praise you, O Lord among the
nations; we will sing unto you among the heavens.
Glorious, everlasting are you, our God! Amen.

Twenty-Sixth Sunday after Pentecost
Chief Elder Festival

Watchword for the Week — Brothers and sisters, do not be weary in doing what is right. 2 Thessalonians 3:13

Sunday, November 13 — Malachi 4:1–2a; Psalm 98
2 Thessalonians 3:6–13; Luke 21:5–19

Chief Elder Festival† — Ezekiel 34:11–16,23–24; Psalm 8
Hebrews 4:14–16; John 10:1–10

The Lord said, "I will defend this city to save it, for my own sake." 2 Kings 19:34

> Fear not, I am with you; O be not dismayed,   709
> for I am your God and will still give you aid;
> I'll strengthen you, help you, and cause you to stand
> upheld by my righteous, omnipotent hand.

God's firm foundation stands, bearing this inscription: "The Lord knows those who are his." 2 Timothy 2:19

> How firm a foundation, you saints of the Lord,   709
> is laid for your faith in his excellent word!
> What more can he say than to you he has said,
> to you who for refuge to Jesus have fled?

Dearest Chief Elder, all praise, honor, and glory are yours. Lord, you are our master as well as our friend. Thank you for guiding us through all that has been and all that is yet to come. In your name we pray. Amen.

† On November 13, 1741, announcement was made to the congregations of the Brethren's Church of the Chief Eldership of Jesus Christ.

Monday, November 14 — Psalm 125
1 Kings 8:17–53; John 14:15–24

This is what the Lord said, "Through those who are near me I will show myself holy, and before all the people I will be glorified." Leviticus 10:3

A charge to keep I have,   645
a God to glorify,
a never-dying soul to save
and fit it for the sky.

You know the message God sent to the people of Israel, preaching peace by Jesus Christ—he is Lord of all. Acts 10:36

Grace and peace from God, our blessed Savior,   444
be with all who love his name;
church of Christ, his service deem a favor,
joyfully his death proclaim;
be prepared for rest or for employment,
from activity derive enjoyment,
serve with zeal and faithfulness,
filled with love his name confess.

Lord God, you are the Lord of all; help us to keep your name holy and to glorify you. Help us to preach peace to all those around us. Amen.

Tuesday, November 15 — Psalm 126
1 Kings 8:54–9:19; John 14:25–15:8

I shall not be put to shame, having my eyes fixed on all your commandments. Psalm 119:6

As it was without beginning,   458
so it lasts without an end;
to their children's children ever
shall God's righteousness extend:
unto such as keep God's cov'nant
and are steadfast in his way,
unto those who still remember
the commandments and obey.

The disciples were urging Jesus, "Rabbi, eat something." But he said to them, "I have food to eat that you do not know about." So the disciples said to one another, "Surely no one has brought him something to eat?" Jesus said to them, "My food is to do the will of him who sent me and to complete his work." John 4:31–34

Take my life that it may be   610
all your purpose, Lord, for me.
Take my moments and my days;
let them sing your ceaseless praise,
let them sing your ceaseless praise.

God, our Father, help us to know and do your will. May all that we do this day be pleasing in your sight. Lord, bless us and keep us all in your loving care. Amen.

Wednesday, November 16 — Psalm 127
1 Kings 9:20–10:29; John 15:9–17

Let all those rejoice who put their trust in you. Psalm 5:11 (NKJV)

Endow us richly with your gifts and grace   377
to fit us for the duties of our place;
so open now our lips, our hearts so raise,
that both our hearts and lips may give you praise.

Although you have not seen Jesus Christ, you love him; and even though you do not see him now, you believe in him and rejoice with an indescribable and glorious joy. 1 Peter 1:8

To God be the glory—great things he has done!   550
so loved he the world that he gave us his Son,
who yielded his life an atonement for sin,
and opened the life-gate that all may go in.
Praise the Lord, praise the Lord,
let the earth hear his voice!
Praise the Lord, praise the Lord,
let the people rejoice!
O come to the Father through Jesus the Son,
and give him the glory—great things he has done!

Our Lord Jesus, though we may not see you face-to-face, help us to show your presence to our neighbors, friends, family, and to all whom we meet. Let us be your hands and feet in the life of someone who needs you today. In Jesus' name we pray. Amen.

Thursday, November 17 — Psalm 128
1 Kings 11:1–25; John 15:18–16:4

Behold, to the Lord your God belong heaven and the highest heavens, the earth and all that is in it. Deuteronomy 10:14 (NASB)

> Holy God, we praise your name: 386
> Lord of all, we bow before you.
> Saints on earth your rule acclaim;
> all in heaven above adore you.
> Infinite your vast domain;
> everlasting is your reign.

Ever since the creation of the world his eternal power and divine nature, invisible though they are, have been understood and seen through the things he has made. Romans 1:20

> We thank you, our Creator,   453
> for all things bright and good,
> the seedtime and the harvest,
> our life, our health, our food;
> accept the gifts we offer
> for all your love imparts,
> and what you most would treasure—
> our humble, thankful hearts.
> All good gifts around us
> are sent from heav'n above;
> then thank the Lord, O thank the Lord
> for all his love.

Lord, you can be seen in all of your creation. Help us to recognize you in all that we see and to hold your creation close to our hearts. Amen.

Friday, November 18 — Psalm 129
1 Kings 11:26–12:24; John 16:5–16

O Lord, I am oppressed; be my security!
Isaiah 38:14

If dangers gather round,   615
still keep me calm and fearless;
help me to bear the cross
when life is bleak and cheerless,
to overcome my foes
with words and actions kind;
O God, your will disclose,
your counsel let me find.

The Spirit helps us in our weakness; for we do not know how to pray as we ought, but that very Spirit intercedes with sighs too deep for words. Romans 8:26

Give patience as we watch and weep,   750
though mercy long delay;
give courage our faint souls to keep,
and trust you though you slay;
give these, and then your will be done;
thus strengthened with all might,
we, by your Spirit and your Son,
shall pray, and pray aright.

Though things in our lives may sometimes be uncertain, help us to keep our hearts and minds focused on you, Holy Spirit. Be our guide this day as we face whatever comes our way. In Jesus' name we pray. Amen.

Saturday, November 19 — Psalm 130
1 Kings 12:25–13:22; John 16:17–33

When they say to you, "Consult the mediums and the spiritists," should not a people consult their God? Isaiah 8:19 (NASB)

Come as a teacher, sent from God,   432
charged his whole counsel to declare;
life o'er our ranks the prophet's rod,
while we uphold your hands with prayer.

Whoever is united with the Lord is one with him in spirit. 1 Corinthians 6:17 (NIV)

'Tis a pleasant thing to see   670
brothers in the Lord agree,
sisters of a God of love
live as they shall live above,
acting each a Christian part,
one in word and one in heart.

Lord, we are united with you when we put our full faith in you. Let us not seek guidance from the world around us, but trust you in all that we do. Amen.

Reign of Christ (Christ the King Sunday)

Watchword for the Week — Be still, and know that I am God! I am exalted among the nations, I am exalted in the earth. Psalm 46:10

Sunday, November 20 — Jeremiah 23:1–6; Psalm 46
Colossians 1:11–20; Luke 23:33–43

Uphold me according to your promise, that I may live, and let me not be put to shame in my hope. Psalm 119:116

> Lord, your body ne'er forsake,   p86
> n'er your congregation leave;
> we in you our refuge take,
> of your fullness we receive:
> ev'ry other help be gone,
> you are our support alone;
> for on your supreme commands
> all the universe depends.

May the God of peace himself sanctify you entirely; and may your spirit and soul and body be kept sound and blameless at the coming of our Lord Jesus Christ. 1 Thessalonians 5:23

> Come, let us all with gladness raise   519
> a joyous song of thanks and praise
> to God who rules the heav'nly host,
> God, Father, Son, and Holy Ghost.

Heavenly King of kings, help us to be still and know that you are the reigning King of our lives. Bless us this day, O Lord, we pray and forever keep us in your love. Amen.

Monday, November 21 — Psalm 131
1 Kings 13:23–14:20; John 17:1–19

Great are the works of the Lord; they are pondered by all who delight in them.
Psalm 111:2 (NIV)

> Children of the heav'nly King, 789
> as you journey, sweetly sing;
> sing your Savior's worthy praise,
> glorious in his works and ways.

Consider the lilies, how they grow: they neither toil nor spin; yet I tell you, even Solomon in all his glory was not clothed like one of these.
Luke 12:27

> When peace, like a river, attendeth my way, 754
> when sorrows like sea billows roll;
> whatever my lot, you have taught me to say,
> it is well, it is well with my soul.
> It is well with my soul,
> it is well, it is well with my soul.

Heavenly Father, your works are great! You constantly show us that you are with us in all that we do. Help us to stop worrying and to put our hopes and fears in your hands, O God. Amen.

Tuesday, November 22 — Psalm 132
1 Kings 14:21–15:8; John 17:20–26

As the mountains surround Jerusalem, so the Lord surrounds his people, from this time on and forevermore. Psalm 125:2

> Through all the tumult and the strife, 701
> I hear that music ringing.
> It sounds and echoes in my soul;
> how can I keep from singing?
> No storm can shake my inmost calm,
> while to that Rock I'm clinging.
> Since love is Lord of heaven and earth,
> how can I keep from singing?

John wrote: I heard a loud voice from the throne saying, "See, the home of God is among mortals. He will dwell with them; they will be his peoples." Revelation 21:3

> They stand, those halls of Zion, 814
> all jubilant with son,
> so bright with many an angel,
> and all the martyr throng.
> The Prince is ever in them,
> the daylight is serene;
> the tree of life and healing
> has leaves of richest green.

Lord, we know that we are yours and yours alone. Help us to reflect the love that you have given to us so that others may join your fold. In Jesus' name we pray. Amen.

Wednesday, November 23 — Psalm 133
1 Kings 15:9–16:14; John 18:1–11

Noah did all that God commanded him. Genesis 6:22

As sure as I prove   608
your mercy and love,
as life you did gain
for me, and my comfort does ever remain,
so may I prove true,
devoted to you,
and cheerfully stand,
prepared to comply with your ev'ry command.

By faith Noah, being warned by God about things not yet seen, in reverence prepared an ark for the salvation of his household. Hebrews 11:7 (NASB)

Faith is a living power from heav'n   700
that grasps the promise God has giv'n,
a trust that can't be overthrown
fixed heartily on Christ alone.

Lord God, faith is our most powerful gift. Just as
Abraham, Noah, Sarah, and Moses put their full
faith in you, let us find the strength to put our full
faith in you with all that we do. Amen.

Thursday, November 24 — Psalm 134
1 Kings 16:15–17:24; John 18:12–24

I know that my Redeemer lives. Job 19:25

Guide me, O my great Redeemer, 790
pilgrim through this barren land.
I am weak, but you are mighty;
hold me with your pow'rful hand.
Bread of heaven, bread of heaven,
feed me now and evermore,
feed me now and evermore.

Paul wrote: The saying is sure and worthy of full acceptance, that Christ Jesus came into the world to save sinners—of whom I am the foremost. 1 Timothy 1:15

Christ is our Master, Lord, and God, 479
the fullness of the Three in One.
His life, death, righteousness, and blood
our faith's foundation are alone;
his Godhead and his death shall be
our theme to all eternity.

Dearest Savior, thank you for coming into the world, living among us, and knowing us inside and out; thank you for being our Savior, conquering for us, and allowing us to follow you. Amen.

Friday, November 25 — Psalm 135:1–12
1 Kings 18; John 18:25–40

The human mind plans the way, but the Lord directs the steps. Proverbs 16:9

> He leadeth me: O blessed thought!   787
> O words with heav'nly comfort fraught!
> Whate'er I do, where'er I be,
> still 'tis God's hand that leadeth me.
> He leadeth me, he leadeth me;
> by his own hand he leadeth me,
> his faithful foll'wer I would be,
> for by his hand he leadeth me.

You ought to say, "If the Lord wishes, we will live and do this or that." James 4:15

> Be with me, Lord, where'er I go;   733
> teach me what you would have me do;
> suggest whate'er I think or say;
> direct me in the narrow way.

Lord, guide our feet so that we will be in your will and do the goodness of your Spirit. Be our sure feet in this life so that we may rejoice with you in the next. In Jesus' name we pray. Amen.

Saturday, **November 26** — Psalm 135:13–21
1 Kings 19; John 19:1–11

The righteous are like trees planted by streams of water, which yield their fruit in its season, and their leaves do not wither. Psalm 1:3

Come, thou Fount of ev'ry blessing,   782
tune my heart to sing thy grace;
streams of mercy, never ceasing,
call for songs of loudest praise.
Teach me some melodious sonnet,
sung by flaming tongues above.
Praise the mount—I'm fixed upon it—
mount of God's redeeming love.

The fruit of the Spirit is love, joy, peace, patience, kindness, generosity, faithfulness, gentleness, and self-control. Galatians 5:22–23

O that Jesus' love and merit   589
filled our hearts both night and day!
May the leading of his Spirit
all our thoughts and actions sway!
Then should we be ever ready
cheerfully to testify
how our spirit, soul, and body
do in God our Savior joy.

God of love, joy, and peace, abide with us this
day in all that we do and say. Take from us the
things that worry us most and let us delight in you
through all of what this day may bring. In Jesus'
name we pray. Amen.

First Sunday of Advent

Watchword for the Week — Come, let us walk in the light of the Lord! Isaiah 2:5

Sunday, November 27 — Isaiah 2:1–5; Psalm 122
Romans 13:11–14; Matthew 24:36–44

My word shall not return to me empty, but it shall accomplish that which I purpose, and succeed in the thing for which I sent it. Isaiah 55:11

Straight shall be what long was crooked,   264
and the rougher places plain!
Let your hearts be true and humble,
as befits his holy reign!
For the glory of the Lord
now on earth is shed abroad,
and all flesh shall see the token
that God's word is never broken.

The disciples went out and proclaimed the good news everywhere, while the Lord worked with them and confirmed the message by the signs that accompanied it. Mark 16:20

I love to tell the story   625
of unseen things above,
of Jesus and his glory,
of Jesus and his love.
I love to tell the story,
because I know it's true;
it satisfied my longings
as nothing else would do.
I love to tell the story;
I'll sing this theme in glory
and tell the old, old story
of Jesus and his love.

Lord, as we go forth today may we spread your word in all that we say and do. May the power of your message not fall upon deaf ears; may we all know that you are God. Amen.

Monday, November 28 — Psalm 136
1 Kings 20:1–21; John 19:12–24

Happy are those who fear the Lord, who greatly delight in his commandments. Psalm 112:1

> Perfect submission, all is at rest, 714
> I in my Savior am happy and blessed,
> watching and waiting, looking above,
> filled with his goodness, lost in his love.
> This is my story, this is my song,
> praising my Savior all the day long.
> This is my story, this is my song,
> praising my Savior all the day long.

**Continue in what you have learned and firmly believed, knowing from whom you learned it, and how from childhood you have known the sacred writings that are able to instruct you for salvation through faith in Christ Jesus.
2 Timothy 3:14–15**

> You are the truth; your word alone 661
> true wisdom can impart;
> you only can inform the mind
> and purify the heart.

Source of all wisdom and truth, teach us to sow words of love and peace instead of hate and war in this world that we call home. Help us to love our neighbors as ourselves as we seek to do your will. Amen.

Tuesday, November 29 — Psalm 137
1 Kings 20:22–21:16; John 19:25–37

I will manifest my holiness among you in the sight of the nations. You shall know that I am the Lord, when I bring you into the land of Israel, the country that I swore to give to your ancestors. Ezekiel 20:41–42

> O seed of Israel's chosen race, 403
> now ransomed from the fall,
> hail him who saves you by his grace,
> and crown him Lord of all!
> Hail him who saves you by his grace,
> and crown him Lord of all!

The gifts and the calling of God are irrevocable. Romans 11:29

> We thank you then, O Father, p162
> for all things bright and good,
> the seedtime and the harvest,
> our life, our health, our food;
> help us to show thanksgiving
> for all you freely give;
> to love you in our neighbor,
> and by the way we live.
> All good gifts around us
> are sent from heav'n above;
> then thank the Lord,
> O thank the Lord for all his love.

Your gifts to us are plentiful, dear Lord. Help us to use them to praise you and to show the nations that you are Lord of our lives. Amen.

Wednesday, November 30 — Psalm 138:1–5
1 Kings 21:17–22:28; John 19:38–20:9

I will not let you go, unless you bless me. Genesis 32:26

> With joyfulness and longing   p13
> we look to you, O Lord;
> receive us in your mercy,
> and cheer us with your word.
> Crown us with love enduring
> and promises of grace,
> and let your holy blessing
> remain within this place.

Devote yourselves to prayer, keeping alert in it with thanksgiving. Colossians 4:2

> Dear Lord and Father of mankind,   739
> forgive our foolish ways;
> reclothe us in our rightful mind;
> in purer lives thy service find,
> in deeper rev'rence, praise.

Lord God, help us to never shy away from conversing with you. Prayer is our way to talk with you. May the conversation never end. Amen.

Thursday, December 1 — Psalm 138:6–8
1 Kings 22:29–53; John 20:10–23

Keep hold of instruction; do not let go; guard her, for she is your life. Proverbs 4:13

> Great God of all wisdom,   p128*
> of science and art,
> O grant us the wisdom
> that comes from the heart.
> Technology, learning,
> philosophy, youth—
> all leave us still yearning
> for your word of truth.

The aim of such instruction is love that comes from a pure heart, a good conscience, and sincere faith. 1 Timothy 1:5

> Blessed are the pure in heart,   584
> for they shall see their God.
> The secret of the Lord is theirs;
> their soul is Christ's abode.

O wondrous source of all knowledge and truth, instill in us a love and yearning for all that is of you. Amen.

---

* © 1984 by Jane Parker Huber from *A Singing Faith*. Used by permission of Westminster John Knox Press.

Friday, December 2 — Psalm 139:1–6
2 Kings 1:1–2:18; John 20:24–31

I lie down and sleep; I wake again, for the Lord sustains me. Psalm 3:5

> In waking, lift our thoughts above,   570*
> in sleeping guard us still,
> that we may rise to know your love
> and prove your perfect will.

Peace to all of you who are in Christ. 1 Peter 5:14

> The peace which God alone reveals   p33
> and by his word of grace imparts,
> which only the believer feels,
> direct, and keep, and cheer our hearts!
> And may the holy Three-in-One,
> the Father, Word, and Comforter,
> pour an abundant blessing down
> on ev'ry soul assembled here!

Prince of peace, whether waking or sleeping, we know that you are with us, sustaining us with your perfect peace. Amen.

Saturday, December 3 — Psalm 139:7–12
2 Kings 2:19–3:27; John 21:1–14

Truly God is good to the upright, to those who are pure in heart. Psalm 73:1

> Lord, we your presence seek;   584
> we ask this blessing true:
> give us a pure and lowly heart,
> a temple fit for you.

Simeon was looking forward to the consolation of Israel. Luke 2:25

> For you, since first the world was made,   280
> All hearts have waited, watched, and prayed;
> prophets and patriarchs, year by year,
> have longed to see your light appear.

O, God, guide our faith. Show us ways of gratitude and teach us to give to others with pure hearts. Hear our songs of praise. Let us rejoice from our hearts in this most blessed Advent season. Amen.

Second Sunday of Advent

Watchword for the Week — Repent, for the kingdom of heaven has come near. Matthew 3:2

Sunday, December 4 — Isaiah 11:1–10; Psalm 72
Romans 15:4–13; Matthew 3:1–12

The Lord lift up his countenance upon you, and give you peace. Numbers 6:26

> The Lord bless and keep you in his favor   446
> as his chosen, cherished heir;
> the Lord make his face shine on you ever
> and enfold you in his care.
> The Lord lift his countenance upon you,
> may where'er you go his Spirit lead you,
> and his peace on you bestow;
> amen, amen, be it so.

May the God of hope fill you with all joy and peace in believing. Romans 15:13

> Sing hallelujah, praise the Lord!   543
> Sing with a cheerful voice;
> exalt our God with one accord,
> and in his name rejoice.
> Ne'er cease to sing, O ransomed host,
> praise Father, Son, and Holy Ghost,
> until in realms of endless light
> your praises shall unite.

Loving God, you are the source of our joy and peace. We believe because of your gift of Jesus Christ and your gift of faith through the Holy Spirit. Hallelujah! Amen.

Monday, December 5 — Psalm 139:13–16
2 Kings 4:1–37; John 21:15–25

Be glad and rejoice in the Lord your God. Joel 2:23

God is love, let heav'n adore him;   463
God is love, let earth rejoice;
let creation sing before him
and exalt him with one voice.
God who laid the earth's foundation,
God who spread the heav'ns above,
God who breathes through all creation:
God is love, eternal love.

Blessed be the Lord God of Israel, for he has looked favorably on his people and redeemed them. He has raised up a mighty savior for us in the house of his servant David. Luke 1:68–69

Rejoice! Our God has come,   p185
in love and lowliness;
the Son of God has come
God's children all to bless;
God with us now descends to dwell,
God in our flesh, Immanuel.

Lord God, we rejoice that you sent your son Jesus to redeem our souls. Let us be glad that in this season of Advent you remain present with us, guiding us daily and preparing us for your second coming. Amen.

Tuesday, **December 6** — Psalm 139:17–24
2 Kings 4:38–5:14; Acts 1:1–14

Elijah said, "How long will you go limping with two different opinions? If the Lord is God, follow him; but if Baal, then follow him." 1 Kings 18:21

> Grant us your truth, your freedom give,   464
> that hearts for you might solely live
> 'til all your living altars claim
> one holy light, one heav'nly flame!

Jesus said, "No one sews a piece of unshrunk cloth on an old cloak; otherwise, the patch pulls away from it, the new from the old, and a worse tear is made." Mark 2:21

> You are the way, the truth, the life;   661
> grant us that way to know;
> that truth to keep, that life to win,
> whose joys eternal flow.

Father, when you sent your Son, you sent a new way of life which offers us a life of redemption and salvation. May we live each day in a way that shows that we are redeemed, saved, and loved by you. Amen.

Wednesday, December 7 — Psalm 140:1–5
2 Kings 5:15–6:23; Acts 1:15–26

Because of the Lord's great love we are not consumed. Lamentations 3:22 (NIV)

> The Lord has promised good to me,   783
> his word my hope secures;
> he will my shield and portion be
> as long as life endures.

The grace of our Lord overflowed for me with the faith and love that are in Christ Jesus. 1 Timothy 1:14

> Through many dangers, toils, and snares,   783
> I have already come;
> 'tis grace has brought me safe thus far,
> and grace will lead me home.

Almighty Father, as we remember the sacrifices that you have made for us, we are thankful for the ultimate sacrifice of your son, Jesus Christ, the Lamb of God. We thank you for the redemption that was paid for by his blood. Amen.

Thursday, December 8 — Psalm 140:6–13
2 Kings 6:24–7:20; Acts 2:1–13

Joshua fell on his face to the earth and worshiped, and he said to him, "What do you command your servant, my Lord?" Joshua 5:14

May we faithful, may we faithful   636
in our service be,
truly careful, truly careful
in our ministry;
keep us to your church fast bound,
in the faith preserve us sound,
often weeping, often weeping
grateful tears of joy.

Blessed are those who hear the word of God and obey it! Luke 11:28

Jesus, Master, will you use   p42
one who owes you more than all?
As you will, I would not choose;
only let me hear your call.
Jesus, let me always be
in your service glad and free.

Christ, we await your leading. You are a voice of courage to those who speak but are not heard. Help us to hear their pleas and to do what you would have us do to ease their distress. Amen.

Friday, December 9 — Psalm 141:1–4
2 Kings 8; Acts 2:14–28

Balaam replied, "Although Balak were to give me his house full of silver and gold, I could not go beyond the command of the Lord my God." Numbers 22:18

> Only be still and wait his pleasure   712
> in cheerful hope with heart content.
> He fills your needs to fullest measure
> with what discerning love has sent;
> doubt not our inmost wants are known
> to him who chose us for his own.

Do not be overcome by evil, but overcome evil with good. Romans 12:21

> Guide me, O my great Redeemer,   790
> pilgrim through this barren land.
> I am weak, but you are mighty;
> hold me with your pow'rful hand.
> Bread of heaven, bread of heaven,
> feed me now and evermore,
> feed me now and evermore.

God of mercy and compassion, overflow our lives with your loving presence and wash away all that would keep us from you. Our worship, love, and service we gladly give in return. Amen.

Saturday, December 10 — Psalm 141:5–10
2 Kings 9; Acts 2:29–47

The days are surely coming, says the Lord, when I will raise up for David a righteous Branch, and he shall reign as king and deal wisely, and shall execute justice and righteousness in the land. Jeremiah 23:5

> Hail to the Lord's anointed!   263
> Great David's greater Son!
> Hail, in the time appointed,
> his reign on earth begun!
> He comes to break oppression,
> to set the captive free,
> to take away transgression
> and rule in equity.

Those who went ahead and those who followed were shouting, "Hosanna! Blessed is the one who comes in the name of the Lord! Blessed is the coming kingdom of our ancestor David! Hosanna in the highest heaven!" Mark 11:9–10

> Hosanna! Blessed is he that comes!   p239
> Hosanna! Hosanna! Blessed is he that comes,
> he that comes in the name of the Lord!
> Hosanna! Blessed is he that comes!
> Hosanna! Hosanna! Hosanna in the highest!

Divine Creator, hear our hosannas for your incarnation amongst your creation who shows us perfect grace and love. Leave us not in our feeble and imperfect efforts to follow your will, but lead us toward divine justice, love, and grace. Amen.

Third Sunday of Advent

Watchword for the Week — Be strong, do not fear! Here is your God.
Isaiah 35:4

Sunday, December 11 — Isaiah 35:1–10; Psalm 146:5–10
James 5:7–10; Matthew 11:2–11

I will gather the exiles. I will give them praise and honor in every land where they have suffered shame. Zephaniah 3:19 (NIV)

O, then what raptured greetings   394
on Canaan's happy shore;
what knitting severed friendships up,
where partings are no more!
Then eyes with joy shall sparkle
that brimmed with tears of late,
no orphans left without a home,
nor mourners desolate.

Jesus saw a great crowd; and he had compassion for them, because they were like sheep without a shepherd. Mark 6:34

Jesus makes my heart rejoice,   662
I'm his sheep and know his voice;
he's a Shepherd, kind and gracious,
and his pastures are delicious;
constant love to me he shows,
yea, my very name he knows.

Shepherd of our souls, we all are exiles in some
way; we long for home. We are connected to others
through the love we have with you and we ask
that you help us to share that love in our daily
interactions. Amen.

Monday, December 12 — Psalm 142
2 Kings 10; Acts 3:1–10

Speak out for those who cannot speak, for the rights of all the destitute. Proverbs 31:8

> Speak thou for us, O Lord,   583r
> in all we say of you;
> according to your word
> let all our teaching be,
> that so your lambs may know
> their own true Shepherd's voice,
> where'er he leads them go,
> and in his love rejoice.

Remember the prisoners as if chained with them —those who are mistreated—since you yourselves are in the body also. Hebrews 13:3 (NKJV)

> We are the hands and feet of Christ,   p46*
> serving by grace each other's need.
> We dare to risk and sacrifice
> with truthful word and faithful deed.

Father, as we walk again the road to Bethlehem, let us remember those who lifted us up on our faith journeys and the trials that revealed your grace, the key to freedom from the prison of sin and death. Amen.

*   © by Jim Strathdee

Tuesday, December 13 — Psalm 143:1–6
2 Kings 11; Acts 3:11–26

Show me your glory, I pray. Exodus 33:18

Lord of glory, God most high,   744
man exalted to the sky,
with your love my heart now fill;
prompt me to perform your will!
Then your glory I shall see;
blessed for all eternity.

Philip said to him, "Lord, show us the Father, and we will be satisfied." Jesus said to him, "Have I been with you all this time, Philip, and you still do not know me?" John 14:8–9

He found them in his house of prayer   396
with one accord assembled,
and so revealed his presence there;
they wept for joy and trembled.
One cup they drank, one bread they broke,
one baptism shared, one language spoke,
forgiving and forgiven.

In the dark and barren depths of our souls, we search for the one source of comfort that can heal and restore. Reveal your glory to us, O God; the light of your love in Christ is our greatest desire. Amen.

Wednesday, December 14 — Psalm 143:7–12
2 Kings 12,13; Acts 4:1–12

The God of heaven is the one who will give us success, and we his servants are going to start building. Nehemiah 2:20

> We are God's house of living stones,   512
> built for his own habitation;
> he fills our hearts, his humble thrones,
> granting us life and salvation.
> Yet to this place, an earthly frame,
> we come with thanks to praise his name;
> God grants his people true blessing.

We are God's fellow workers. 1 Corinthians 3:9 (NKJV)

> The task your wisdom has assigned   638
> here let me cheerfully fulfill,
> in all my work your presence find
> and prove your good and perfect will.

Omnipotent God, through your mighty works you created us, your workers. In all that we busily do to prepare for your coming this Advent season, remind us that our work is for your good and perfect will. Amen.

Thursday, December 15 — Psalm 144:1–4
2 Kings 14; Acts 4:13–22

Fathers make known to children your faithfulness. Isaiah 38:19

> How shall the young direct their way?   510
> What light shall be their perfect guide?
> Your word, O Lord, will safely lead
> if in its wisdom they confide.

Every scribe who has been trained for the kingdom of heaven is like the master of a household who brings out of his treasure what is new and what is old. Matthew 13:52

> We'll bring him hearts that love him,   658
> we'll bring him thankful praise,
> and souls forever striving
> to follow in his ways:
> and these shall be the treasures
> we offer to the King,
> and these are gifts that even
> our grateful hearts may bring.

Gracious God, we give thanks for the wisdom of your word that fills our minds and breathes life into our hearts. Lead us to know your way, so that our lives shine with the light of your love and presence. Amen.

Friday, December 16 — Psalm 144:5–8
2 Kings 15; Acts 4:23–37

Have I any pleasure in the death of the wicked, says the Lord God, and not rather that they should turn from their ways and live? Ezekiel 18:23

> Father, now your sinful child   779
> through your love is reconciled.
> By your pard'ning grace I live;
> daily still I cry, forgive.

Do you not realize that God's kindness is meant to lead you to repentance? Romans 2:4

> Love divine, all loves excelling,   474
> joy of heav'n, to earth come down!
> Fix in us your humble dwelling,
> all your faithful mercies crown.
> Jesus, you are all compassion,
> pure, unbounded love impart!
> Visit us with your salvation,
> enter ev'ry trembling heart.

Loving Savior, we confess that we are a sinful people. We know that it is only through your loving kindness that we can come to you, ask your forgiveness, and receive your pardoning grace. Amen.

Saturday, December 17 — Psalm 144:9–15
2 Kings 16:1–17:6; Acts 5:1–11

I love the Lord, because he has heard my voice and my supplications. Psalm 116:1

> Glorious Lord, yourself impart!   558
> Light of light, from God proceeding,
> open now our ears and heart,
> help us by your Spirit's pleading;
> hear the cry that we are raising;
> hear, and bless our prayers and praising.

The angel said to him, "Do not be afraid, Zechariah, for your prayer has been heard. Your wife Elizabeth will bear you a son, and you will name him John." Luke 1:13

> Wondrous birth! O wondrous child   265
> of the Virgin undefiled!
> Mighty God and Mary's son,
> human and divine in one.

Gracious God, there is much in our world to make us afraid. We give thanks that your Holy Spirit intercedes for us; we know you never forsake us. We lift our praise to you as your love overcomes all that we fear. Amen.

Fourth Sunday of Advent

Watchword for the Week — Restore us, O Lord God of hosts; let your face shine, that we may be saved. Psalm 80:19

Sunday, December 18 — Isaiah 7:10–16; Psalm 80:1–7,10–14
Romans 1:1–7; Matthew 1:18–25

Who is like the Lord our God, who is seated on high, who looks far down on the heavens and the earth? He raises the poor from the dust. Psalm 113:5–7

My pow'r is faint and low   604
'til I have learned to serve;
It lacks the needed fire to glow,
it lacks the breeze to nerve;
it cannot drive the world
until itself be driv'n;
its flag can only be unfurled
when you shall breathe from heav'n.

Paul wrote: Though Christ was crucified in weakness, yet he lives by the power of God. For we also are weak in him, but we shall live with him by the power of God toward you. 2 Corinthians 13:4 (NKJV)

My heart is weak and poor   604
until it master find;
it has no spring of action sure,
it varies with the wind.
It cannot freely move
'til you have wrought its chain;
enslave it with your matchless love,
and deathless it shall reign.

Forgiving God, remind us that our preparations
to receive and celebrate the birth of your Son, no
matter how creative or extravagant, are for naught
if not moved by and infused with your power.
Amen.

Monday, December 19 — Psalm 145:1–7
2 Kings 17:7–41; Acts 5:12–16

Light dawns for the righteous, and joy for the upright in heart. Psalm 97:11

The brightness of the Light divine   56r
does now into our darkness shine;
it breaks upon sin's gloomy night
and makes us children of the light.

When they saw the star, they rejoiced with exceedingly great joy. Matthew 2:10 (NKJV)

As with gladness men of old   p190
did the guiding star behold;
as with joy they hailed its light,
leading onward, beaming bright;
so, most gracious Lord, may we
evermore your splendor see.

Glorious God, lead us to receive Christ Jesus, who upon himself bears all our sins. Then, with hearts and desire more pure, the light of your presence will be our guide, our comfort, and our joy. Amen.

Tuesday, December 20 — Psalm 145:8–16
2 Kings 18; Acts 5:17–40

God does great things beyond understanding, and marvelous things without number. Job 9:10

Praise to the Lord, who o'er all things   530
    is wondrously reigning,
shelt'ring you under his wings,
    O, so gently sustaining.
Have you not seen
all you have needed has been
met by his gracious ordaining.

From his fullness we have all received, grace upon grace. John 1:16

Born your people to deliver,   262
born a child and yet a king,
born to reign in us forever,
now your gracious kingdom bring.
By your own eternal Spirit
rule in all our hearts alone;
by your all-sufficient merit
raise us to your glorious throne.

Creator, too often we are blind to the wonders of this world. We are your people of faith. Help us to see your wonder in the faces of everyone we meet. Amen.

Wednesday, December 21 — Psalm 145:17–21
2 Kings 19:1–28; Acts 5:41–6:7

Woe to those who acquit the guilty for a bribe, but deny justice to the innocent. Isaiah 5:22,23 (NIV)

He comes with rescue speedy   263
to those who suffer wrong,
to help the poor and needy,
and bid the weak be strong,
to give them songs for sighing,
their darkness turn to light,
whose souls, condemned and dying,
were precious in his sight.

With the judgment you make you will be judged, and the measure you give will be the measure you get. Matthew 7:2

Once he came in blessing   270
all our sins redressing,
came in likeness lowly,
Son of God most holy;
bore the cross to save us,
hope and freedom gave us.

You, O God, are the judge of all things. Thank
you for not holding us to the law, but for giving us
grace through Jesus Christ, our salvation, our hope
fulfilled. Amen.

Thursday, December 22 — Psalm 146:1–5
2 Kings 19:29–37; Acts 6:8–7:3

Not by might, nor by power, but by my spirit, says the Lord of hosts. Zechariah 4:6

Spirit of God, who dwells within my heart,   490
wean it from sin, through all its pulses move.
Stoop to my weakness, mighty as you are,
and make me love you as I ought to love.

By faith the walls of Jericho fell. Hebrews 11:30

If you but trust in God to guide you   712
and place your confidence in him,
you'll find him always there beside you
to give you hope and strength within;
for those who trust God's changeless love
build on the rock that will not move.

Father, it can be troubling to see anger, strife, and
dissension around us. You created this beautiful
world for love of your children so that we may love
one another. With our faith and your grace, all
things can be healed. Amen.

Friday, December 23 — Psalm 146:6–10
2 Kings 20:1–21; Acts 7:4–16

All the ends of the earth shall turn to the Lord. Psalm 22:27

> O Holy Spirit, stir us now,   299*
> inspire our hearts to make this vow:
> we will go forth into the night
> and share with all your gift of light.

The true light, which enlightens everyone, was coming into the world. John 1:9

> Light of light, we humbly pray,   276**
> shine upon your world today;
> break the gloom of our dark night,
> fill our souls with love and light,
> give your blessed word rebirth,
> "Peace, good will to all on earth."

Light of the world, we pause to give you thanks for showing us the image of God through your presence. You lighten our dark world and enrich our lives through the fruits of the Holy Spirit. Amen.

*   © James V. Salzwedel

** © by Eleanor R. Roller

Christmas Eve

Saturday, December 24 — Psalm 147:1–6
2 Kings 21:1–22:10; Acts 7:17–29

I kept my faith, even when I said, "I am greatly afflicted." Psalm 116:10

Sing, pray, and keep his ways unswerving,   712
offer your service faithfully,
and trust his word; though undeserving,
you'll find his promise true to be.
God never will forsake in need
the soul that trusts in him indeed.

If the Son makes you free, you will be free indeed. John 8:36

Come, O long-expected Jesus,   262
born to set your people free;
from our fears and sins release us;
O, in you our rest shall be.
Israel's strength and consolation,
hope to all the earth impart,
dear desire of ev'ry nation,
joy of ev'ry longing heart.

Father, you use life's challenges to strengthen our faith. May we live our faith in ways that show the world the love that you showed to us through the gift of your Son. No other gift will ever be as precious. Amen.

Nativity of the Lord (Christmas Day)

Watchword for Christmas Day — The law was given through Moses; grace and truth came through Jesus Christ. John 1:17

Sunday, December 25 — Isaiah 52:7–10; Psalm 98
Hebrews 1:1–4,(5–12); John 1:1–14

The bows of the mighty are broken, but the feeble gird on strength. 1 Samuel 2:4

Blessed are the poor in spirit,   595
claiming nothing as their own,
but as giv'n them by their Father
that his goodness may be shown.
Blessed are they who share the sorrow
of their God's unchanging love;
they shall know his presence with them
and his promised comfort prove.

Mary said, "He has brought down the powerful from their thrones, and lifted up the lowly; he has filled the hungry with good things, and sent the rich away empty." Luke 1:52–53

He came down to earth from heaven   292
who is God and Lord of all,
and his shelter was a stable,
and his cradle was a stall;
with the poor and meek and lowly
lived on earth our Savior holy.

Creator of all that shall be, we're blessed by your incarnation. Separated from you, alone and in darkness, we languished until you came, gave us good things, and lifted us up. Comfort us. Set our feet upon the path toward your kingdom. Amen.

Monday, December 26 — Psalm 147:7–14
2 Kings 22:11–23:20; Acts 7:30–43

The Lord opens the eyes of the blind. Psalm 146:8

> Amazing grace! How sweet the sound   783
> that saved a wretch like me!
> I once was lost, but now am found,
> was blind, but now I see.

The eyes of your heart may be enlightened in order that you may know the hope to which he has called you. Ephesians 1:18 (NIV)

> Open my eyes, that I may see   452r
> glimpses of truth you have for me;
> place in my hands the wonderful key
> that shall unclasp and set me free.
> Silently now I wait for you,
> ready, my God, your will to see;
> open my eyes, illumine me,
> Spirit divine!

O great Physician of our hearts, our hope is built on your blood and righteousness. Thank you for opening our eyes through the birth of our Savior so that we may see your truth. Amen.

Tuesday, December 27 — Psalm 147:15–20
2 Kings 23:21–24:20; Acts 7:44–60

Turn, O Lord, save my life; deliver me for the sake of your steadfast love. Psalm 6:4

> For God, in grace and tenderness,   519
> regarded us in our distress;
> yea, to our aid himself he came;
> let all adore God's holy name.

Jesus turned, and seeing her he said, "Take heart, daughter; your faith has made you well." And instantly the woman was made well. Matthew 9:22

> Abide among us ever,   451r
> Lord, with your faithfulness;
> Jesus, forsake us never,
> Help us in all distress.

In faith we journey with uncertain steps to greet our Savior and Lord. Jesus is born into our world and meets us wherever we are found. We give thanks that God's love in Christ heals and saves us. Amen.

Wednesday, December 28 — Psalm 148:1–6
2 Kings 25; Acts 8:1–8

The Lord said to Jeremiah, "Now I have put my words in your mouth." Jeremiah 1:9

Keep me from saying words 615
that later need recalling;
guard me, lest idle speech
may from my lips be falling;
but when, within my place,
I must and ought to speak,
then to my words give grace,
lest I offend the weak.

From the cloud there came a voice, "This is my Son, the Beloved; listen to him!" Mark 9:7

Great things he has taught us, 550
    great things he has done,
And great our rejoicing through Jesus the Son:
but purer, and higher, and greater will be
our wonder, our transport when Jesus we see.
Praise the Lord, praise the Lord,
    let the earth hear his voice!
Praise the Lord, praise the Lord,
    let the people rejoice!
O come to the Father through Jesus the Son,
and give him the glory—great things he has done!

Dear Lord, daily we struggle and strive to make the words from our thoughts and mouths to be words that are acceptable in your sight. Please keep your hand on our mouths so that we may speak your words. Amen.

Thursday, December 29 — Psalm 148:7–14
1 Chronicles 1:1–37; Acts 8:9–17

Do not be afraid, for I am with you to deliver you, says the Lord. Jeremiah 1:8

Father, your name be praised,   575
    your kingdom given,
your will be done on earth as 'tis in heaven;
keep us in life, forgive our sins, deliver
us now and ever.

The Son of Man came to seek out and to save the lost. Luke 19:10

This is the time, when he was born to save us,   830*
who set us free from sins that would enslave us;
for Mary's child and all his coming gave us;
to God be endless praise!

Glorious God, you sent your precious Son to deliver and save us. Your gift of grace enables us to live in your light day by day. Thank you for your blessings and love. Amen.

Friday, December 30 — Psalm 149
1 Chronicles 1:38–2:17; Acts 8:18–25

More majestic than the thunders of mighty waters, more majestic than the waves of the sea, majestic on high is the Lord! Psalm 93:4

O tell of his might, O sing of his grace,   566
whose robe is the light, whose canopy space.
His chariots of wrath the deep thunderclouds form,
and dark is his path on the wings of the storm.

Jesus Christ says, "In the world you face persecution. But take courage; I have conquered the world!" John 16:33

When we suffer, God sends healing;   534*
when we sin, the Lord forgives;
from the grave the Lord redeems us,
and, by grace, we rise to live!

Majestic living Water, you have washed us in your saving grace; blessed is your name. Amen.

Saturday, December 31 — Psalm 150
1 Chronicles 2:18–55; Acts 8:26–40

How very good and pleasant it is when kindred live together in unity! For there the Lord ordained his blessing, life forevermore. Psalm 133:1,3

> 'Til sons of men shall learn your love,   532r
> and follow where your feet have trod;
> 'til glorious from your heaven above
> shall come the city of our God.

Agree with one another, live in peace; and the God of love and peace will be with you. The grace of the Lord Jesus Christ, the love of God, and the communion of the Holy Spirit be with all of you. 2 Corinthians 13:11,13

> Lord Jesus, 'mid your flock appear;   311
> your ransomed congregation bless;
> we meet to close another year;
> accept the thanks our hearts express.
> We are not able to record
> the countless favors we have known;
> they show that we, most gracious Lord,
> 'mid all our sins remain your own.

Almighty Father, we give you thanks for the blessing of another year. We ask for the Spirit to be in us as we start the new year. Thank you for your love, grace, and mercy. Amen.

DIRECTORY
AND STATISTICS

Moravian Church in North America
Northern and Southern Provinces

2016

THE MORAVIAN CHURCH IN NORTH AMERICA

1021 Center Street, Bethlehem, PA 18018
459 South Church Street, Winston-Salem, NC 27101

Published by the Interprovincial Board of Communication
Moravian Church in North America

www.moravian.org

CONTENTS

ADDRESSES OF CHURCHES

Churches are listed alphabetically by state and then alphabetically by city of physical location.

NP = Northern Province
SP = Southern Province

CD = Canadian District
ED = Eastern District
WD = Western District

ALBERTA, CANADA (NP, CD):
BRUDERHEIM -
Bruderheim Church
Highway 45
Mail: Box 208
Bruderheim, AB T0B 0S0
Canada
O: 780.796.3775
F: 780.796.9736
email:
admin.bruderheimmoravian@shaw.ca
www.bruderheimmoravian.org

CALGARY -
Christ Church
600 Acadia Drive SE
Calgary, AB T2J 0B8
Canada
O: 403.271.2700
F: 403.271.2810
email: moravian@nucleus.com
www.christmoravian.com

Good Shepherd Community Church
6311 Norfolk Drive NW
Calgary, AB T2K 5J8
Canada
O: 403.274.4888
F: 403.451.1556
email:
admin@goodshepherdmoravian.org
www.goodshepherdmoravian.org

EDMONTON -
Edmonton Church
9540 83 Avenue NW
Edmonton, AB T6C 1B9
Canada
O: 780.439.1063
F: 780.756.7898
email: edmontonmoravian@shaw.ca
www.edmontonmoravian.com

Millwoods Church
2304 38th Street NW
Edmonton, AB T6L 4K9
Canada
O: 780.463.7427
F: 780.461.3058
email: office@mcchurch.ca
www.mcchurch.ca

Rio Terrace Church
15108 76 Avenue NW
Edmonton, AB T5R 2Z9
Canada
O/F: 780.487.0211
email: rioterracechurch@shaw.ca
www.rioterracechurch.org

LEDUC COUNTY -
Heimtal Church
51117 Range Road 250
Leduc County, AB T9G 0B3
Canada
O: 780.955.7305
email: heimtal@telus.net
www.heimtal.com

SHERWOOD PARK -
Good News Church
2 Primrose Boulevard
Sherwood Park, AB T8H 1G2
Canada
O: 780.467.0337
email: goodnewschurch@yahoo.com
www.goodnewschurch.ca

CALIFORNIA (NP, WD):
BANNING -
Morongo Church
47765 Foothill Road
Banning, CA 92220
Mail: PO Box 352
Banning, CA 92220-0352
O: 951.849.3067
email: morongomoravian@verizon.net

DOWNEY-
Downey Church
10337 Old River School Road
Downey, CA 90241-2057
O: 562.927.0718
email: downeymoravian10337@gmail.com
www.downeymoravian.org

DISTRICT OF COLUMBIA
(NP, ED):
WASHINGTON -
Faith Church
405 Riggs Road NE
Washington, DC 20011-2515
O: 202.635.9012/9013
F: 202.635.9014
email:
writetous@faithmoravianchurch.org
www.faithmoravianchurch.org

FLORIDA (SP):
LONGWOOD-
Rolling Hills Church
1525 State Road 434 W
Longwood, FL 32750-3877
O: 407.332.8380
email: rhmcoffice@centurylink.net
www.rhmoravian.org

MIAMI-
King of Kings Church
1880 NW 183rd Street
Miami, FL 33056
email: kokmoravian@att.net

New Hope Church
6001 SW 127th Avenue
Miami, FL 33183-1427
O/F: 305.273.4047
email: nhmiami@yahoo.com

Prince of Peace Church
1880 NW 183rd Street
Miami, FL 33056
O: 305.628.2061
F: 305.625.5365
email: popmc@bellsouth.net
www.princeofpeacemoravianchurch.org

WEST PALM BEACH -
Palm Beach Church
297 27th Street
West Palm Beach, FL 33407
O: 561.832.1363
F: 561.832.1363 (call first)
email: pbmoravian@yahoo.com

GEORGIA (SP):
STONE MOUNTAIN -
First Church of Georgia
4950 Hugh Howell Road
Stone Mountain, GA 30087
O: 770.491.7250
F: 770.414.5678
email: firstmoravianga@gmail.com
www.gamoravian.org

ILLINOIS (NP, WD):
WEST SALEM -
West Salem Church
257 E. Church Street
West Salem, IL 62476
Mail: PO Box 27
West Salem, IL 62476-0027
O: 618.456.8532
email: wsmor12@gmail.com
www.westsalemmoravianchurch.webs.com

INDIANA (NP, WD):
HOPE -
Hope Church
202 Main Street
Hope, IN 47246
O: 812.546.4641
email:
office@hopemoravianchurch.org or
pastor@hopemoravianchurch.org
www.hopemoravianchurch.org

MARYLAND (NP, ED):
NEW CARROLLTON -
Trinity Church
7011 Good Luck Road
New Carrollton, MD 20784
O: 301.441.1814
email:
trinitymoravianoffice@gmail.com
www.trinitymoravianchurch.org

THURMONT -
Graceham Church
8231-A Rocky Ridge Road
Thurmont, MD 21788
O: 301.271.2379
F: 301.271.4241
email:
secretary@gracehammoravian.org
or
pastorsue@gracehammoravian.org
www.gracehammoravian.org

UPPER MARLBORO -
St. Paul's Church
8505 Heathermore Boulevard
Upper Marlboro, MD 20772
O: 301.627.4200
F: 301.627.4204
email: spmoravian@gmail.com
www.spmoravian.org

MICHIGAN (NP, WD):
DAGGETT -
Daggett Church
102 Old US Highway 41
Daggett, MI 49821
Mail: c/o G. Straughan
2201 Libal Street
Green Bay, WI 54301
O: 906.753.6995
email: daggett@new.rr.com

UNIONVILLE -
Unionville Church
2711 Cass Street
Unionville, MI 48767
O: 989.674.8686
email: office@unionvillemoravian.org
www.unionvillemoravian.org

WESTLAND -
Grace Church
31133 Hively Avenue
Westland, MI 48185
O/F: 734.721.9290
email: gracemoravian@gmail.com

MINNESOTA (NP, WD):
ALTURA -
Our Savior's Church
37 Chapel Drive NW
Altura, MN 55910
Mail: PO Box 161
Altura, MN 55910-0161
O: 507.796.5612
email: osmoravian@centurylink.net
www.oursaviorsmoravian.org

CHASKA -
Chaska Church
115 E 4th Street
Chaska, MN 55318
O: 952.448.4000
F: 952.448.6016
email: chaskamoravian@embarqmail.com
www.chaskamoravian.org

MAPLE GROVE -
Christ's Community Church
13250 93rd Avenue
Maple Grove, MN 55369
O: 763.420.7187
email:
christscommunitymoravian@gmail.com
www.ccc-mg.org

NORTHFIELD -
Northfield (Main Street) Church
713 Division Street
Northfield, MN 55057
O: 507.645.7566
email:
mainstreetmoravianchurch@yahoo.com
www.mainstreetmoravian.org

SAINT CHARLES -
Berea Church
1270 Berea Drive
St. Charles, MN 55972
Mail: PO Box 402
Saint Charles, MN 55972-0402
O: 507.932.3584

VICTORIA -
Lake Auburn Church
7460 Victoria Drive
PO Box 160
Victoria, MN 55386
O/F: 952.443.2051
email:
lakeauburnchurch@centurylink.net
www.lakeauburnchurch.embarqspace.com

WACONIA -
Waconia Church
209 East 2nd Street
Waconia, MN 55387
O: 952.442.2920
email: wmoravian@gmail.com
www.waconiamoravian.org

NEW JERSEY (NP, ED):
CINNAMINSON -
Palmyra Church
1921 Cinnaminson Avenue
Cinnaminson, NJ 08077
O: 856.829.2886
email: palmyramoravian@gmail.com
www.palmyramoravian.org

EGG HARBOR -
Egg Harbor City Church
245 Boston Avenue
Egg Harbor City, NJ 08215
O: 609.965.1920
email: wknt03@aol.com
www.eggharborcitymoravian.weebly.com

RIVERSIDE -
First Church
228 East Washington Street
Riverside, NJ 08075-3629
O: 856.461.0132
F: 856.764.7032
email: riversidemoravian@verizon.net
www.riversidemoravian.org

UNION -
Battle Hill Church
777 Liberty Avenue
Union, NJ 07083
O: 908.686.5262
F: 908.378.5866
email: bhmoravian@verizon.net

NEW YORK (NP, ED):
BRONX -
Tremont Terrace Church
1621 Pilgrim Avenue
Bronx, NY 10461
O: 718.829.2156
F: 718.829.0044
email: tremontterrace@verizon.net

BROOKLYN -
Fellowship Church (Meeting at
Church of the Evangel U.C.C.)
1950 Bedford Avenue
Brooklyn, NY 11225
O: 718.287.7200

John Hus Church
153 Ocean Avenue
Brooklyn, NY 11225
O: 718.856.2200
F: 718.856.2201
email: johnhusmoravian@optonline.net
www.johnhusmoravianchurch.com

NEW YORK -
First Church
154 Lexington Avenue
New York, NY 10016
Mail: PO Box 1874
Murray Hill Station
New York, NY 10156-0609
O: 212.683.4219
F: 212.683.9734
email: firstmoravian@verizon.net

United Church
200 East 127th Street
New York, NY 10035
Mail: PO Box 90
New York, NY 10035-0090
O: 212.722.2109
F: 212.987.2818
email: unitedmoravian@gmail.com
www.unitedmoravian.org

QUEENS -
Grace Church
178-38 137th Avenue
Springfield Gardens
Queens, NY 11434
O: 718.723.2681
F: 718.723.4288
email: gracemoravian@verizon.net
www.gracemoravianchurchny.org

STATEN ISLAND -
Castleton Hill Church
1657 Victory Boulevard
Staten Island, NY 10314
O: 718.442.5215 or 718.442.5309
F: 718.442.5211
email: office@castletonhill.org
www.castletonhill.org

Great Kills Church
62 Hillside Terrace
Staten Island, NY 10308
O: 718.317.7788
F: 718.356.2826
email: office@greatkillsmoravian.org
www.greatkillsmoravian.org

New Dorp Church
2205 Richmond Road
Staten Island, NY 10306-2557
O: 718.351.0090
F: 718.351.0290
email:
ndmcthree.moravian@verizon.net
www.newdorpmoravian.org

Vanderbilt Avenue Church
285 Vanderbilt Avenue
Staten Island, NY 10304
O: 718.447.2966
email: office@vanderbiltmoravian.org
www.vanderbiltmoravian.org

NORTH CAROLINA (SP):
ADVANCE -
Macedonia Church
700 NC Highway 801 N
Advance, NC 27006
O: 336.998.4394
F: 336.940.5317
email: macedonia@yadtel.net
www.macedoniamoravian.org

BETHANIA -
Bethania Church
5545 Main Street
Bethania, NC 27010
Mail: PO Box 170
Bethania, NC 27010-0170
O: 336.922.1284
F: 336.922.1294
email:
bethaniamoravian@triad.twcbc.com
www.bethaniamoravian.org

CHARLOTTE -
Little Church on the Lane
522 Moravian Lane
Charlotte, NC 28207
O: 704.334.1381
F: 704.333.2281 (call first)
www.littlechurchonthelane.com

Peace Church
4418 Rea Road
Charlotte, NC 28226
O: 704.759.9939
F: 704.927.1688
email: general@peacemoravian.com
www.peacemoravian.com

CLEMMONS -
Clemmons Church
3535 Spangenberg Avenue
Clemmons, NC 27012
Mail: PO Box 730
Clemmons, NC 27012
O: 336.766.6273
F: 336.766.3794
email: Office@clemmonsmoravian.org
www.clemmonsmoravian.org

DURHAM -
Christ the King Church
4405 Hope Valley Road
Durham, NC 27707
O: 919.489.1711
F: 919.419.0032
email: office@ctkhome.org
www.ctkhome.org

EDEN -
Leaksville Church
712 McConnell Street
Eden, NC 27288
Mail: PO Box 35
Eden, NC 27289
O: 336.623.9440
email: leaksvillemoravian@gmail.com
www.leaksvillemoravianchurch.org

GREENSBORO -
First Church
304 South Elam Avenue
Greensboro, NC 27403
O: 336.272.2196
F: 336.275.7800
email: office@greensboromoravian.org
www.greensboromoravian.org

HUNTERSVILLE -
New Beginnings Church
203 Seagle Street
Huntersville, NC 28078
Mail: PO Box 2278
Huntersville, NC 28070-2278
O: 704.992.2003
F: 704.992.2002
email: newbeginnings100@bellsouth.net
www.newbeginningsmoravian.org

KERNERSVILLE -
Kernersville Church
504 South Main Street
Kernersville, NC 27284
O: 336.993.3620
F: 336.993.7052
email: kmchurch@embarqmail.com
www.kernersvillemoravian.org

KING -
King Church
228 West Dalton Road
King, NC 27021
O: 336.283.5322
email: office@kingmoravianchurch.org
www.kingmoravianchurch.org

LEWISVILLE -
Unity Church
8300 Concord Church Road
Lewisville, NC 27023
O: 336.945.3801 or 336.945.3877
email: unitymc@windstream.net
www.unitymoravian.org

LEXINGTON -
Enterprise Church
2733 Enterprise Road
Lexington, NC 27295-9233
O: 336.764.1281
email: emcpastor@bellsouth.net

MAYODAN -
Mayodan Church
104 South 3rd Avenue
Mayodan, NC 27027
Mail: PO Box 245
Mayodan, NC 27027-0245
O: 336.548.2645
F: 336.548.2645 (call first)
email:
mayodanmoravian@triad.twcbc.com

MT. AIRY -
Grace Church
1401 North Main Street
Mt. Airy, NC 27030
O: 336.786.5627
F: 336.786.2896
email:
office@gracemoravianchurch.org
www.gracemoravianchurch.org

NEWTON -
New Hope Church
2897 Sandy Ford Road
Newton, NC 28658
O: 828.294.4802
F: 828.294.1237
email: newhopemoravian@gmail.com
www.newhopemoravian.org

OAK RIDGE -
Moravia Church
2920 Oak Ridge Road
Oak Ridge, NC 27310
O/F: 336.643.5166
email: moraviamoravian@att.net
www.moraviachurch.org

RALEIGH -
Raleigh Church
1816 Ridge Road
Raleigh, NC 27607
O: 919.787.4034
F: 919.787.4250
email: office@raleighmoravian.org
www.raleighmoravian.org

RURAL HALL -
Mizpah Church
3165 Mizpah Church Road
Rural Hall, NC 27045
O: 336.924.1661
email:
mizpahmoravianchurch@windstream.net
www.mizpahmoravianchurch.org

Rural Hall Church
7939 Broad Street
Rural Hall, NC 27045
Mail: PO Box 487
Rural Hall, NC 27045-0487
O: 336.969.9488
F: 336.450.1535
email: secretary@rhmc.org
www.rhmc.org

WALNUT COVE -
Fulp Church
1556 US 311 Highway South
Walnut Cove, NC 27052
O/F: 336.591.7940
email: fulpmoravian@embarqmail.com
www.fulpmoravian.org

WILMINGTON -
Covenant Church
4126 South College Road
Wilmington, NC 28412
O/F: 910.799.9256
email: office@covenantmoravian.org

WINSTON-SALEM -
Advent Church
1514 West Clemmonsville Road
Winston-Salem, NC 27127
O: 336.788.4951
F: 336.788.0739
email: amchurch@triad.rr.com
www.adventmoravian.org

Ardmore Church
2013 West Academy Street
Winston-Salem, NC 27103
O: 336.723.3444
F: 336.723.5710
email: office@ardmoremoravian.org
www.ardmoremoravian.org

Bethabara Church
2100 Bethabara Road
Winston-Salem, NC 27106
O/F: 336.924.8789
email: bethabaraoffice@windstream.net
www.bethabara.com

Bethesda Church
740 Bethesda Road
Winston-Salem, NC 27103
O: 336.765.1357
F: 336.768.6977

Calvary Church
600 Holly Avenue
Winston-Salem, NC 27101
O: 336.722.3703
F: 336.724.1956 (call first)
email: office@calvarymoravian.org
www.calvarymoravian.org

Christ Church
919 West Academy Street
Winston-Salem, NC 27101-5103
O: 336.722.2007
F: 336.724.1704
email: office@christmoravianchurch.org
www.christmoravianchurch.org

Fairview Church
6550 Silas Creek Parkway
Winston-Salem, NC 27106
O: 336.768.5629
F: 336.768.5637
email:
fmc@fairviewmoravianchurch.org
www.fairviewmoravianchurch.org

Friedberg Church
2178 Friedberg Church Road
Winston-Salem, NC 27127-9073
O: 336.764.1830
F: 336.764.4524
email: info@friedbergmoravian.org
www.friedbergmoravian.org

Friedland Church
2750 Friedland Church Road
Winston-Salem, NC 27107
O: 336.788.2652
F: 336.784.1534
email: lindalyons2@triad.rr.com

Fries Memorial Church
251 North Hawthorne Road NW
Winston-Salem, NC 27104
O: 336.722.2847
F: 336.722.2132
email: frieschurch@gmail.com
www.frieschurch.org

Home Church
529 South Church Street
Winston-Salem, NC 27101
O: 336.722.6171
F: 336.723.5085
email: home1771@homemoravian.org
www.homemoravian.org

Hope Church
2759 Hope Church Road
Winston-Salem, NC 27127
O: 336.765.8017
email: hopemoraviannc@triad.rr.com
www.hopemoraviannc.org

Hopewell Church
701 Hopewell Church Road
Winston-Salem, NC 27127
O: 336.788.2289
email: hmc701@triad.twcbc.com
www.hopewellmoraviannc.org

Immanuel New Eden Church
3680 Old Lexington Road
Winston-Salem, NC 27127
O: 336.788.1561

Konnoak Hills Church
3401 Konnoak Drive
Winston-Salem, NC 27127
O: 336.788.9321
F: 336.785.0211
email: khmc3401@bellsouth.net
www.khmoravian.org

Messiah Church
1401 Peace Haven Road
Winston-Salem, NC 27104-1397
O: 336.765.5961
F: 336.659.6642
email: messiah1401@gmail.com
www.messiahmoravian.org

New Philadelphia Church
4440 Country Club Road
Winston-Salem, NC 27104
O: 336.765.2331
O: 336.768.5961
F: 336.765.5536
email: pastor@newphilly.org
www.newphilly.org

Oak Grove Church
120 Hammock Farm Road
Winston-Salem, NC 27105
O: 336.595.8167
email:
oakgrovemoravian@embarqmail.com

Olivet Church
2205 Olivet Church Road
Winston-Salem, NC 27106
O: 336.924.8063
F: 336.922.9005
email: olivet@windstream.net
www.olivetmoravian.org

Pine Chapel
324 Goldfloss Street
Winston-Salem, NC 27127
O: 336.723.7118
email: pinechapelmoravian@att.net

Providence Church
929 Old Hollow Road
Winston-Salem, NC 27105
O/F: 336.767.8234

St. Philips Church
3002 Bon Air Avenue
Winston-Salem, NC 27105
O: 336.770.5933
email: office@stphilipsmoravian.org
www.stphilipsmoravian.org

Trinity Church
220 East Sprague Street
Winston-Salem, NC 27127
O: 336.724.5541 or 336.724.5542
F: 336.724.1246
email: office@trinitymoravian.org
www.trinitymoravian.org

Union Cross Church
4295 High Point Road
Winston-Salem, NC 27107
O: 336.769.2411
email: ucmc@unioncrossmoravian.org
www.unioncrossmoravian.org

NORTH DAKOTA (NP, WD):
DAVENPORT -
Canaan Church
4465 159th Avenue SE
Davenport, ND 58021
O: 701.347.4730
email: canaannews@aol.com
www.moraviannd.com

DURBIN -
Goshen Church
4201 153rd Avenue SE
Durbin, ND 58059
Mail: PO Box 336
Leonard, ND 58052
O: 701.645.2466
email: pastor@bethelgoshen.com
www.bethelgoshen.com

FARGO -
Shepherd of the Prairie
6151 25th Street South
Fargo, ND 58104
O: 701.235.5711
email: office@shepherdfargo.org
www.shepherdfargo.org

LEONARD -
Bethel Church
State Highway 18
Leonard, ND 58052
Mail: PO Box 336
Leonard, ND 58052
O: 701.645.2466
email: pastor@bethelgoshen.com
www.bethelgoshen.com

OHIO (NP, ED):
DOVER -
First Church
319 North Walnut Street
Dover, OH 44622
O: 330.364.8831
email:
pastor@firstmoravianchurch.org
www.firstmoravianchurch.org

DUBLIN -
Church of the Redeemer
3883 Summitview Road
Dublin, OH 43016-8426
O: 614.766.5030
or 614.766.5032
email: info@redeemermoravian.org
www.redeemermoravian.org

GNADENHUTTEN -
Gnadenhutten Church
133 South Walnut Street
Gnadenhutten, OH 44629
Mail: PO Box 126
Gnadenhutten, OH 44629-0126
O: 740.254.4374
email: gnadenmor2@yahoo.com

NEW PHILADELPHIA -
Fry's Valley Church
594 Fry's Valley Road SW
New Philadelphia, OH 44663-7830
O: 740.254.9373
email: fvmc1857@gmail.com

Schoenbrunn Community Church
2200 East High Avenue
New Philadelphia, OH 44663
O: 330.339.1940
email: pastor@scmchurch.org
www.scmchurch.org

Sharon Church
4776 Moravian Church Road SE
New Philadelphia, OH 44663
O: 740.922.5507
email: sharonsec@roadrunner.com
www.sharonmoravian.org

UHRICHSVILLE -
First Church
315 North Water Street
Uhrichsville, OH 44683
Mail: PO Box 249
Uhrichsville, OH 44683
O: 740.922.0886
email: uhrichsvillemoravian@gmail.com

ONTARIO, Canada (NP, ED):
TORONTO -
New Dawn Church
7 Glenora Avenue
Toronto, ON M6C 3Y2
Canada
O: 416.656.0473
email: newdawnmoravian@bellnet.ca
www.newdawnmoravianchurch.org

PENNSYLVANIA (NP, ED):
ALLENTOWN -
Calvary Church
948 North 21st Street
Allentown, PA 18104-3785
O: 610.435.6881
email: calvarym@ptd.net
www.calvarymoravian.net

BETHLEHEM -
Advent Church
3730 Jacksonville Road
Bethlehem, PA 18017
O: 610.866.1402 or 610.868.0477
F: 610.868.0507
email:
office@adventmoravianbethlehem.org
www.adventmoravianchurch.com

Central Church
73 West Church Street
Bethlehem, PA 18018-5821
O: 610.866.5661 or 610.866.0607
F: 610.866.7256
email:
office@centralmoravianchurch.org
www.centralmoravianchurch.org

College Hill Church
72 West Laurel Street
Bethlehem, PA 18018
O: 610.867.8291
F: 610.865.3067
email:
church@collegehillmoravian.org
www.collegehillmoravian.org

East Hills Church
1830 Butztown Road
Bethlehem, PA 18017
O: 610.868.6481
F: 610.868.6219
email: office@easthillsmc.org
www.easthillsmc.org

Edgeboro Church
645 Hamilton Avenue
Bethlehem, PA 18017
O: 610.866.8793
F: 610.866.8583
email:
churchoffice@edgeboromoravian.org
www.edgeboromoravian.org

West Side Church
402 Third Avenue
Bethlehem, PA 18018-5699
O: 610.865.0256
email: mail@westsidemoravian.org
www.westsidemoravian.org

CANADENSIS -
Canadensis Church
4791 Route 447
Canadensis, PA 18325
Mail: PO Box 209
Canadensis, PA 18325-0209
O: 570.595.7114

COOPERSBURG -
MorningStar Church
234 South Main Street
Coopersburg, PA 18036
O/F: 610.282.1908
email: coopmoravian@aol.com

EASTON -
First Church
225 North 10th Street
Easton, PA 18042
O: 610.258.6317
email: eastonmoravian@rcn.com
www.firstmoravianeaston.org

Palmer Township Church
2901 John Street
Easton, PA 18045-2544
O: 610.253.2510
F: 610.253.7401
email: pmc@palmermoravian.org
www.palmermoravian.org

EMMAUS -
Emmaus Church
146 Main Street
Emmaus, PA 18049
O: 610.965.6067
F: 610.966.5420
email: pastor@emmausmoravian.org
www.emmausmoravian.org

HELLERTOWN -
Mountainview Church
331 Constitution Avenue
Hellertown, PA 18055
O: 610.838.9344
F: 610.838.2807
email:
mountainviewmoravian@verizon.net
www.mountainviewmoravianchurch.com

LANCASTER -
Lancaster Church
227 North Queen Street
PO Box 1327
Lancaster, PA 17608
O: 717.397.9722
email: office@lancastermoravian.org
www.lancastermoravian.org

LEBANON -
Lebanon Church
1115 Birch Road
Lebanon, PA 17042-9123
O: 717.273.5864
F: 717.273.0255
email: lebmoravian@comcast.net
www.freewebs.com/lebanonmoravian

Lititz -
Lititz Church
8 Church Square
Lititz, PA 17543
O: 717.626.8515
F: 717.626.8258
email: office@lititzmoravian.org
www.lititzmoravian.org

Nazareth -
Nazareth Church
4 South Main Street
Center Square
Nazareth, PA 18064
Mail: PO Box 315
Nazareth, PA 18064-0315
O: 610.759.3163
F: 610.759.3175
email: nazmoroffice@rcn.com
www.nazarethmoravian.org

Schoeneck Church
316 North Broad Street Extension
Nazareth, PA 18064
O: 610.759.0376
F: 610.759.9762
email:
schoeneck@schoeneckmoravian.org
www.schoeneckmoravian.org

Newfoundland -
Newfoundland Church
Route 191
Newfoundland, PA 18445
Mail: PO Box 221
Newfoundland, PA 18445-0221
O: 570.676.8201

Philadelphia -
Redeemer Church
2950 South 70th Street
Philadelphia, PA 19142
O: 215.365.6448
email: 2950redeemer@gmail.com
www.redeemermoravianphiladelphia.net

Reading -
Reading Church
1116 Perry Street
Reading, PA 19604-2005
O: 610.374.0886
email:
readingmoravianpa@gmail.com
www.readingmoravian.org

York -
Covenant Church
901 Cape Horn Road
York, PA 17402
O: 717.755.3269
email: covenantyork@gmail.com
www.covenantyork.org

First Church
39 North Duke Street
York, PA 17401
O: 717.843.2239
email: firstmoravianchurch@verizon.net
www.firstmoravianchurch.worthyofpraise.org

VIRGINIA (SP):
Ararat -
Willow Hill Church
577 Willow Hill Road
Ararat, VA 24053
email: info@willowhillmoravian.org
www.willowhillmoravian.org

Cana -
Crooked Oak Church
3574 Bear Trail Road
Cana, VA 24317
email: ijeaster@ccpsd.k12.va.us

Mt. Bethel Church
127 Mt. Bethel Church Road
Cana, VA 24317
O: 276.755.4690
www.mountbethelmoravianchurch.com

WISCONSIN (NP, WD):
APPLETON -
Freedom Church
W3471 Center Valley Road
Appleton, WI 54913-8937
O: 920.734.1278
email: freedommoravian@gmail.com
www.freedommoravianchurch.com

CAMBRIDGE -
London Church
N5610 Hwy. O
Cambridge, WI 53523
Mail: PO Box 45
Cambridge, WI 53523-0045
O: 608.764.1482
email:
janefz@charter.net

DEFOREST -
Christian Faith Church
805 East Holum Street
DeForest, WI 53532-1320
O: 608.846.5876
email: cfmcoffice@gmail.com
www.cfmoravianchurch.org

EPHRAIM -
Ephraim Church
9970 Moravia Street
Ephraim, WI 54211
Mail: PO Box 73
Ephraim, WI 54211-0073
O: 920.854.2804
email: worship@ephraimmoravian.org
www.ephraimmoravian.org

GREEN BAY -
West Side Church
1707 South Oneida Street
Green Bay, WI 54304
O: 920.499.4433
F: 920.499.9966
email: office@wsmoraviangb.org
www.wsmoraviangb.org

LAKE MILLS -
Lake Mills Church
301 College Street
Lake Mills, WI 53551-1494
O: 920.648.5412
F: 920.648.3669
email: lmmc3@frontier.com
www.lakemillsmoravianchurch.org

MADISON -
Glenwood Church
725 Gilmore Street
Madison, WI 53711
O: 608.233.8709
F: 608.233.2595
email: glenwoodmoravian@gmail.com
www.glenwoodmoravian.org

Lakeview Church
3565 Tulane Avenue
Madison, WI 53714
O: 608.249.1973
email: lakeviewrev@sbcglobal.net
www.lakeviewmoravianchurch.org

PITTSVILE -
Veedum Church
County Road E
Pittsville, WI 54466
Mail: PO Box 244
Pittsville, WI 54466-0244
O: 715.884.6911

RUDOLPH -
Rudolph Church
Mail: PO Box 144
Rudolph, WI 54475-0144

SISTER BAY -
Sister Bay Church
10924 Old Stage Road
Sister Bay, WI 54234
Mail: PO Box 1010
Sister Bay, WI 54234
O: 920.854.4080
email: sbmcoffice@dcwis.com
www.sisterbaymoravianchurch.org

STURGEON BAY -
Sturgeon Bay Church
323 South 5th Avenue
Sturgeon Bay, WI 54235
O: 920.743.6218
F: 920.743.0440
email: sbmc@sbmoravian.org
www.sbmoravian.org

WATERTOWN -
Ebenezer Church
N8095 High Road
Watertown, WI 53094
Mail: N8071 High Road
Watertown, WI 53094
O: 920.206.0222
email: emc1853@aol.com
www.ebenezermoravianchurch.org

Watertown Church
510 Cole Street
Watertown, WI 53094
O: 920.261.7494
F: 920.206.9030
email:
watertownmoravianchurch@yahoo.com
www.watertownmoravianchurch.org

WISCONSIN RAPIDS -
Kellner Church
Junction of County Hwys U and W
Wisconsin Rapids, WI 54494
Mail: 8016 County Road FF
Wisconsin Rapids, WI 54494
O: 715.423.2688

Wisconsin Rapids Church
310 First Avenue South
Wisconsin Rapids, WI 54495-4155
O: 715.423.0180
email: moravian@wctc.net
www.wrmoravian.org

NEW AND EMERGING MINISTRIES

ALBERTA, CANADA:
Sherwood Park
The Connection
The Common Ground Alberta
Community Cafe
The Rev. Ian Edwards &
The Rev. Dr. Eileen Edwards
Church Planters
50 Brentwood Boulevard, Suite 101
Sherwood Park, AB T8H 1P3
Canada
O: 587.269.4808
email:
commongroundcommunitycafe@gmail.com
www.commongroundcommunitycafe.org

MINNESOTA:
St. Michael
Safe Harbor Church
The Rev. David Glasser
Church Planter
9702 41st Street NE
St. Michael, MN 55376

Meeting location:
10904 57th Street NE
Albertville, MN 55301
O: 763.497.9024
email: dave@safeharbor-church.net
www.safeharbor-church.net

NORTH CAROLINA:
Winston-Salem
Come and Worship
The Rev. Brad Bennett
395 Janet Avenue
Winston-Salem, NC 27104

Meeting location:
Liberty Arts Center
526 N Liberty Street
Winston-Salem, NC 27101
Sundays at 10:00am
email: bsj3bennett@earthlink.net
sam@moravianantioch.org

Winston-Salem
Anthony's Plot
The Rev. Russ May
2323 Sunnyside Ave.
Winston-Salem, NC 27127

Meeting location:
Anthony's Plot Community
2323 Sunnyside Ave.
Winston-Salem, NC
O: 336-306-3562
email: info@anthonysplot.org
russ@anthonysplot.org
volunteer@anthonysplot.org
www.anthonysplot.org

PENNSYLVANIA:
Lehigh Valley
Iglesia Esperanza for Bethlehem
The Rev. Tracy Robinson
The Rev. Rhonda Robinson
Church Planters
724 East 6th Street
Bethlehem, PA 18015

Meeting location:
617 East 4th Street
Bethlehem, PA 18015
O: 610.504.9127
email: pastortracy@
esperanzaforbethlehem.org or
pastorrhonda@
esperanzaforbethlehem.org
www.esperanzaforbethlehem.org

WISCONSIN:
Milwaukee
Tricklebee Cafe
The Rev. Christie Melby-Gibbons
Church Planter
2339 N. Sherman Boulevard
Milwaukee, WI 53210

Meeting location: TBD
email: tricklebeecafe@gmail.com

MORAVIAN FELLOWSHIPS

CALIFORNIA:
Hope Fellowship
Gina Antonio
1147 Hollyburn Avenue
Menlo Park, CA 94025

Meeting Location:
1199 East Bay Shore Road
East Palo Alto, CA 94303

FLORIDA:
Margate Fellowship
The Rev. Joe Nicholas
1880 NW 183rd Street
Miami, FL 33056
O: 305.628.2061, F: 305.625.5365

Meeting Location:
Prince of Peace Lutheran Church
6012 NW 9 Court
Margate, FL 33063
email:
margatemoravian@gmail.com

New Covenant Fellowship
The Rev. Ofreciano Julias
1621 Quail Drive Bldg 203
West Palm Beach, FL 33409
H: 561.313.3651

Meeting Location:
Executive Centre
Palm Beach Lakes Boulevard
West Palm Beach, FL 33409

Nueva Esperanza Fellowship
Illovis Gonzalez, *Provincial Acolyte*
c/o 6001 SW 127 Avenue
Miami, FL 33183

Meeting Location:
New Hope Moravian Church

Suriname Moravian Fellowship
Armand Sabar, *Coordinator*
245 NE 191 Street Unit #3009
Miami, FL 33179
O: 305.401.5479

Meeting Location:
Prince of Peace Moravian Church

Rayaka Ingnika Fellowship
Elizabeth Bolaños, *Coordinator*
4921 81st Avenue Terrace East
Sarasota, FL 34243
H: 941.539.2740
email: eli_bolanos@msn.com

Meeting Location:
Primera Iglesia Bautista
4445 South Lockwood Ridge Road
Sarasota, FL 34231

Tampa Fellowship
Federico Velasquez, *Coordinator*
6602 North 24th Street
Tampa, FL 33610-1310
O: 813.476.7969
C: 813.431.1917

Meeting Location:
St. Paul Lutheran Church
5103 North Central Avenue
Tampa, FL 33610

MORAVIAN FELLOWSHIPS CONTINUED

NORTH CAROLINA:
Community Fellowship
Jack Nance, *Coordinator*
3733 Konnoak Drive
Winston-Salem, NC 27127
H: 336.784.5252

Welcome-Arcadia Road
Welcome, NC 27374
O: 336.731.8265
Mail: PO Box 397
Welcome, NC 27374-0397

Mountain Laurel Fellowship
Julia Simmons, *Coordinator*
563 Rector Road
Ennice, NC 28623
H: 336.657.3032
email: ghb43@skybest.com

Meeting Location:
Transou UMC
Sundays at 11:00am
Laurel Springs, NC 28644

SOUTH CAROLINA:
Palmetto Fellowship
Patricia L. Bald, *Coordinator*
223 North Church Street
Spartanburg, SC 29306
O: 864.582.7263
email:
palmettomoravianfellowship@gmail.com
www.palmettomoravianfellowship.org

Meeting Location:
Cannon Memorial Chapel
Central United Methodist Church
233 North Church Street
Spartanburg, SC 29306

WASHINGTON:
Northwest Fellowship
Joan Thomas
20904 3rd Avenue South
Des Moines, WA 98198
O: 206.824.6411
email: mimisgiftbooksjoan@gmail.com

WISCONSIN:
Mamre Fellowship
Don Wegner, *Coordinator*
W5884 Church Road
Johnson Creek, WI 53038-9736
H: 920.699.3272

Meeting Location:
N9015 County Highway Q
Watertown, WI 53094

MORAVIAN CHURCH IN NORTH AMERICA
PROVINCIAL AND DISTRICT OFFICES

The Provincial Elders' Conference
Northern Province

The Rev. Dr. Elizabeth D. Miller, President
Office: 1021 Center St., PO Box 1245, Bethlehem, PA 18016-1245
O: 610.867.7566, 800.732.0591, F: 610.866.9223
email: betsy@mcnp.org
www.mcnp.org

Northern Province District Executive Boards

Eastern District
The Rev. David E. Bennett, President
1021 Center St., PO Box 1245, Bethlehem, PA 18016-1245
O: 610.865.0302, 800.732.0591, F: 610.866.9223
email: edeb@mcnp.org
www.moravian.org/moravian-church-eastern-district/

Western District
The Rev. James T. Hicks, President
PO Box 12677, Green Bay, WI 54307-2677
O: 920.883.2212
email: jamesthicks@aol.com
www.moravian.org/moravian-church-western-district/

Canadian District
Bryan Peacock, President
600 Acadia Dr. SE, Calgary, Alberta T2J 0B8, Canada
O: 403.271.2700
email: bryan@mcnp.org
http://www.moravian.org/canada/moravian-church-in-canada/

The Provincial Elders' Conference
Southern Province

The Rev. David B. Guthrie
459 S. Church St., Winston-Salem, NC 27101
O: 336.725.5811, 888.725.5811, F: 336.723.1029
email: dguthrie@mcsp.org
www.mcsp.org

CHURCH CAUSES
Northern Province

Members and friends of the Moravian Church can show continuing interest in its work by making the Church a beneficiary in their will or by making an outright monetary gift. For the address of any corporation listed below, please see pages immediately preceding. The programs of the Northern Province are administered by the following incorporated boards:

The Board of Elders of the Canadian District of the Moravian Church in America, Northern Province

Board of World Mission of the Moravian Church

Canadian Moravian Foundation

The Executive Board of the Eastern District of the Moravian Church in America, Northern Province

The Executive Board of the Eastern District of the Moravian Church in America, Northern Province for the Foster Fund

The Executive Board of the Western District of the Moravian Church in America, Northern Province

Hope Conference and Renewal Center

Interprovincial Board of Communication

Linden Hall School for Girls at Lititz, Pennsylvania

Marquardt Memorial Manor, Inc.

Moravian Academy

The Moravian Archives

Moravian Care Ministries, Inc.

Moravian Church, Northern Province

Moravian College

Moravian Hall Square Historic District, Inc.

Moravian Hall Square Retirement Community, Inc.

Moravian Manors, Inc.

Moravian Music Foundation, Inc.

Moravian Open Door, Inc.

Moravian Theological Seminary

Mt. Morris Camp and Conference Center

The Provincial Women's Board

The Society for Promoting the Gospel

Sperling-Zimmerman Memorial Home

Trustees of the Moravian Larger Life Foundation

Van-Es Camp and Conference Centre

Southern Province

The programs of the Southern Province are administered by the following boards and agencies:

The Board of Cooperative Ministries*
Board of World Mission of the Moravian Church
Interprovincial Board of Communication
Laurel Ridge, Moravian Camp, Conference, & Retreat Center*
Mission Society of the Moravian Church, South, Inc.
Moravian Music Foundation, Inc.
Moravian Theological Seminary
The Provincial Elders' Conference
Provincial Support Services*
Provincial Women's Board*
Salem Academy and College
Salemtowne
Sunnyside Ministry*

Not incorporated. Bequests to these boards and agencies should be made for their use to the Moravian Church in America, Southern Province.

REMITTANCES
Contributions for provincial or general church causes should be sent to the provincial treasurer:

NORTHERN PROVINCE: Christina Giesler, Controller
1021 Center Street, PO Box 1245, Bethlehem, PA 18018-1245

SOUTHERN PROVINCE: Dennis Stanfield, Treasurer
459 South Church Street, Winston-Salem, NC 27101

PLANNED GIFTS AND BEQUESTS: For information about estate plans or information about charitable trusts, annuities and other forms of planned gifts to support one or more of the above ministries or your church, contact
Paul McLaughlin, President
Moravian Ministries Foundation
119 Brookstown Ave., Suite 305,
Winston-Salem, NC 27101
Phone: 1.888.722.7923

PRAYER DAYS AND SPECIAL EMPHASES

The following prayer days or special emphases have been authorized by the Northern Provincial Synod or by the Provincial Elders' Conferences of the Northern and Southern Provinces of the Moravian Church in North America:

Ecumenical Sunday: The last Sunday in January.

For Retired Ministers (optional): The last Sunday in January.

For Moravian Unity Work: The first Sunday in March.

Moravian Music Sunday: Fifth Sunday of Easter (fourth Sunday after Easter).

For Moravian Retirement Community (Southern Province):
> The second Sunday in May.

For Outdoor Ministries (Northern Province): The Sunday after Trinity.

For Camps & Conferences (Southern Province): The Sunday after Trinity.

For World Peace and Nuclear Disarmament (Northern Province):
> The first Sunday in August.

For Public Education and Moravian Educational Institutions
> (Southern Province): The last Sunday in August.

For Public Education (Northern Province): The last Sunday in August.

For Christian Education: The second Sunday in September.

For Church Development (Northern Province): The third Sunday in September.

For the Church's Ministry to Older Adults (Northern Province):
> The fourth Sunday in September.

For Older Adults (Southern Province): The fourth Sunday in September.

For Children: A Sunday in October.

For World Mission: The second Sunday in October.

For Peace with Justice and Freedom (Northern Province):
> The third Sunday in October.

Moravian Women's Sunday (Northern Province):
> The first Sunday in November (date optional).

For the Bible Society: The Sunday before Thanksgiving.

For Moravian College and Theological Seminary (Northern Province):
> The Sunday on or immediately after November 20.

World AIDS Day: December 1.

THE UNITAS FRATRUM
(International Moravian Church)
for the year ending December 31, 2014 Provided by the Chair of the Unity Board

Province	C	O	M	COM	T
Alaska*	22	2	---	---	1,900
America, North	93	3	104	16,688	20,690
America, South	56	10	50	13,012	15,423
Burundi***	---	---	45	---	40,000
Congo	80	---	---	---	21,600
Costa Rica*	2	3	4	---	600
Cuba***	8	15	4	---	600
Czech Republic	28	---	46	---	5,211
Czech Mission Province**/*	9	7	11	---	650
Eastern West Indies	51	3	46	---	15,400
European Continental*	24	28	50	---	15,000
Garifuna***/*	---	---	---	---	9,000
Great Britain	30	---	22	---	1,500
Guyana**	8	---	3	---	1,026
Haiti*	7	---	---	---	4,500
Honduras*	125	---	30	---	25,000
Honduras Mission Province**/*	74	---	27	---	16,868
Jamaica & Cayman Islands	65	---	34	5,446	7,897
Kenya***	---	---	---	---	600
Labrador**/*	4	---	---	---	1,900
Malawi**	10	11	5	---	5,190
Nicaragua*	226	---	100	---	97,000
Peru***	---	5	4	---	50
Ruvuma & Njombe***	9	4	12	1,389	1,552
Rwanda***	---	---	5	---	5,000
Sierra Leone**	---	3	1	---	37
South Africa	87	176	67	32,672	42,000
South Asia*	5	---	3	---	385
Suriname	67	---	28	---	60,000
Tanzania, East**	56	10	58	10,431	23,683
Tanzania, Kigoma	30	---	43	---	30,204
Tanzania, Northern**	25	3	34	---	3,905
Tanzania, Rukwa*	51	405	---	33,832	60,037
Tanzania, Southern*	164	---	153	109,544	180,124
Tanzania, South West	208	42	469	---	530,008
Tanzania, Western*	61	270	85	---	110,000
Uganda***/*	5	3	---	---	102
Zambia**	17	49	13	---	7,884
Zanzibar***	1	4	1	---	155
Total, Dec, 31, 2014	**1,708**	**1,056**	**1,557**	**223,014**	**1,362,681**

C = Congregations
O = Outstations
M = Ordained Ministers
COM = Communicants
T = Total Membership

* no membership statistics received for 2014
** Mission Province
*** Mission Area

OFFICIAL HEADS OF FULL UNITY PROVINCES
COMPRISING THE MORAVIAN UNITY

Phone numbers do not include international access code numbers. The international direct dial access code from U.S. phones is 011 except for calls to Labrador, Eastern West Indies, and Jamaica.

President of the Unity Board
The Rev. Robert Hopcroft
President, Great Britain and Ireland
Moravian Church House
5-7 Muswell Hill
London N10 3TJ United Kingdom
O: 44.208.883.3409
F: 44.208.365.3371
email:
Robert.Hopcroft@moravian.org.uk
www.unitasfratrum.org

Unity Business Administrator
The Rev. Dr. Jørgen Bøytler, Ph.D.
Lindegade 26
DK–6070 Christiansfeld
Denmark
O: 45.7456.1420
C: 45.4036.1420
email: boytler@ebu.de

Alaska
The Rev. Isaac Amik
PO Box 545
371 Third Avenue
Bethel, AK 99559-0545
O: 907.543.2478
F: 907.543.3942
email:
isaacamik@alaskamoravianchurch.org
www.alaskamoravian.org

America (North)
The Rev. Dr. Elizabeth D. Miller
1021 Center Street
PO Box 1245
Bethlehem, PA 18016-1245
O: 610.865.3137
F: 610.866.9223
email: betsy@mcnp.org
www.mcnp.org

America (South)
The Rev. David Guthrie
459 South Church Street
Winston-Salem, NC 27101
O: 336.725.5811
F: 336.723.1029
email: dguthrie@mcsp.org
www.mcsp.org

D. R. Congo
The Rev. Moise M. Tshimanga
Eglise Morave au Congo
PO Box 126
Muene-Ditu, Congo
O: 24.381.603.0558
email: tshimangamoise@yahoo.fr

Costa Rica
Dr. Leopold Pixley, Ph.D.
Iglesia Morava en Costa Rica
Apartado Postal 2140-1002
Paseo de los Estudiantes
San José, Costa Rica
Central America
O/F: 506.227.1542
email: lpixley@costarricense.cr

Czech Republic
The Rev. Peter Krasny
Bozeny Nemcove 54/9
CZ 460 05 Liberec V
Czech Republic
O: 420.484.847916
email: krasny@jbcr.info
www.jbcr.info

Eastern West Indies
The Rev. Dr. Cortroy Jarvis
Cashew Hill
PO Box 504
St. John's Antigua, West Indies
O: 268.560.0185
F: 268.462.0643
email: cjarvis.ewip@gmail.com
www.moravians.net

European Continental
The Rev. Raimund Hertzsch
Badwasen 6
D–73087 Bad Boll, Germany
O: 49.7164.942130
F: 49.7164.942199
email: raimund.hertzsch@bb.ebu.de
www.ebu.de

Great Britain and Ireland
Gillian Taylor
Moravian Church House
5-7 Muswell Hill
London N10 3TJ United Kingdom
O: 44.208.883.3409
F: 44.208.365.3371
email:
Gillian.Taylor@moravian.org.uk
www.moravian.org.uk

Honduras
The Rev. Harlan Maclin Kley
Iglesia Morava, Puerto Lempira
Depto. Gracias a Dios
Honduras, Central America
O: 504.8886.9295
F: 504.441.0627
email: harlancley@yahoo.com

Jamaica & the Cayman Islands
The Rev. Dr. Paul Gardner
The Moravian Church Office
PO Box 8369
3 Hector Street
Kingston CSO
Jamaica, West Indies
O: 876.928.1861
F: 876.928.8336
email: moravianchurch@cwjamaica.com
www.jamaicamoravian.org

Malawi
The Rev. Henry Mwakibinga
Moravian Church in Malawi
PO Box 119
Karonga, Malawi
email: moravian_cmm@yahoo.com

Nicaragua
The Rev. Cora Antonio
Iglesia Morava en Nicaragua
Puerto Cabezas RAAN Nicaragua
Central America
O/F: 505.792.2222
M: 505.835547
email: gonzalomoravo@gmail.com

South Africa
The Rev. Brian Abrahams
PO Box 24111
Lansdowne
7780 South Africa
O: 27.21.761.4030
F: 27.21.761.4046
email: mcsa@iafrica.com

Suriname
The Rev. Hesdie Zamuel
Evangelische Broeder Gemeente
PO Box 1811 Maagdenstraat 50
Paramaribo, Suriname
South America
O: 597.473073
F: 597.475794
email: ebgs@sr.net or
renoldpansa@yahoo.com
www.moravianchurch.sr

Tanzania, Kigoma
The Rev. Charles Katale
Lake Tanganyika Mission Province
PO Box 1267
Kigoma, Tanzania
email: revckatale@yahoo.com

Tanzania, Northern
The Rev. Peter Malema
PO Box 12320
Arusha, Tanzania
O/F: 255.27.250.7901
email: mcnt2007@yahoo.com

Tanzania (Rukwa)
The Rev. Nebort Kipeta Sikazwe
PO Box 378
Sumbawanga Rukwa
Tanzania, East Central Africa
O: 255.25.280.2714
F: 255.25.280.2079
email: sikazwenebort@yahoo.com

Tanzania (Southern)
The Rev. Samwel Kabigi
Moravian Church in Tanzania
PO Box 32
Rungwe Tukuyu
Tanzania, East Central Africa
O: 255.25.255.2030
F: 255.25.255.2298
email: samwel.kabigi@yahoo.com

Tanzania (Southwest)
The Rev. Z. E. Sichone
PO Box 377
2643 Mbeya
Tanzania, East Central Africa
O: 255.25.250.2643
email: mctswp@hotmail.com

Tanzania (Western)
The Rev. Ezekiel Yona
PO Box 29
Tabora, Tanzania
East Central Africa
O/F: 255.26.260.4822
email: ezekielyoha@yahoo.com

MISSION AREAS

*(Parenthesis indicate the supervising province -
correspondence should be directed to the supervising province)*

Moravian Church in Belize
(Honduras)

Moravian Church in Burundi
(Tanzania - Western)

Moravian Church in Cuba
(USA - Southern Province)

Moravian Church in Fr. Guiana
(Suriname)

Moravian Church in Garifuna
(Honduras)

Moravian Church in Haiti
(Jamaica)

Moravian Church in Kenya
(Tanzania - Western)

Moravian Church in Peru
(USA - Board of World Mission)

Moravian Church in Rwanda
(Tanzania - Western)

Moravian Church in Sierra Leone
(USA - Southern Province)

Moravian Church in South Asia
(Great Britain)

Moravian Church in Uganda
(Tanzania - Western)

Moravian Church in Zanzibar
(Tanzania - Eastern)

MISSION PROVINCES

Czech Republic
The Rev. Jiri Polma, *Chairman*
Komenskeho 603
CZ - 46822 Zelezny Brod
Czech Republic
O: 420.483.38923
email: jiri.polma@seznam.cz

Guyana
The Rev. Brinmore Phaul
The Moravian Church in Guyana
53 New Garden Street
Queenstown Georgetown
Guyana, South America
O: 592.226.2524
F: 592.227.4590
email: brinmorep@yahoo.com

Honduras
Rev. Salomon Ordonez
Ahuas, Honduras
email: ordonezsalomon@yahoo.com.mx

Labrador
Sarah Jensen
PO Box 220 Station B
Happy Valley-Goose Bay
Labrador A0P 1E0 Canada
O: 709.923.2262
email: moravianhv@hotmail.com
www.labradormoravian.blogspot.com

Tanzania, Eastern
(supervised by Tanzania, Southern)
The Rev. Samuel Mwaiseje
Eastern Tanzania Mission Province
PO Box 16416
Dar Es Salaam, Tanzania
O: 255.715.391929
email: samuelmwaiseje@yahoo.com
or moravian07@gmail.com

Zambia
(supervised by Tanzania, Southwest)
The Rev. Happy Crodwel Sikafunda
Moravian Church in Zambia
PO Box 38508
Lusaka, Zambia
O: 260.262.1215 or 260.976.051433
email: sikafunda2000@yahoo.com

UNITY UNDERTAKINGS

(Parenthesis indicate the supervising province)

**Star Mountain
Rehabilitation Center**
(European Continental Province)
Ms. Ghada Naser, *Director*
PO Box 199
Ramallah, Palestine
O: 972.2.296.2705
F: 972.2.296.2715
email: starmountaincenter@gmail.com
www.starmountain.org

**Unity Archive of the Moravian
Church**
Dr. Rüdiger Kröger, *Director*
PO Box 21
Zittauerstrasse 24
D-02745 Herrnhut
Germany
O: 49.358.734.8731
F: 49.358.734.8766
email: unitaetsarchiv@ebu.de

UNITY AGENCIES

Unity Women's Desk

459 South Church St., Winston-Salem, NC 27101
O: 1.336.725.6413, C: 336.416.2337
Rev. Patricia Garner, Coordinator
email: unitywomen2011@gmail.com
www.unitywomensdesk.org

Advisory Board:
Angelene Swart, *Africa Region*
email: angeleneswart@absamail.co.za

Sallie Greenfield, *American Region*
email: unitywomen2011@gmail.com

Muriel Held, *Caribbean Region*
email: muriheld@gmail.com

Erdmute Frank, *European Region*
email: e.enkelmann@gmx.net

RELATED TO THE AMERICAN PROVINCES

Unity of the Brethren in Texas

James Marek, President of Synodical Committee
1304 TH Johnson Dr.
Taylor TX 76574

HISTORICAL NOTES

Organization dates of congregations in the United States and
Canada and dates of the worldwide Moravian Church:

JANUARY

1-	1815	Sharon, Tuscarawas, Ohio
	1858	Chaska, Minnesota
	1915	Waconia, Minnesota
	1968	United, New York, New York, merger of New York III and IV
	2010	MorningStar, Coopersburg, Pennsylvania, merger of Coopersburg and Grace
3-	1856	Ordination of John Andrew Buckley, the first Moravian minister of African descent, Antigua, West Indies
	1932	First service of confirmation of Moravians in Honduras
5-	1992	New Hope, Miami, Florida
12-	1757	The first Moravian convert baptized on Antigua, West Indies
19-	1964	Rio Terrace, Edmonton, Alberta, Canada
20-	1889	Wisconsin Rapids, Wisconsin
21-	1951	Konnoak Hills, Winston-Salem, North Carolina
28-	1996	Palm Beach, West Palm Beach, Florida
30-	1864	Sturgeon Bay, Wisconsin
31-	1971	St. Paul's, Upper Marlboro, Maryland

FEBRUARY

2-	1891	Bethel, Leonard, North Dakota
	1964	Trinity, New Carrollton, Maryland
3-	1957	Official organization of Morongo Moravian Church, Banning, California; result of Indian mission work begun in 1889
9-	1749	Warwick, now Lititz, Lititz, Pennsylvania
12-	1978	Covenant, Wilmington, North Carolina
	1989	Good Shepherd, Kernersville, North Carolina
13-	1870	Unionville, Michigan
	1983	New Hope, Newton, North Carolina

MARCH

1- 1457   Date observed in commemoration of the founding in Bohemia of the Unitas Fratrum, now known as the Moravian Church

5- 1939   Calvary, Allentown, Pennsylvania

14- 1849   Arrival of first Moravian missionaries in Bluefields, Nicaragua

1886   Great Kills, Staten Island, New York

1951   Mountainview, Hellertown, Pennsylvania

15- 1925   Grace, Mount Airy, North Carolina

21- 1993   King of Kings, Miami, Florida

23- 1975   First, Stone Mountain, Georgia

24- 1799   The first Moravian converts baptized on Tobago, West Indies

25- 1752   First, York, Pennsylvania

1995   Morning Star, Asheville, North Carolina

27- 1966   John Hus, Brooklyn, New York

28- 1954   Lakeview, Madison, Wisconsin

APRIL

1- 1756   Arrival on Antigua, West Indies, of Samuel Isles, the first Moravian missionary on that island

1888   First, Easton, Pennsylvania

3- 1896   Sister Bay, Wisconsin

4- 1773   Friedberg, Winston-Salem, North Carolina

6- 1851   Olivet, Winston-Salem, North Carolina

7- 1929   Glenwood, Madison, Wisconsin

9- 1917   Veedum, Pittsville, Wisconsin

10- 1949   Palmer Township, Easton, Pennsylvania

1988   Good News, Sherwood Park, Alberta, Canada

11- 1898   Enterprise, Arcadia, North Carolina

13- 1732   The first Easter sunrise service of the Moravians conducted in the Hutberg cemetery at Herrnhut, Germany

1760   Bethania, North Carolina

1859   Egg Harbor City, New Jersey

1885   Windsor, now Christian Faith, DeForest, Wisconsin

21- 1929 Leaksville, Eden, North Carolina

1976 Our Savior's, Altura, Minnesota, merger of Bethany and Hebron

25- 1890 Arrival on Trinidad, West Indies, of Samuel Thaeler and John Holmes to organize Moravian work on that island

27- 1790 Arrival on Tobago, West Indies, of John and Mary Montgomery (parents of hymnwriter James Montgomery) to begin Moravian work on that island

1852 New York II, now Tremont Terrace, Bronx, New York

1969 Christ, Calgary, Alberta, Canada

MAY

3- 1728 Beginning of Losungen (Daily Texts) in Herrnhut, Germany

1931 Rural Hall, North Carolina

5- 1822 St. Philip's, Winston-Salem, North Carolina

1895 Fairview, Winston-Salem, North Carolina

6- 1860 West Side, Bethlehem, Pennsylvania

1895 Bruderheim, Alberta, Canada

9- 1760 Count Zinzendorf dies. (b. May 26, 1700)

12- 1727 Unanimous adoption of the first statutes, or Brotherly Agreement, by the settlers at Herrnhut, Germany, the first definite step toward reorganization of the Unitas Fratrum

17- 1863 Palmyra, Cinnaminson, New Jersey

18- 1902 Calgary, now Good Shepherd, Calgary, Alberta, Canada

19- 2002 New Beginnings, Huntersville, North Carolina

22- 1966 Redeemer, Philadelphia, Pennsylvania

1983 Christ's Community Church, Maple Grove, Minnesota

24- 1856 Macedonia, Advance, North Carolina

1878 Goshen, Durbin, North Dakota

25- 1844 West Salem, Illinois

1986 Faith Church of the Nation's Capital, Washington, D.C.

26- 1853 Ephraim, Wisconsin

1963 Acceptance of Saratoga Union, Wisconsin Rapids, Wisconsin, as a Moravian congregation

JUNE

1- 1895   Rudolph, Wisconsin

5- 1898   Willow Hill, Ararat, Virginia

6- 1954   Downey, California

9- 1957   East Hills, Bethlehem, Pennsylvania

11- 1857   Fry's Valley, New Philadelphia, Ohio

12- 1905   Edmonton, Alberta, Canada

     1943   Fargo, now Shepherd of the Prairie, Fargo, North Dakota

     1955   Battle Hill, Union, New Jersey, continuing the Elizabeth, New Jersey, congregation begun in 1866

14- 1777   Arrival of the first Moravian missionaries on St. Kitts, West Indies

17- 1722   Beginning of the building of Herrnhut, Germany, by the emigrants from Moravia

     1830   Hope, Indiana

     1853   Ebenezer, Watertown, Wisconsin

18- 1932   Hopewell, Winston-Salem, North Carolina

20- 1884   Arrival of first Moravian missionaries in Bethel, Alaska

21- 1621   The Day of Blood, so called because on that day 27 patriots, most of them members of the Brethren's Church, were executed at Prague, Bohemia

     1924   Advent, Winston-Salem, North Carolina

     1958   Grace, Westland, Michigan

25- 1742   Central, Bethlehem, Pennsylvania

     1747   Nazareth, Pennsylvania

     1876   Fries Memorial, Winston-Salem, North Carolina

26- 1988   Fellowship, Brooklyn, New York

27- 1895   Bruderfeld, now Millwoods, Edmonton, Alberta, Canada

29- 1924   Ardmore, Winston-Salem, North Carolina

JULY

6- 1415   Burning at the stake of John Hus, Bohemian martyr and forebear of the Unitas Fratrum

     1763   New Dorp, Staten Island, New York

     1800   Gnadenhutten, Ohio

14- 1912   Trinity, Winston-Salem, North Carolina

17- 1927   Crooked Oak, Cana, Virginia

26- 1846 New Philadelphia, Winston-Salem, North Carolina

1896 Heimtal, South Edmonton, Alberta, Canada

30- 1747 Emmaus, Pennsylvania

31- 1752 Arrival of first Moravian missionaries in Labrador

AUGUST

13- 1727 Manifestation of the unity of the Spirit, at the Holy Communion service held in the Berthelsdorf, Germany, church; regarded as the spiritual birthday of the Renewed Moravian Church

1837 Newfoundland, Pennsylvania

1900 Clemmons, North Carolina

21- 1732 Departure of the first Moravian missionaries from Herrnhut for St. Thomas in the West Indies; the beginning of Moravian missions and of the modern missionary movement of the Protestant church

26- 1780 Hope, Winston-Salem, North Carolina

2001 The Promise, Lewis Center, Ohio

27- 1727 Beginning of the Hourly Intercession

1872 Formation of the Moravian Prayer Union

31- 1873 Castleton Hill, Staten Island, New York

SEPTEMBER

3- 1780 Friedland, Winston-Salem, North Carolina

5- 1869 Northfield, Minnesota

10- 1911 Daggett, Michigan

11- 1854 Watertown, Wisconsin

13- 1893 Union Cross, Winston-Salem, North Carolina

1896 Mizpah, Rural Hall, North Carolina

16- 1741 Recognition and acceptance of Christ as the Chief Elder of the Moravian Church

1858 Canadensis, Pennsylvania

1984 New Dawn, Toronto, Ontario, Canada

18- 1768 Baptism of the first Moravian convert on Barbados, West Indies

25- 1887 Oak Grove, Winston-Salem, North Carolina

26- 1765 Arrival of John Wood and Andrew Rittsmansberger on Barbados, West Indies, from Herrnhut to begin Moravian work

OCTOBER

2- 1807 Beginning of the Moravian Theological Seminary at Nazareth, Pennsylvania, in 1858 transferred to Bethlehem

3- 1762 Schoeneck, Nazareth, Pennsylvania

1896 Moravia, Summerfield, North Carolina

4- 1953 Raleigh, North Carolina

5- 1908 First, Greensboro, North Carolina

1924 King, North Carolina

6- 1889 London, Cambridge, Wisconsin

7- 2002 Immanuel-New Eden, merger of Immanuel (1912) and New Eden (1923)

8- 1758 Graceham, Thurmont, Maryland

1967 Rolling Hills, Longwood, Florida

10- 1885 Moving into the first house in Bethel, Alaska, by missionaries John Kilbuck and William Weinland

18- 1889 Stapleton, now Vanderbilt Avenue, Staten Island, New York

20- 1985 Church of the Redeemer, Dublin, Ohio

22- 1899 Bethesda, Winston-Salem, North Carolina

23- 1881 Canaan, Davenport, North Dakota

24- 1874 First, Uhrichsville, Ohio

25- 1896 Christ, Winston-Salem, North Carolina

1914 Edgeboro, Bethlehem, Pennsylvania

31- 1858 Lake Auburn, Victoria, Minnesota

NOVEMBER

7- 1920 The Little Church on the Lane, Charlotte, North Carolina

9- 1980 Grace, Queens, New York

10- 1867 Kernersville, North Carolina

11- 1893 Fulp, Walnut Cove, North Carolina

12- 1909 Kellner, Wisconsin Rapids, Wisconsin

13-	1741	Formal announcement to the congregations of the Moravian Church of the immediate Headship of the Lord Jesus Christ in his church on earth
	1771	Home, Winston-Salem, North Carolina
	1893	Calvary, Winston-Salem, North Carolina
	1965	Covenant, York, Pennsylvania, merger of Bethany and Olivet
14-	1779	Baptism of the first Moravian convert on St. Kitts, West Indies
16-	1924	Pine Chapel, Winston-Salem, North Carolina
	1980	Unity, Lewisville, North Carolina
17-	1753	Arrival of the first Moravians from Bethlehem, Pennsylvania, on the Wachovia Tract in North Carolina to establish a settlement; observed as the anniversary of Bethabara, the first congregation of the Southern Province
	1850	Fort Howard, now West Side, Green Bay, Wisconsin
18-	1930	Beginning of Moravian work in Honduras by George Heath in Cauquira
	1951	Messiah, Winston-Salem, North Carolina
21-	1880	Providence, Winston-Salem, North Carolina
24-	1963	Park Road, Charlotte, North Carolina, name Peace adopted in 1999
	1991	Christ the King, Durham, North Carolina
25-	1852	Mt. Bethel, Cana, Virginia
29-	1896	Mayodan, North Carolina
30-	1746	Lancaster, Pennsylvania
	1986	Prince of Peace, Miami, Florida

DECEMBER

4-	1874	Berea, St. Charles, Minnesota
7-	1754	Missionaries arrived in Kingston, Jamaica.
11-	1887	College Hill, Bethlehem, Pennsylvania
13-	1732	Arrival of Leonard Dober and David Nitschmann, the first foreign missionaries of the Moravian Church, on St. Thomas, West Indies

DECEMBER (continued)

16-	1877	Fries Memorial, Winston-Salem, North Carolina
17-	1914	Reading, Pennsylvania
19-	1747	Lebanon, Pennsylvania
21-	1856	Lake Mills, Wisconsin
22-	1866	Freedom, Appleton, Wisconsin
25-	1862	First, South Bethlehem, Pennsylvania, now Advent, Bethlehem, Pennsylvania
27-	1748	First, New York, New York
	1842	First, Dover, Ohio
31-	1865	First, Riverside, New Jersey
	1947	Schoenbrunn, New Philadelphia, Ohio

To Order *Moravian Daily Texts* Contact:
Interprovincial Board Of Communication
Moravian Church In North America
PO Box 1245 • 1021 Center Street
Bethlehem, Pa 18016-1245
610.867.0593 Or 610.867.7566, Ext. 38

Or Order Online At:
store.moravian.org